Alberto Flores Galindo

Historical Materialism Book Series

The Historical Materialism Book Series is a major publishing initiative of the radical left. The capitalist crisis of the twenty-first century has been met by a resurgence of interest in critical Marxist theory. At the same time, the publishing institutions committed to Marxism have contracted markedly since the high point of the 1970s. The Historical Materialism Book Series is dedicated to addressing this situation by making available important works of Marxist theory. The aim of the series is to publish important theoretical contributions as the basis for vigorous intellectual debate and exchange on the left.

The peer-reviewed series publishes original monographs, translated texts, and reprints of classics across the bounds of academic disciplinary agendas and across the divisions of the left. The series is particularly concerned to encourage the internationalization of Marxist debate and aims to translate significant studies from beyond the English-speaking world.

For a full list of titles in the Historical Materialism Book Series available in paperback from Haymarket Books, visit: www.haymarketbooks.org/ series_collections/1-historical-materialism.

Alberto Flores Galindo

Utopia, History, and Revolution

Carlos Aguirre

Charles Walker

Haymarket Books
Chicago, IL

First published in 2024 by Brill Academic Publishers, The Netherlands
© 2025 Koninklijke Brill NV, Leiden, The Netherlands

Published in paperback in 2025 by
Haymarket Books
P.O. Box 180165
Chicago, IL 60618
773-583-7884
www.haymarketbooks.org

ISBN: 979-8-88890-573-9

Distributed to the trade in the US through Consortium Book Sales and Distribution (www.cbsd.com) and internationally through Ingram Publisher Services International (www.ingramcontent.com).

This book was published with the generous support of Lannan Foundation, Wallace Action Fund, and the Marguerite Casey Foundation.

Special discounts are available for bulk purchases by organizations and institutions. Please call 773-583-7884 or email info@haymarketbooks.org for more information.

Cover art and design by David Mabb. Cover art is a development of *Painting 15, Rhythm 69 (William Morris Block Printed Pattern Book, with Hans Richter Storyboard, developed from Richter's* Rhythmus 25 *and Kazimir Malevich's film script* Artistic and Scientific Film—Painting and Architectural Concerns—Approaching the New Plastic Architectural System). Paint and wallpaper on canvas (2007).

Printed in the United States.

Library of Congress Cataloging-in-Publication data is available.

Contents

Acknowledgements VII

Introduction 1
    Carlos Aguirre and Charles Walker

1 Between the Andean Utopia and the Socialist Utopia 7
    Carlos Aguirre and Charles Walker
  1 Rethinking Mariátegui and Peruvian Marxism 11
  2 Andean Utopia as History and Memory 20
  3 Intellectual and Methodological Dialogues 22
  4 The Andean Utopia under Debate 24

2 'More Than One Alternative': Alberto Flores Galindo and Peru's War of Independence 28
    Charles Walker
  1 Searching for New Paths 31
  2 Túpac Amaru 33
  3 Aristocracy, the Plebe, and Historians 37
  4 Searching and Searching 42
  5 More Than One Alternative 45

3 Leftwing Political Culture and Print Culture in Contemporary Peru: The Making of a Public Intellectual 47
    Carlos Aguirre
  1 The Making of an Intellectual: Flores Galindo and the Generation of 1968 56
  2 The Printed Word as an Intellectual Weapon 60
  3 Conclusion: The Public Intellectual and Print Culture 73

4 'Theres Is No Happy Island': Flores Galindo, Cuba, and the Socialist Utopia 75
    Carlos Aguirre
  1 Latin American Intellectuals Respond to Reagan 78
  2 The 1986 Casa De Las Américas Prize 87
  3 Return Visit to Cuba 91
  4 (Re)Thinking the Revolution 96
  5 Friendship and Solidarity 102
  6 Conclusion 104

5 'Historians Cannot Overlook the Present': Alberto Flores Galindo on the Shining Path, Violence, and the 1980's Crisis   108
   Charles Walker
   1   The Art of Doing Research and Writing Essays   109
   2   The Boiling Point   111
   3   The Silent War   118
   4   Debates, Controversies, and Polemics   124
   5   Time of Plagues   131
   6   Human Rights   134
   7   Conclusions   137

6 A Requited Passion: Flores Galindo and Literature   139
   Carlos Aguirre
   1   A Passion for Reading   139
   2   Literature and the Historical Craft   148
   3   The Forging of a Style   153
   4   The Impossible Library   155
   5   Signs of a Bygone Era   157

   Bibliography   167
   Index   187

Acknowledgements

This book is a translation of our 2020 *Alberto Flores Galindo: Utopía, historia y revolución*. We have made some corrections and small changes, and edited some sections to introduce Flores Galindo to a larger, non-Peruvian audience. We want to express our gratitude to Pablo Sandoval, general editor of La Siniestra Ensayos, who published the original version of this book in Lima and has enthusiastically supported this edition. Several people helped us during the research and writing of these essays. They are acknowledged in each chapter. In addition, we want to thank Laura Pérez Carrara, who translated Chapters 3, 4, and 6, and Kique Bossio, who provided incisive suggestions while translating chapters 2 and 5 for the original Spanish edition in Lima. At Brill, we thank Sebastian Budgen, Danny Hayward, Jason Prevost, Simona Casadio, and Bart Nijsten for their support during the different stages of production of this book. We also thank Lisa Rivero for creating the index.

Carlos Aguirre and Charles Walker

Introduction

Carlos Aguirre and Charles Walker

'A storm swept the world in 1968'. That is how noted activist and writer Tariq Ali summarised the wave of protests and mobilisations that shook Paris and Berkeley, Mexico City and Prague, London and Chicago in that extraordinary year.[1] Two ideas are most frequently associated with those events: revolution and utopia. Radical and revolutionary change seemed just around the corner, although it was not always the change Marxists and socialists had dreamed about. This time the agenda for change included ideas and practices about sex, religion, culture, gender paradigms, generational relations, art, drugs, and music, not only (or mainly) working-class emancipation and the pursuit of socialism. Although its importance is hard to deny, the legacy of 1968 is still a matter of dispute: was it truly revolutionary and emancipatory, or merely a frivolous and superficial outburst by spoiled kids in blue jeans?[2]

Changes in the world and at home affected a new generation of radicalised students in Peru. The Cuban revolution and the recent death of Che Guevara; anticolonial struggles in Africa; the civil rights and anti-Vietnam war movements in the United States; the writings of Jean-Paul Sartre, Franz Fanon, Paulo Freire, and Herbert Marcuse; guerrilla movements in Latin America; and the initial formulations of Liberation Theology all helped define the ideological contours of a generation of students and, less often, workers. Heeding the call to 'go to the masses' (*acercarse al pueblo*), they engaged in 'revolutionary' activities, even if these were often limited to militancy in small, semi-clandestine parties, distributing fliers in factories, and endless theoretical debates that deployed the canonical works of Marx, Lenin, Mao, and Guevara as weapons not only to destroy capitalism and imperialism, but also (and sometimes especially) to discredit competing factions on the left.[3]

In Peru, 1968 was the year the military broke its role as guardian of the status quo and, after a coup on 3 October, launched a process of reforms to end foreign domination, destroy the oligarchic system, advance social justice, and promote

---

1 Ali 2008.
2 For overviews of 1968 and the 1960s more generally, see Kurlansky 2004 and DeGroot 2008. For Latin America, Sorensen 2007, Gould 2009, and Zolov 2009. For the case of Peru, Arroyo 1986 and Flores Galindo 1987a.
3 Martínez 1997, Cáceres Valdivia 1993.

popular participation. Under the leadership of General Juan Velasco Alvarado, the Revolutionary Government of the Armed Forces, as it was dubbed by its ideologues and leaders, nationalised industries, implemented a radical land reform, promoted workers' autogestion, and created an entity (SINAMOS) to help mobilise the rural and urban masses. As such, it presented a challenge to the Left: while the pro-Soviet Communist Party offered the military regime critical support and Maoist factions rejected it as fascist, the groups that comprised the 'New Left' opposed it as a corporatist and bourgeois expression of nationalism. Whatever the label was, the Left had to compete with an unexpected rival for popular support.[4]

A young, relatively shy, and brilliant student at the still small and elitist Pontificia Universidad Católica del Perú (hereafter PUCP or Catholic University) could not remain indifferent to these developments. Alberto Flores Galindo, called Tito by virtually everyone, began his undergraduate education in 1966 and quickly immersed himself in the exciting political and intellectual climate. Born in 1949 to a middle-class family and educated at a private Catholic school, he was an avid reader as a child and later developed a deep social consciousness and a seemingly endless intellectual curiosity. He enrolled in the History undergraduate programme at the Catholic University, then largely a bastion of political conservatism and historiographical traditionalism. Searching for new intellectual challenges, he took courses with Liberation Theology founder Gustavo Gutiérrez, a relationship that helped him rethink religion, spirituality, and the connection between intellectuals and the oppressed and marginalised sectors of society. The works of Sartre, Antonio Gramsci, and especially the Peruvian José Carlos Mariátegui introduced Flores Galindo to Marxism. He participated in reading and discussion groups and established friendships and contacts beyond the walls of the Catholic University and the rather small community of historians and history students. Not surprisingly, he became an unequivocal militant of the left, first through radicalised but relatively small groups – FRES (Socialist Students Revolutionary Front), MIR (Leftist Revolutionary Movement), and VR (Revolutionary Vanguard) – and later as an independent and critical public intellectual. Socialism in those years, he asserted, 'was more a myth than a proposal or a project, but it possessed the mobilising passion to promote a sort of "march to the people" … that took many university students to peasant communities, mining camps, sugarcane cooperatives, urban slums, and especially factories'.[5]

---

4 See Aguirre and Drinot 2017.
5 Flores Galindo 1987a, p. 218.

After completing his undergraduate degree at the Catholic University in 1972, he spent two years in Paris (1972–4) undertaking doctoral studies, where he took classes with prominent French historians such as Fernand Braudel and Pierre Vilar.[6] Once back in Lima, he started teaching at the Catholic University and participating in public debates. This coincided with the fall of general Velasco in August 1975 and the beginning of the 'second phase' of the military regime, a period marked by a shift towards a conservative and anti-communist agenda and a process of intense mobilisation on the part of the Left and the labour movement. Within leftist intellectual circles, this was a period of intense debates on socialism, Marxism, and the 'national question'. Flores Galindo wrote articles on a variety of topics for newspapers, literary supplements, and academic journals, which reflected his intellectual and political interests and his passionate engagement with debates in the public sphere. He became a public intellectual compelled 'to speak truth to power' and used any available forum and space (the labour union and the university podium, the modest student-owned magazine, and the more established academic journal) to make his work visible and his voice heard.[7]

The 1980s, the last decade of his life, during which he produced his most important books and essays, coincided with the irruption of the Maoist group known as Shining Path and the brutal response by the Peruvian state, a conflict that produced tens of thousands of casualties and heinous human rights violations from both sides.[8] He passed away on 26 March 1990, at the age of 40.

Despite his untimely death he left a vast oeuvre consisting of monographs, essays, edited volumes, and articles that continues to attract widespread readership for its brilliance, originality, and versatility. He was also an unrepentant socialist intellectual for whom the study of the past was justified only if it helped build a more just and egalitarian society. Dozens of publications in Peru and elsewhere mourned his passing and the tragic loss to brain cancer of a brilliant thinker in the prime of his life. Many noted a gaping hole in intellectual and political circles at a critical moment when the Shining Path guerrilla movement was escalating its violent campaigns and targeting union leaders, leftists, and community activists; when leftist parties (and socialism on a world scale) entered into profound crisis and Neo-Liberalism and the right advanced; and

---

6 In the first footnote of *Arequipa y el sur andino* (Flores Galindo 1977a), he recognised the work of French historians Pierre Vilar, François Furet, and Pierre Goubert as informing his approach to 'regional history'.
7 On this, see Chapter 3 of this book.
8 Truth and Reconciliation Commission 2014.

when Peruvian society began to suffer from Alberto Fujimori's ruthless dictatorship. Flores Galindo's voice had been leading the fight against these forces.[9]

Flores Galindo conceived and executed his intellectual and political project within a society that faced enormous challenges: the legacy of colonialism and racism, the social and political exclusion of large segments of society, and the systematic aggression against Andean cultures and values, threatened by the forces of capitalist globalisation and Peru's own longue durée inequalities and stratification. He always conceived his work as a contribution to both historiographical and political debates. He studied and wrote about a startlingly wide range of topics: the Spanish conquest and its impact on Andean societies; the assault on native religions through the 'extirpation of idolatries' campaign; the anticolonial rebellions of Túpac Amaru and Juan Santos Atahualpa; the colonial crisis and the wars of independence; racism and nation-state formation in the nineteenth century; peasant communities and revolts; José Carlos Mariátegui and the origins and history of Marxism and the left; the guerrillas of the 1960s; the fictional and ethnographic work of Peruvian author José María Arguedas; and the war between Shining Path and the Peruvian state.

Intellectually, he was strongly influenced by Marxist thinkers such as José Carlos Mariátegui and the Italian Antonio Gramsci, French historians Pierre Vilar and Fernand Braudel, and British Marxist historians like Eric Hobsbawm and E.P. Thompson. He also felt close to critical historians such as the Cuban Manuel Moreno Fraginals and the Catalan Josep Fontana. He ascribed to a critical, heterodox, and eclectic form of Marxism, distant from the rigidities of economism and determinism. He paid close attention to human agency, culture, and mentalities. His familiarity with literature, and his efforts to work across disciplines (he spent much of his career teaching in the Sociology Department of the Catholic University in Peru) also contributed to his unique blending of rigour, creativity, and a captivating writing style.

In Peru and Latin America, his work has been influential not only among historians but also sociologists, anthropologists, and cultural studies scholars. He has inspired efforts to rethink colonialism, the historical roots of racism and authoritarianism, and the centrality of Indigenous cultures and peoples. Current debates on decolonial thought have also invoked Flores Galindo's interventions.[10] His books have circulated widely: *Buscando un Inca. Identidad y utopía en los Andes* (1986) (*In Search of an Inca. Identity and Utopia in the*

---

9 'Homenaje a Alberto Flores Galindo. "Otro mundo es posible"', a special issue of *Libros & Artes* (Lima) 11 (September 2005), includes a loving collection of essays about Flores Galindo.
10 Rivera 2019, Vallega 2024.

Andes), arguably his most important and mature contribution, has Spanish-language editions in Peru, Mexico, and Cuba, as well as English and Italian translations; *La agonía de Mariátegui* (1980) (*Mariátegui's Agony*), his widely acclaimed study of the founder of Peruvian Marxism, has multiple editions in Peru and has been released in Spain, Venezuela, and Cuba; a compilation of some of his seminal essays, *Los rostros de la plebe* (*The Faces of the Plebe*), organised by Magdalena Chocano, was published in Spain in 2001.[11] His trajectory as a socialist historian was the subject of an important book by Brazilian historian Marcos Sorrilha Pinheiro.[12] A short introduction to his work has been published in Argentina.[13] For Cuban Marxist intellectual Fernando Martínez Heredia (1939–2017), Flores Galindo was 'one of the best historians of the continent' and 'a notable Marxist'.[14]

Besides the two years he spent in France, a semester of teaching in Barcelona (1987), and brief absences to attend conferences, Flores Galindo spent his entire life in Peru, pursuing an intellectual and political agenda that became ever more urgent as the dramas of the 1980s unfolded. He was never just a scholar: he was a journalist, an activist, an organiser, a mentor, and a provocateur. In the best tradition of Latin American public intellectuals, he fulfilled that role with endless energy until his untimely death.

His relationship with the English-speaking world was tenuous, although he engaged with scholars in the US such as John Coatsworth, Friedrich Katz, Steve Stern, Florencia Mallon, Deborah Poole, and Karen Spalding. Only one of his books has been translated into English, which has prevented him from reaching a wider audience in the anglophone world. We hope that this book will familiarise English-speaking readers with Flores Galindo's radical and imaginative approach to the study of the past, his energetic presence as a public intellectual, and his efforts towards building a socialist society.

This volume is comprised of six chapters written in different circumstances.[15] They address different facets of his work as a historian and as a socialist intellectual. Chapter 1, 'Alberto Flores Galindo: Between the Andean Utopia and the Socialist Utopia', is a revised and enlarged version of the introduction

---

11   Flores Galindo 2001.
12   Sorrilha Pinheiro 2013.
13   Trimboli 2024.
14   Suárez and Kruijt 2012.
15   The authors have tried to minimise the inevitable repetitions of information and arguments that appear throughout the book, which are explained by the different origins of the six chapters and because we envisioned that they could be read independently from each other.

we wrote for *In Search of an Inca. Identity and Utopia in the Andes*, the English translation of his most important book.[16] It offers a general overview of Flores Galindo's contributions and places them within the political and intellectual coordinates in which they were produced. Chapter 2, '"More than One Alternative": Alberto Flores Galindo and Peru's War of Independence', examines his contributions to the study of Peru's rupture with Spain, highlighting their originality and relevance as well as some of their limitations. Chapter 3, 'Leftwing Political Culture and Print Culture in Contemporary Peru: The Making of a Public Intellectual', reconstructs Flores Galindo's vigorous participation in scholarly and political debates and emphasises his intense and creative use of print materials, a feature that was central to political culture of the time. Chapter 4, '"There is No Happy Island": Flores Galindo, Cuba, and the Socialist Utopia', analyses the relationship between Flores Galindo and the Cuban Revolution, marked by his sympathy and solidarity but also by unresolved tensions between his conception of a democratic version of socialism and the authoritarian features of the Cuban regime. Chapter 5, '"Historians Cannot Overlook the Present": Alberto Flores Galindo on the Shining Path, Violence, and the 1980's Crisis', reviews his frequently overlooked work on the authoritarian project of the Shining Path, the brutal response by the Peruvian State and armed forces, and the emergence of a human rights community. Finally, Chapter 6, 'A Requited Passion: Flores Galindo and Literature', focuses on his close relationship with fiction and poetry and explores the ways in which it contributed to his work as a historian.

---

16   Flores Galindo 2010.

CHAPTER 1

Between the Andean Utopia and the Socialist Utopia

Carlos Aguirre and Charles Walker

For Alberto Flores Galindo, the emancipation of the oppressed and the construction of a socialist society were intimately connected to the intellectual and ideological battles over the knowledge and interpretation of the past. Like José Carlos Mariátegui, Antonio Gramsci, Walter Benjamin, or E.P. Thompson, Flores Galindo saw himself as an intellectual whose mission was to question the status quo, contribute to the forging of a new society, and help rethink the past as a weapon in the ideological and political battles needed to move socialism forward. He viewed history as one of the most important battlefields, and he never ceased looking at the past with a critical eye or engaging in hard-fought polemics against those who, in his view, manipulated history in the service of a conservative agenda.[1] However, Flores Galindo did not merely 'apply' Marxist theory to the reconstruction of the past to produce superficial and ideological accounts to serve a political agenda, as was common in those days. Rather, he was a rigorous and creative historian whose work was grounded in solid archival research and a nondogmatic use of theory, Marxist and others.

The counterpoint between past and present and between theory and archival research was a signature throughout his fertile intellectual career. His first monograph explored the political organisation, mobilisation, and struggle of Andean mine workers (1900–30). Influenced by recent labour history, Flores Galindo examined not only the exploitation of Cerro de Pasco Copper Corporation workers, but also the role daily life and culture played in working-class consciousness.[2] Next he employed French *Annales* school methodology, including the *longue durée* and the use of the 'region' as a unit of historical analysis, in a study of Arequipa. He focused on the economic exchanges and commercial circuits that articulated the 'Andean south' between the eighteenth and twentieth

---

1 On numerous occasions he attacked the view of history as a 'dialogue with the dead', for it would mean that 'we stop thinking about the present, we amputate our future, and transform historians into guardians of a cemetery'. Flores Galindo 1983a, pp. 39–40.
2 Flores Galindo 1974.

centuries, but he also remained mindful of the actors (landowners, merchants, and peasants) behind those processes.³ Flores Galindo consciously attempted to de-centre the formulation of historical problems in Peru by adopting a regional and rural perspective. 'The Andean south' ('el sur Andino') was central to this effort and informed most of his subsequent work and that of many historians. In addition, *Arequipa y el sur andino* briefly but convincingly criticised Dependency Theory, still fashionable among Peruvian and Latin American intellectuals and scholars in the second half of the 1970s.

Two historical figures began to attract Flores Galindo's attention: Túpac Amaru, the leader of a massive 1780 anticolonial Andean rebellion, and José Carlos Mariátegui, the founder of Peruvian Marxism and one of the most important Marxist intellectuals of the twentieth century. It is not difficult to identify some of the motivations behind this interest. The military government that took over in 1968 used Túpac Amaru as a symbol of its alleged emancipatory programme, as a 'precursor' of its 'military revolution', a notion that Flores Galindo and most of the Peruvian left found debatable.⁴ Historicising Túpac Amaru would help demystify his role and legacy by answering a deceptively simple question: 'What does Túpac Amaru II represent in colonial history? Or in other words, was the 1780 insurrection a mere rural riot, a hopeless rebellion, a revolution, an ethnic expression, or a national movement?'⁵ Flores Galindo also asked why Peru, a tumultuous viceroyalty and country with much insurgency, had never experienced a revolution. From 1975 on he wrote various articles and edited an anthology of essays on Túpac Amaru and began to use the concept of *utopia* to refer to a host of ideas and projects behind insurrectionary movements.

Flores Galindo's interest in the study of Mariátegui, on the other hand, came mostly from his engagement in debates within the Peruvian left. How should the left respond to the military appropriation of 'revolution' and 'socialism'? What was the place of indigenous peoples in a socialist project? What was the relationship between the construction of socialism and the so-called national problem, that is, the idea that Peru had not 'completed' its formation as a nation? And more urgently, who was the 'revolutionary agent' that would carry on socialist transformations? Leftist intellectuals passionately debated these issues, all of which concerned Mariátegui in the 1920s. Although many commentators tended to canonise Mariátegui and make him the 'precursor' of

---

3   Flores Galindo 1977a.
4   On the uses of Túpac Amaru by the military regime, see Walker 2017.
5   Flores Galindo 1976a, p. 7.

various branches of the Peruvian left, Flores Galindo aimed to historicise Mariátegui and illuminate the person, his circumstances, and the ways in which his intellectual method might inspire new ways of thinking about Peruvian society. He did that in a series of articles and in two important books, the first with friend and collaborator Manuel Burga – a multi-layered study of Peru's history between 1895 and 1930 – and the second a superb intellectual and political biography of Mariátegui, that will be discussed in detail below.[6]

Túpac Amaru and Mariátegui represented, in the eyes of Flores Galindo, attempts to navigate against the current, the imaginative creation of projects of radical social transformation and alternative visions of the nation. These ultimately unsuccessful projects most clearly articulated in Peru the related themes of utopia and revolution that characterised the spirit of 1968. Those themes reappeared, widely amplified, when in 1980 a Maoist movement known as Shining Path started an insurrection allegedly under the guidance of Mariátegui's thought.[7] Shining Path promised to make communism a reality – not only in Peru but in the entire world – through the 'correct' application of revolutionary violence. Utopian communism, unapologetic violence (including against rivals on the left), and the transformation of a small and isolated guerrilla group in the heart of Andean rural societies to a nationwide threat to the Peruvian state challenged leftist intellectuals and parties that once again engaged in urgent debates about the relationship between revolution, socialism, and Andean peoples and cultures. Few intellectuals were better equipped to tackle those issues than Flores Galindo. His most ambitious contribution was the notion of 'Andean utopia', a concept that he would use as an entryway into the fractured history of Peru from the Spanish conquest to the present. We will come back to this.

The 1980s were a decade of dizzying intellectual productivity for Flores Galindo. He completed his doctoral thesis in 1983, a social history of Lima in the transition from colonialism to independence, which was published as a book in 1984.[8] *Aristocracia y plebe*, a highly innovative study of the class structure and social dynamics of Lima, attempted to explain why, at a time when riots, rebellions, and other social movements shook the Andean region, the capital of the Viceroyalty of Peru remained relatively quiet. He found the explanation

---

6 Burga and Flores Galindo 1980, Flores Galindo 1980a.
7 Although its official name was 'Communist Party of Peru', the movement led by philosopher Abimael Guzmán was widely known as 'Sendero Luminoso' (Shining Path). It started its armed insurrection in May 1980. Chapter 5 of this book discusses Flores Galindo's (and others') views on the Shining Path.
8 Flores Galindo 1984a.

in Lima's peculiar class structure and the confluence of vertical forms of despotism, social control, and horizontal manifestations of violence and tension among the lower orders. Flores Galindo also produced a series of chapters and articles exploring the notion of 'Andean utopia' that later made up *Buscando un Inca. Identidad y utopía en los Andes* (*In Search of an Inca. Identity and Utopia in the Andes*), whose first edition was published in Havana in 1986.[9] His output also included numerous essays, edited volumes, and books on a variety of topics, all while he continued teaching, lecturing, and consolidating a centre of socialist studies (SUR, Casa de Estudios del Socialismo) and *Márgenes*, a journal of cultural and political commentary.[10]

By the late 1980s, Flores Galindo had embarked on a major study of José María Arguedas (1911–69), the Peruvian anthropologist and writer who in his view best represented the dilemmas and tensions of Peruvian society. Arguedas, the son of a mestizo lawyer, was raised among indigenous servants, grew up speaking Quechua, and later attempted to depict Peru's fractured reality in ethnographic and fictional works. He also struggled against depression until committing suicide in 1969. As many other authors have suggested, Arguedas's oeuvre offers a fascinating laboratory in which to explore Andean culture and its conflictive relationship with the 'western' world, precisely the central theme in Flores Galindo's own historical work, particularly in *In Search of an Inca*. Arguedas, wrote Flores Galindo, 'is one of those exceptional characters who, in his linguistic trajectory and his work as a writer, condensed the tensions and preoccupations of a given society'.[11] In addition, Flores Galindo found in Arguedas's work a peculiar 'precursor and futurist' content, a sort of visionary 'anticipation' of the paths that Peruvian society would (or could) take.[12] Unfortunately, Flores Galindo's sudden illness in February 1989 and death in March 1990, at age 40, interrupted this project.

---

9   Flores Galindo 1986a. Henceforth, all citations from this book, unless otherwise noted, will be taken from the English translation, Flores Galindo 2010.
10 His articles and essays of this period are included in volumes V and VI of his *Obras Completas* (Flores Galindo 1997 and 2007).
11 Flores Galindo 1986h, p. 395. This is one of the two manuscript essays that Flores Galindo wrote about Arguedas and that were published posthumously. The other one is Flores Galindo 1988f. Both were first published together in Flores Galindo 1992.
12 Flores Galindo 1986h, p. 392.

1 Rethinking Mariátegui and Peruvian Marxism

As mentioned above, the 1970s were years of intense debates within the Peruvian left: the routes to access power, the type of party that would lead the revolution, the necessary but complex articulation of socialism with what was called 'the national question' and the role of the peasantry and Andean culture in the construction of socialism, among others, demanded attention and generated endless discussions. Velasco's experiment had shown the possibilities and limits of a revolution from above carried out by the military and technocrats. The fall of Allende in Chile had painfully demonstrated the difficulties of building socialism through democracy. The multiple currents of the Peruvian left – pro-Moscow, Maoists, Trotskyists, Guevaristas, Polpotians and others – used to invoke, in addition to Marx, Lenin, Trotsky, and Mao, the name of José Carlos Mariátegui, the founder of Marxism in Peru, to whose writings they flocked, like the faithful Christians to the Bible, in search of the sacred word that would show the path to follow. The most dogmatic group of all (although in this they had serious competition) used a slogan from which their nickname would later be derived: 'Following the Shining Path of José Carlos Mariátegui'. Mariátegui had become a 'model kit', as Flores Galindo used to repeat, a phrase with Cortazarian resonances.[13] Each party or faction came up with 'their' Mariátegui. The controversies of those years, in the cold nights of Plaza San Martín or in crowded university auditoriums, pitted political leaders, intellectuals, and students armed with books and ready to throw at each other the precise quotes from Mariátegui that 'proved' their truth. They were the *mariategueros*, as José Ignacio López Soria branded them.[14]

At the same time, through different but confluent paths, Peruvian and foreign scholars were engaged in an effort to offer a more complex image of Mariátegui and his time, through a revaluation of Leguía's 'oncenio', working-class struggles, the founding of the Socialist Party and APRA, and the controversy and breakup with Haya de la Torre.[15] Authors such as Piedad Pareja, Denis Sulmont, César Germaná, Baltazar Caravedo, Wilfredo Kapsoli and others, with varying rigour and originality, excavated archives and contemporary newspapers to

---

13 Cortázar 1972.
14 López Soria 1982a, p. 104.
15 APRA (American Popular Revolutionary Alliance) was a movement founded in 1924 by Peruvian ideologist Víctor Raúl Haya de la Torre. Although initially Mariátegui and Haya de la Torre were ideologically close and collaborated on various projects, a radical rupture took place in 1928 when Mariátegui clearly defined his socialist option.

offer a much richer understanding of the period and its protagonists.[16] Flores Galindo was part of that collective effort, both with his already mentioned book about the Cerro de Pasco mine workers and with a series of texts about Mariátegui.[17] On the other hand, a group of foreign scholars also began to rigorously analyse Mariátegui: they include Antonio Melis in Italy, Robert Paris in France, Harry Vanden and Jesús Chavarría in the United States, and José Aricó in Argentina and later in Mexico, where he was exiled.[18] They offered innovative interpretations that went beyond *mariateguería*. Aricó (1931–91) had embarked for some time on a two-pronged theoretical and political project. First, he wanted to contribute to rethinking the Marxist tradition through a process of translation and systematisation of texts, both classic and lesser known, culminating in the series Cuadernos de Pasado y Presente, a collection of 98 titles published over a period of fifteen years.[19] Second, Aricó forcefully put forward the notion of 'Latin American Marxism', that is, a way of interrogating Marxism and offering interpretations and solutions in accordance with the specific conditions of the region. It was in this effort that Aricó discovered Mariátegui. In an interview in 1986 he would recall that, although he had dealt with Marx and Mariátegui long before his trip to Mexico in 1976, 'the new turn of the research, the paths it followed to advance in such a shifting terrain, the results that it may have achieved, all this was done during the Mexican exile and I think they owe a lot to it'.[20] During those years he was working on a book that he never finished and which he referred to colloquially as 'the mamotreto' (or hefty volume): a history of Latin American Communism and socialism, the title and focus of which varied over time.[21]

In 1978, in the Cuadernos de Pasado y Presente series, Aricó published a collective volume he organised, *Mariátegui y los orígenes del marxismo lati-*

---

16   Sulmont 1975, Kapsoli Escudero 1976, Caravedo 1977, Pareja 1978, Germaná 1980.
17   In 1975 Flores Galindo published a brief article on the polemic between Haya de la Torre and Mariátegui and was interviewed in the magazine *Mundial* on the foundation of the Peruvian Communist Party; in 1976, he published an article on Communists and the 1930 crisis; in 1978, two additional texts in *Amauta*; in 1979 he penned an essay on Marxism and Andean societies, published in *Allpanchis*; and addressed the place of intellectuals, the national question, and the Haya de la Torre-Mariátegui debate in the already-mentioned book he cowrote with Manuel Burga (1980). In a 1986 interview he said that the book could have been titled 'The Peru of Mariátegui and Haya de la Torre'. Oshiro 1990.
18   Melis 1968, Paris 1973, Vanden 1975, Aricó 1978, Chavarría 1979.
19   On this impressive editorial project led by Aricó, that included several titles translated by him, see Cortés 2019 and Crespo 2023.
20   Aricó 2014, p. 241.
21   Cortés 2019, pp. 55–61.

noamericano, which was to generate important debates and helped renew the field of Mariátegui studies.[22] Aricó's extensive introduction began with a forceful statement: *Seven Interpretive Essays*, Mariátegui's 1928 seminal book, 'with all the errors or limitations it may contain ... remains, fifty years after its publication, the only significant theoretical work of Latin American Marxism'.[23] For Aricó, Mariátegui endorsed an 'anti-economistic and anti-dogmatic' interpretation of Marxism, 'at a time when attempting it from the Communist ranks was theoretically inconceivable and politically dangerous'.[24] Aricó visited Lima that same year, 1978, invited by Sinesio López and other sociology professors at the PUCP to lead a seminar on Gramsci and the possibilities of formulating an 'open Marxism'. Once in Lima, Aricó changed his mind and dedicated the seminar to Mariátegui: 'His presentations on Mariátegui – López recalled in 1991 – left deep marks and, above all, gave rise to valuable products. The most brilliant of all was, without a doubt, *La agonía de Mariátegui* by Alberto Flores Galindo, with whom he established a solid friendship'.[25] In a note commenting on those presentations, Flores Galindo highlighted the 'special passion' with which Aricó projected 'an unconventional image of Mariátegui', a thinker 'unattached to dogma'.[26] Aricó's interpretations were also subjected to harsh criticism from intellectuals linked to the Communist Party: some, like César Lévano, accused him of promoting a 'rapprochement to Aprismo', while Ricardo Luna Vegas would chastise Aricó's reading of Mariátegui as 'malicious' and 'distorting'.[27]

Aricó's influence on Flores Galindo is undeniable, although we need to dispel any temptation to see their relationship as akin to teacher and disciple. Sinesio López is correct in emphasising Aricó's 'footprints', but we should keep in mind that Flores Galindo had been writing and reflecting on Mariátegui since the early 1970s. They coincided in their vision of Mariátegui as a heterodox, critical thinker with a strong culturalist mark, far from the rigidities of the Third International and deeply rooted in the Peruvian experience. They also shared the conviction that to properly understand Mariátegui he had to be placed in precise historical coordinates. *La agonía de Mariátegui* contains numerous references to Aricó, generally to underline points of agreement:

---

22 Aricó 1978.
23 Aricó 1978, p. xix, Mariátegui 1971 [1928].
24 Aricó 1978, p. xiv.
25 López 1991, p. 6.
26 Flores Galindo 1978a, p. 99.
27 Both quotes taken from Ricca 2015, p. 305.

Trying to recover the daily image of Mariátegui as a politician, with his tensions and conflicts, his errors and his successes, discovering the man behind the tangle of rhetoric, was the purpose that I had outlined for myself in this book. This places me in the steps of Jesús Chavarría and José Aricó, as I started noticing that Mariátegui developed his own independent way of thinking Marx.[28]

The encounter with Aricó – erudite in Marxist traditions and texts, a sharp reader of Mariátegui, and a legendary editor of journals and collections – confirmed to the young Peruvian historian that his approach and many of his interpretations were on the right track. Aricó was, without a doubt, a decisive influence in the conception and writing of *La agonía de Mariátegui*.

On a date that we have not been able to specify, towards the end of 1979, Flores Galindo participated in a sociology congress in Ayacucho, where he presented a paper on Mariátegui whose title is unknown and whose original text, apparently, has not survived. At that congress, according to the testimony of Maruja Martínez, Flores Galindo 'argued in particular with some Ayacucho professors belonging to what would later be known as the Shining Path', and it was there, Martínez adds, that the idea of writing *La agonía de Mariátegui* was conceived.[29] Martínez suggests that the motivation behind the project of writing the book stemmed from the confrontation with members of the Shining Path. The anecdote is indeed very revealing, given the accusations Flores Galindo received of being pro-Shining Path in the 1980s. Upon his return to Lima and for the next six months, according to Martínez, Flores Galindo would become immersed in the writing of the book.

Flores Galindo himself places the origin of the book not in Ayacucho but in a conversation, also towards the end of 1979, with Óscar Dancourt, director of *Amauta*, a radical left magazine. Different groups of the left were at that time immersed in heated discussions with a view to the May 1980 elections. Several parties of diverse ideological affiliations, including Trotskyists and Maoists, formed the coalition Alianza Revolucionaria de Izquierda (ARI, Left Revolutionary Alliance) which, in Flores Galindo's view, sought to build 'a mass leftist movement ... rooted in Peruvian society'.[30] Dancourt asked Flores Galindo to

---

28 They also had discrepancies, both in their interpretations of Mariátegui and in the political projects they sought to articulate. One of them was the relationship between Mariátegui and Haya de la Torre: Flores Galindo perceived in Aricó an effort to bring them closer, something that according to him was not supported by the evidence.
29 Martínez's testimony is taken from Flores Galindo 1994b, p. 605.
30 Flores Galindo 1994b, p. 595.

write a series of articles about 'the defence of similar positions that Mariátegui had made, in 1929, in confrontation with the Communist International'.[31] Flores Galindo, as noted previously, had been reflecting for some time on Mariátegui, socialism, and the elusive constitution of Peru, a country with an indigenous majority, into a nation. Flores Galindo accepted Dancourt's invitation and in January 1980 began publishing a series of articles in *Amauta* whose titles and content anticipate some of the themes he would address in *La agonía de Mariátegui*.[32]

This was a book, thus, conceived and forged in the debates within the left and written with a sense of urgency that was nothing less than agonising. While Flores Galindo was thinking and writing about Mariátegui, some events contributed to fuelling that sense of urgency. On the internal political front, the ARI broke up due to a lack of agreement among its members on who should lead the alliance. On 17 May, on the eve of the general elections, Sendero Luminoso, waving the ideological flags of Mao and Mariátegui, began its bloody war to conquer power. In terms of intellectual debates in Marxist circles, a decisive milestone was the holding of the International Colloquium 'Mariátegui and the Latin American Revolution', organised by José Aricó at the Autonomous University of Sinaloa, in Culiacán, Mexico, 14–18 April 1980, to mark the 50th anniversary of Mariátegui's death.[33]

Flores Galindo presented a paper on the young Mariátegui, his intellectual formation, and his extensive journalistic output.[34] At that event, which brought together the most important Mariátegui scholars, intense discussions pitted critical, innovative, and heterodox views on Mariátegui against more orthodox ones. In an article written after the colloquium, Flores Galindo sharply criticised those who 'went exclusively to "celebrate" Mariátegui (the fifty years since his death), making all sorts of concessions to rhetoric and bad taste'. Instead, he applauded the presence of those 'more interested in "discussing" his ideas, placing them within the conflictive history of socialism and the Communist movement'.[35] One of the topics of discussion was Mariátegui's relationship with APRA and the Third International. Flores Galindo, according to the tran-

---

[31] Ibid.
[32] Flores Galindo 1980b, Flores Galindo 1980c, Flores Galindo 1980d, Flores Galindo 1980e, Flores Galindo 1980f, Flores Galindo 1980g. He published two more articles in other outlets. Flores Galindo 1980h, Flores Galindo 1980i.
[33] Cortés 2018. The contributions and debates have been compiled in Cortés and García 2023.
[34] The paper was incorporated as a chapter into *La agonía de Mariátegui* from the second edition forward. See Flores Galindo 1994b, pp. 517–48.
[35] Flores Galindo 1980j, p. 137.

script of the debates, 'strive[d] to place Mariátegui at a distance from both the International and Haya de la Torre's positions'.[36]

Flores Galindo returned to Peru after that colloquium not only intellectually energised by the presentations, debates, and conversations, but more convinced than ever of the need to systematise in a book the reconstruction of Mariátegui as a heterodox, independent, critical, and original Marxist thinker and politician, thus at odds with those who represented dogma, intellectual and political rigidity, and the imposition of agendas drawn up from afar Peruvian reality. The controversy with the Komintern[37] would be the central knot that allowed Flores Galindo to reconstruct the final period of Mariátegui's life during which, as his ideas matured, he collided with the dogmatic positions of the Third International.

Where do the originality and contributions of *La agonía de Mariátegui* lie? What are the virtues that make it stand out within the abundant bibliography on Mariátegui? In the appendix to the book Flores Galindo summarised the purpose that guided him in writing the book:

> The goal was to undertake *the critique of the mythologised image of Mariátegui* – that kind of icon and inevitable reference used to endorse any political position – and *find instead the human being, the historical character*; it was then necessary to place the controversy with the Komintern in the context of Peruvian society during the final years of the Leguía regime, reread it from the biography of Mariátegui, and reconstruct the links between him and his contemporaries. Historical analysis would provide a certain 'distancing effect' that is essential *to not subordinate interpretation to current political tactics*. It happens that, alongside his image as an icon, Mariátegui had become a sort of 'megaphone' through which the left propagated its political positions, regardless of any respect for the fidelity to Mariategui's thought.[38] (emphases added)

This exercise in demystifying and historicising the character translated into a series of arguments that were sometimes audacious, always ingenious, and often controversial. Regarding the relationship with the Komintern, Flores Galindo presented a forceful and provocative thesis: Mariátegui was a victim of the sectarianism of Komintern officials who did not conceive of the possib-

---

36 Cortés 2018, p. 79.
37 Flores Galindo used Komintern instead of Comintern in his writings. We will do the same throughout this book. The name Third International is also used.
38 Flores Galindo 1994b, pp. 595–6.

ility of a self-made ('propia') Peruvian or Indo-American way of thinking about Marxism, the revolution, and the party. Mariátegui was seen as a dilettante intellectual rather than as a party man, and for that very reason he became suspicious: his main book included in the title the terms 'essays' and 'Peruvian reality', unacceptable for those who conceived Marxism as a closed ideology that did not allow interpretations or adaptations.[39] Isolated and abandoned, even by some of his closest collaborators, Mariátegui was preparing, at the time of his death, to leave Peru to settle in Buenos Aires, where he planned to continue to publish the journal *Amauta*, that he founded in 1926.

Mariátegui's Marxism, on the other hand, 'developed far from any academicism, surrounded instead by events, immersed in daily life, an offspring of those same streets and crowds that informed the young Mariátegui's journalistic craft'.[40] Mariátegui, according to Flores Galindo, was not an ideologue and never wanted to write a manual or a doctrinal treatise; his version of Marxism was made at the 'fast, short, and hammering rhythm of his typewriter', as Flores Galindo used to repeat, and in close relationship with the events that surrounded him: mass movements, daily life, readings and gatherings, journalism, and direct contact with workers. For this reason, it is a fluid Marxism, sometimes incoherent but always original and critical. For Mariátegui, writes Flores Galindo, 'Marxism was never a "theory" nor a set of 'concepts' but, above all, an attitude, a way of life, a worldview'.[41] Mariátegui's Marxism was forged, Flores Galindo suggests, amid debates and confrontations of ideas: 'Controversy was an everyday occurrence in his biography but it also ended up being the privileged instrument for the development of his thought, an essential standard of truth, a necessity'.[42]

Unlike what Komintern officials (and Haya de la Torre followers) thought, Mariátegui was not just an intellectual: he was, despite the limitations of mobility, a man of action and an organiser – of a journal, a publishing house, a party project – activities that must be seen, according to Flores Galindo, as part of the same project. *Amauta*, in that sense, was 'the prelude' to the party. But what type of party was Mariátegui proposing? Certainly not one with a closed and rigid structure, much less one that responded submissively to the dictates of a supranational organisation like the Communist International. Nor one that followed the Peruvian caudillista tradition, one that, starting in 1928, Haya de la Torre would imprint on his APRA project. If it was neither one nor the other,

---

39   Flores Galindo 1994b, p. 407.
40   Flores Galindo 1994b, p. 391.
41   Flores Galindo 1994b, p. 438.
42   Flores Galindo 1994b, p. 511.

then what would be the party 'model' that Mariátegui wanted for Peruvian socialism? Flores Galindo, in another provocative interpretation, suggests that Mariátegui, in fact, did not know. Actually, he did not need to know given that 'he rejected the definition of a plan designed in advance, because otherwise the workers' experiences and lessons could not be collected: it was not a question of imposing an organisation outside the mass movement'.[43] 'Se hace partido al andar', 'You make your own party as you walk', Mariátegui could have written, paraphrasing the Spanish poet Antonio Machado, not only at the organisational but also at the programmatic level. The party that Mariátegui imagined had to be revolutionary and inspired by Marxism, but also one that would find its direction and its form in the popular movement and the contingencies of politics.

This mass movement, in a country like Peru, necessarily involved incorporating the peasantry, which was of mostly indigenous extraction. A 'proletarian' party could not be organised only with the still incipient industrial working class. Peruvian socialism, for Mariátegui, had to incorporate – and be nourished by – the experience of the Andean world: here was another point of disagreement between Mariátegui and the Komintern, reflected in the coldness and even hostility with which his essay on 'The Problem of Race in Latin America' was received at the 1929 Communist conference in Buenos Aires.[44]

The first edition of *La agonía de Mariátegui* was published in November 1980, a little less than a year after the sociology congress in Ayacucho and the conversation with Óscar Dancourt mentioned above. Its release did not leave the intellectual and political left indifferent. It was not common in Peru (and it is not common today) for a history book to be reviewed, commented on, and criticised so widely and in political more than scholarly publications, but this was not just any history book: it was a text that challenged the left and did so by dismantling a series of commonplaces related to the life and legacy of Mariátegui, who had become a kind of untouchable guru for groups of intellectuals and militants. Flores Galindo's book, inevitably, was read in connection with the present. After all, it had been conceived – as Mariátegui himself would have wanted – in the heat of ongoing debates about the revolution and socialism. Carlos Iván Degregori, writing several years later, considered Flores Galindo's 'the ideal Mariátegui for a generation marked by the Cuban revolution, Che's adventure, the French May 1968 and, above all, by the tsunami of peasants, workers, migrants, and organised regions movements that shook the

---

43   Flores Galindo 1994b, p. 476.
44   Mariátegui 2011.

country, breaking down structures and prejudices', and thanked Flores Galindo 'for rescuing that Mariátegui at the very moment when other intellectuals were inventing another one to suit them: Marxist-Leninist, dogmatic to the point of caricature and, in any case, farther away than the one that documents of the time and the testimonies of his contemporaries reveal'.[45] As seen in Chapter 5, Degregori and Flores Galindo energetically disagreed on many other topics.

The reactions were varied, as expected, and almost all included criticisms of different caliber. Carlos Franco, author of the most extensive commentary on *La agonía de Mariátegui*, observed that 'only those who understand the meaning of the myth [of Mariátegui] and the ideological, political, and personal identification of the traditional left with him, will be able to understand the depth of the wound caused by the book'.[46] This 'wound' generated extremely harsh criticism. César Lévano would say, paraphrasing Borges, that 'intimately, this book suffers from death'.[47] One of the most frequently questioned topics was the image of an isolated and defeated Mariátegui, at odds with the Third International, and ready to leave Peru and begin a new stage, more intellectual than organisational. Others pointed out that the image of the Komintern offered by Flores Galindo was too static and monolithic. The always thorny issue of the relationship between Mariátegui and APRA was also the subject of discussion: for some, Flores Galindo's book did not sufficiently emphasise the radical difference between Mariátegui and Haya de la Torre, especially after 1928, while, for others, on the contrary, Flores Galindo omitted or undervalued the points of convergence between the two. In that same area, Flores Galindo was criticised for presenting a supposed 'equidistance' between the Third International and APRA: since he confronted both, Mariátegui would appear, according to this reproach, seeking an intermediate position, equally distant from APRA's reformism and the orthodox Communism of the International. The question of the party – including its character, affiliation, program, and even the name – was also a subject of discussion.[48]

La agonía de Mariátegui is, in a certain sense, the chronicle of a defeat: the party that Mariátegui helped found became something very different and could not 'clearly preserve its irreducible autonomy: to differentiate itself from

---

45 Degregori 2005, p. 3.
46 Franco 1981, p. 56.
47 Lévano 1981, p. 39.
48 Most interventions in this debate are reproduced in the dossier included in the commemorative edition of *La agonía de Mariátegui* (Flores Galindo 2021).

Aprismo without being absorbed by the Communist International'.[49] But leaving it there does not do justice to either Flores Galindo's book, a portrait of Mariátegui in which his life, 'epoch', and oeuvre are beautifully intertwined, or to Mariátegui himself, who fought until the end to make socialism a reality and produced a truly original way of thinking through and about Marxism from the periphery of capitalism.

2 Andean Utopia as History and Memory

Flores Galindo developed the notion of 'Andean utopia' in collaboration with fellow historian Manuel Burga. It emerged in 1978 when the two were discussing millenarianism and messianism in the Andes while working on their respective projects and coauthoring *Apogeo y crisis de la república aristocrática*.[50] Financial support from UNESCO later funded a long-term project on the Andean utopia. In 1982 they coauthored 'The Andean Utopia: Ideology and Peasant Struggle in the Andes, 16th–20th Centuries', and although their collaboration continued, divergent interpretations led to the publication of two different books.[51] Flores Galindo published *Buscando un Inca. Identidad y utopía en los Andes* in 1986, two years before Burga's *Nacimiento de una utopia. Muerte y resurrección en los Andes*.[52]

In Search of an Inca is a sweeping reinterpretation of key developments in Peruvian history covering more than 500 years. In Flores Galindo's view, the relationship between Andean societies and the western world shaped the entire period and articulated Peru's central historical problem. The ways in which Andean people rationalised, coped with, and responded to challenges generated by that encounter are central to his work. Peru's historical and contemporary social, racial, and regional fractures or divisions resulted from an asymmetrical, traumatic, and conflictive relationship between those two worlds. To understand the historical formation of those fissures and contribute to a political project to overcome them, Flores Galindo identified the

---

49 Flores Galindo 1994b, p. 509.
50 Burga 2005, p. 116. An early formulation of some of the ideas connected to 'Andean utopia' appeared in Flores Galindo 1977b. The first time 'Andean utopia' appeared in print was in Flores Galindo 1981a.
51 Burga and Flores Galindo 1982a.
52 As mentioned above, the first edition of Flores Galindo's book was published by Casa de las Américas in Havana (Flores Galindo 1986a). The first edition of Burga's book was published by Instituto de Apoyo Agrario (Burga 1988).

recurrence of the Andean utopia, that is, the idealised depiction of the pre-Hispanic past, especially the Inca Empire, as an era of social justice, harmony, and prosperity. The Andean utopia functioned not only as a discourse about 'the past' but also as the foundation for extremely relevant political and social agendas for the future. Various historical actors imagined the social and political structures of the pre-Hispanic Andean world – or at least what they considered as such – as models for their societies. The ideal society of the future was thus a return to a glorious past. 'A distinctive feature of the Andean utopia', according to Flores Galindo, was that 'the ideal city did not exist outside history or at the remote beginning of time. On the contrary, it was a real historic fact that had a name (Tahuantinsuyo);[53] a ruling class (the Incas); and a capital (Cusco)'.[54]

Flores Galindo found this construction in the writings of the Indigenous chronicler Felipe Guaman Poma de Ayala and mestizo writer Inca Garcilaso de la Vega, in religious practices that resisted Catholic evangelisation, and among the masses who followed Túpac Amaru's call for rebellion in the 1780s. He identified it as a mobilising force behind indigenous and peasant unrest in the 1920s and 1960s and as inspiration for various forms of political discourse and agency in the twentieth century (including Marxism, Aprismo, and others). And he saw it in José María Arguedas's literary expressions of the beauty and tragedy of Andean cultures and in the messianic and authoritarian undertones of the Maoist movement known as Shining Path. He did not postulate equivalency between these constructions, nor did he suggest that the Andean utopia was a rigid and inflexible set of beliefs uniformly appropriated by different historical agents. In fact, he insisted that it was more appropriate to talk about 'Andean utopias', for the plural reflected the contested and wide-ranging nature of these constructions. But he did see in all those formulations instruments with which 'people without hope' (the vanquished, the subaltern, the oppressed) 'challenge[d] a history that condemned them to the margins'.[55]

In Search of an Inca therefore scrutinises history and memory in the pursuit of an understanding of past and contemporary Andean people and culture. It looks at myths, dreams, memories, and imaginaries, but also at the ways in which they informed concrete political projects and actions. No other book had ever attempted such an ambitious interpretive framework to understand Andean societies.

---

53 Tahuantinsuyo is the Quechua name for the Inca empire.
54 Flores Galindo 2010, p. 27.
55 Flores Galindo 2010, p. 247.

Flores Galindo wrote the book not as a scholarly monograph but as a series of connected and independent essays, many of which were first published in journals or collective volumes and later revised for inclusion in this book. The urgency of releasing some of these materials in the context of intense ideological debates and rather dramatic political conditions in Peru explains the peculiar composition of *In Search of an Inca*. But it is also related to the author's following in the steps of many other Peruvian intellectuals and historians – Mariátegui, Jorge Basadre, Pablo Macera, and Raúl Porras Barrenechea, to mention but a few – who made ample use of the essay genre to produce influential works.[56] Flores Galindo's use of the essayist style helps explain the virtues and the shortcomings of this volume. It allowed Flores Galindo the freedom to cover hundreds of years of Peruvian history, combine different methodological traditions (history, ethnography, psychoanalysis, cultural and literary studies), and make ample and creative use of secondary materials. His talent as a historian and writer is displayed in the brilliance of these pages and in the sharpness of his observations about a wide variety of historical topics. As several critics have pointed out, however, the essayist style led to an uneven treatment of the book's many topics and to some flaws in his arguments, as we will see.[57]

3 Intellectual and Methodological Dialogues

The concept of Andean utopia introduced new themes and novel methodologies to Peruvian historical and social scientific circles. Nonetheless, Burga and Flores Galindo built upon and contributed to Peruvian debates of the 1980s or those of the 'Generation of 1968'. In discussions that varied widely in tone and sophistication, the left debated violence, revolution, and the role of the indigenous peasantry in a class society. Flores Galindo participated actively, stressing the need for the Peruvian left to return to Mariátegui's 'heterodox' Marxism. He underlined Mariátegui's sensitivity to religion and culture and his attentiveness to the peculiarities of Peruvian reality, particularly its indigenous majority and pre-Colombian past. Flores Galindo pushed the left to avoid

---

56 Flores Galindo highlighted Mariátegui preference for the essay form: 'Mariátegui was not an essayist by default or because he was unable to develop an alternative approach to national reality. He chose that option early on'. Flores Galindo 1984b, p. 98. This tradition extends to other Latin American countries and has been frequently studied as an important genre with its own intellectual characteristics and narrative strategies. On this, see Weinberg 2002 and 2007.

57 Readers have also noticed a few cases of repetition of certain arguments in different chapters.

dogma and imagine creative possibilities for political action. With its focus on how Andean people and others conceived of or invented the Incas to rethink and change the present, *In Search of an Inca* addressed keystone issues of the left while nudging the debate toward history and questions of identity, the imaginary, and representation. Flores Galindo never abandoned his quest to reinvigorate Marxism and wrest it from the hands of those who saw it as a fundamentalist doctrine rather than a creative tool for interpretation and change. While challenging Eurocentrism, he sought to use Marxism and other theoretical schools of thought to interpret and transform Peru.

Flores Galindo's opening to interdisciplinary research, editorship of *Allpanchis* (1978–82), and long-standing position on the editorial board of *Revista Andina* – journals based in the highland city of Cusco – put him in close contact with anthropological and ethnohistorical studies of the Andes. He was convinced of the need to overcome the unfortunate divide between Lima and the provinces and between anthropologists and historians. *In Search of an Inca* reflects Flores Galindo's familiarity with scholarship on the Quechua language, rituals, archaeology, and the precolonial period, topics that most Lima historians in this period did not study. At the same time, Flores Galindo sharply criticised the tendency – common among some ethnohistorians and anthropologists – to think of Andean societies and people as homogenous, frozen in time, and trapped in the mental structures of 'Andean thought'. In the introduction to this book and in several other works, he chastised some scholars for wanting to put Andean people into an 'impossible museum'.[58]

Flores Galindo did not just build on and recast Peruvian and Andean debates. He also incorporated readings and discussions on memory, utopianism, tradition, and modernity, making his own contributions to each. In doing so, he borrowed from a wide array of authors, intellectual traditions, and academic fields and called upon an eclectic selection of readings to develop his arguments. Besides the *Annales* school, innovative cultural historians such as Italian Carlo Ginzburg, unconventional Marxist thinkers such as Benjamin, and rediscovered authors such as Russian philosopher and semiotician Mikhael Bakhtin (1895–1975) were especially important. The Italian thinker Gramsci (1891–1937) proved influential, particularly as Flores Galindo explored Mariátegui, a Gramsci contemporary with whom he shared a similar unorthodox reading of Marxism and tragic life. *Mentalités* studies and the work of English Marxist historians and other members of the New Left also were part of his intellectual repertoire. Flores Galindo built on E.P. Thompson to refine

---

58   Flores Galindo 2010, p. 2.

views on Andean uprisings, particularly Thompson's critique of interpretations of peasant outbreaks as mere 'spasmodic' reactions to material woes. He clearly appreciated Thompson's able pen, political engagement, and effort to create culturalist definitions of class.[59] Studies on popular ideologies by historians Christopher Hill, Eric Hobsbawm, and George Rudé were also influential.

Writing *In Search of an Inca* in the early and mid-1980s brought Flores Galindo into contact with many of the same subjects as Cultural Studies and Subaltern Studies, two schools of thought then in gestation. His attention to lower-class agency; the cultural dimensions of subaltern experiences; and societal forms of consent, control, and cultural domination paralleled the work of cultural critics such as Stuart Hall, Dick Hebdige, and Paul Gilroy. Flores Galindo was familiar with some of them – through Spanish or French translations – but his work betrayed a confluence of approaches and styles more than a Cultural Studies or Subaltern Studies 'influence'. Ranajit Guha published *Elementary Aspects of Peasant Insurgency in Colonial India* in 1983, and *Selected Subaltern Studies*, edited by Guha and Gayatri Chakravorty Spivak, appeared in 1988.[60] They were not widely read in Peru or elsewhere when Flores Galindo was drafting his ideas and were not translated into Spanish until the 1990s.[61] Readers familiar with these and other authors will recognise that Flores Galindo also questioned and reworked Marxism and other western narratives and sought alternative voices, discourses, and paths. Like Guha, Chatterjee, Chakrabarty, and others, Flores Galindo read colonial documentation against the grain to counter conventional interpretations of the Conquest and the 'defeat' of indigenous people. He also looked beyond the traditional notion of the archive, incorporating oral traditions, contemporary rituals, and other sources.

4   The Andean Utopia under Debate

When Flores Galindo published the first edition of *In Search of an Inca*, he already enjoyed prestige in Peru and, to a certain extent, in academic circles in Spain, France, and the United States. *In Search of an Inca* consolidated his

---

59   See Flores Galindo 1982a for a brief appraisal of Thompson's historiographical and political contributions.
60   Guha 1983, Guha and Spivak, 1988.
61   The first Spanish translation of some of Guha's and his collaborators' work was Rivera Cusicanqui and Barragán 1997.

reputation, especially after he won the prestigious Cuban Casa de las Américas Essay Prize in 1986 and (posthumously) the Clarence Haring Prize in 1991 from the American Historical Association.[62] The book has nine Spanish-language editions (seven in Peru, one in Cuba, and one in Mexico) as well as Italian and English translations.[63]

Reviewers in Peru and elsewhere have lauded *In Search of an Inca* for its originality, breadth, importance, and style. They applauded Flores Galindo's search for utopias in the plural and his broad notion of messianic, millenarian, and other counter-hegemonic movements. Although this ample interpretation of Andean utopias made writing (and reading) *In Search of an Inca* more challenging, it allowed him to explore a variety of uses and inventions of the Incas and avoid a restrictive definition that overlooked the creative and heterogeneous invocation of the pre-Colombian past.[64]

In Search of an Inca had a great impact in Peru, and virtually every Peruvian intellectual considers it to be one of the essential books, if not *the* essential book, on Peru in recent decades. Nelson Manrique, a historian and close friend of Flores Galindo, cited its 'surprising reception' in terms of the passion it provoked and the 'amplitude' of the debate it prompted.[65] In a review of key works of Peruvian historiography and sociology since the 1960s, Sinesio López – after calling Flores Galindo 'the greatest historian of the 1970s generation' as well as 'the historian of the vanquished' – praised *In Search of an Inca* as 'the most serious attempt' at understanding Andean world dynamics through the study of 'internal social and political changes and the enormous repertoire of its cultural imaginary, which gave it its unity and identity'.[66] Peruvian sociologist Gonzalo Portocarrero called Flores Galindo's work on Andean utopia 'an intellectual tour de force' that built upon and continued earlier contributions by Mariátegui and Arguedas.[67]

Not surprisingly, the book generated intense debates even among intellectuals close to Flores Galindo's own political and academic circles. Much of the criticism targeted his treatment of the most recent periods in Peruvian history. Anthropologist Carlos Iván Degregori, for instance, contended that the argument lost power as it moved into the twentieth century. According

---

62   This is a prize awarded to the 'Latin American author who has written what is considered the best book in Latin American history in the previous five years'.
63   For details on the different editions of the book, see Chapter 3, pp. 71–2.
64   Chocano 2001, Cáceres Valdivia 2000.
65   Manrique 1986–88, p. 202.
66   López 2009, pp. 8–10.
67   Portocarrero 2005.

to Degregori, Flores Galindo found few examples of the Andean utopia in recent decades, specifically after the weakening of the peasant movement in the 1960s. Degregori faulted his characterisation of tradition and modernity as polar opposites and his failure to understand how vast societal changes since the 1960s, with the spread of technology, modern media, and markets, affected or weakened 'the search for an Inca'.[68] In contrast, anthropologist Henrique Urbano questioned his understanding of the early colonial period. Ever critical, Urbano censured Flores Galindo for overlooking the European roots of Andean messianism, which led to a misunderstanding of key figures such as Guaman Poma and Garcilaso de la Vega, and for an overly capacious definition of utopia. On this latter point, Urbano argued that if any idealisation of the past is utopianism, then virtually every author in early modern Europe created utopias.[69] Manrique questioned Flores Galindo's evidence for the 'pan-Andean' nature of the Andean utopia and argued for a more geographically restricted understanding. In addition, Manrique found that after the Túpac Amaru rebellion, which he describes as the 'apotheosis' of the Andean utopia, its traces are more difficult to document.[70]

The political undertones of the book also generated heated discussions. Flores Galindo vehemently denied promoting the Andean utopia for socialist or neo-indigenista projects. He noted its limitations as a foundation for transformative alternatives and underlined the authoritarian impulses behind some of its variants. Although he clearly sympathised with some of the people who embraced the Andean utopia, he recognised that it could not sustain an alternative project for contemporary Peru: 'It should be clear, therefore, that we are not advocating the Andean utopia. History should liberate us from the past, not seal us off – as [Aníbal] Quijano argued – within 'longue durée' prisons of ideas'.[71] Thus, despite the title, *In Search of an Inca* pushed social scientists, intellectuals, and readers to abandon the pursuit of a pristine Inca past, its remnants in the present, or a project for the future inspired by its traces. Instead, they should explore the creative appropriation, re-creation, and synthesis of the multiple cultural influences that make up Andean societies. It was time to stop searching for an Inca, Flores Galindo asserted, and to embrace instead

---

68 Degregori 2005, p. 4. The differing views of Flores Galindo and Degregori are discussed in greater detail in chapter 5.
69 Urbano 1982, pp. 48–52. See also Urbano 1986.
70 Manrique 1986–88, pp. 205, 207. In a commentary written in 1988, Flores Galindo concurred with these observations. See Flores Galindo 1988a.
71 Flores Galindo 2010, p. 248.

'modern socialism', the only way to channel passions and dreams toward the construction of a better future.[72]

Indeed, Flores Galindo never retreated from his socialist convictions. At a time when the left was in crisis and many leftist intellectuals were abandoning socialism, he remained stubbornly loyal to the ideals that inspired him and his generation two decades before. 'I continue to believe that the ideals that gave rise to socialism – justice, freedom, humanity – are still alive', he stated in his final intellectual manifesto. But socialism, he warned, had a future only 'if we are capable of rethinking it and imagining it with new contents'. For him, socialism should not be confined to just one path, one already traced; echoing Mariátegui, he saw socialism as 'a challenge to creativity' ('un desafío para la creatividad'). In addition – and here the influence of thinkers such as Thompson is clear – socialism meant forging 'a new morality and new values'. He questioned intellectuals and militants who had lost their capacity to 'feel the indignation' ('sentir la indignación') when confronted with the injustices of capitalism or the violence of authoritarian solutions such as Shining Path.[73] Many pages of *In Search of an Inca*, especially in the later chapters, can be read as an enraged indictment of the fallacies of Peruvian democracy, the various forms of social and racial discrimination inflicted upon the most vulnerable sectors of Peruvian society, and the egregious violations of human rights committed in the name of counterterrorism efforts.

Was Flores Galindo a utopian thinker? No doubt. He founded his entire intellectual project on the pursuit of a utopia – not the Andean utopia but a socialist one. That was his lifelong project. As anthropologist Nancy Postero has written, 'If we think of utopia as a consciously constructed political vision for the future, rather than a fruitless return to a fictitious past, then perhaps utopias are just what are needed in the Andes'.[74] Flores Galindo would have agreed.

---

72   His views are clearly stated in Flores Galindo 1989a and 1989b.
73   The quotes are taken from his farewell letter, Flores Galindo 1989f.
74   Postero 2007, p. 21.

CHAPTER 2

'More Than One Alternative': Alberto Flores Galindo and Peru's War of Independence

Charles Walker

> Leaving behind determinisms, we are inclined to think that in the past as well as in the present, there is always more than one alternative.
> ALBERTO FLORES GALINDO[1]

∴

> History does not work for predicting the future, but it does help pose uncomfortable questions.
> ALBERTO FLORES GALINDO[2]

∴

Peru's independence from Spain in the 1820s has been the subject of intense debate for the last two hundred years. For some, it marked the glorious launching of the nation state and deserves wholesale commemoration and celebration, while for others it was a lost opportunity, when continuity rather than change dominated. Two sets of concerns fuelled these polemics: the war of independence itself (platforms, leaders, participants, and results) and broader, persistent questions such as the place of Indigenous peoples within the Peruvian nation, the authoritarian nature of the emerging political system, and the possibilities and challenges of building a democratic and inclusive society. Alberto Flores Galindo addressed many of these questions and, as he did in most of his historical work, connected them to burning contemporary issues.

---

1 Flores Galindo 1987b, I, p. 15.
2 Flores Galindo 1985a, p. 39.

A new project has led me to read or reread the historical work on Peru's transition from colony to republic, the period from 1780 to the 1840s. I am not particularly impressed by the more recent work. Although Peru's bicentennial in 2021 (or 2024 as some contend) shifted attention (yet little research resources) towards the period, the production has been characterised by the rather traditional search for nationalist heroes and gap-filling studies on specific institutions, periods, or towns and cities. In the last quarter century, no single monograph has been published that rethought the period or transformed the field. When I am asked for recent 'must reads', I struggle to answer.[3]

Peruvian or Peruvianist independence-era historiography pales when compared to that of Argentina and Colombia, where historians have prompted a major rethinking of the concept of the nation and traditional chronology. They continue to enrich enduring debates about the significance of the wars of independence and the role of the lower classes in these struggles, while also incorporating new perspectives on space and geography as well as gender and history from below. In addition, many of the best social historians in these countries, taking advantage of the rise in interest with the bicentennials, have written accessible yet deep books for a broad public, beyond specialists. The interest in reaching a broader audience has not sacrificed quality.[4]

In Peru in the last couple decades, no book has been published that has reshaped our understanding of the period as did works by Heraclio Bonilla and Karen Spalding, Scarlett O'Phelan Godoy, and, as will be argued here, Flores Galindo in the 1970s and 1980s.[5] Nor have we seen the vibrant debates in the press that marked these decades, particularly following the publication of

---

3 I disagree with the statement by the editors of one of the best volumes of recent work, Manuel Chust and Claudia Rosas, who sustain that 'It is notorious and notable that there is a potent Peruvian and Peruvianist historiography on independence, particularly in recent decades. It can be proven. Furthermore, it stands out for its excellence'. Their book includes some strong and much-needed work on regional history (i.e. non-Lima) and is without a doubt an important contribution. Nonetheless, this and other recent work have not prompted far-reaching debates; no single monograph has been published that, in my mind, changes the field. Chust and Rosas 2017, p. 11.
4 For some primary examples, Di Meglio 2016, Fradkin 2015, Fradkin and Gelman 2015, Goldman 2016, Wasserman 2011. For an excellent sample of the work on Colombia, see Echeverri, Ortega, and Straka 2018.
5 Bonilla 1972. A second edition, published in 1981, did not have the original 'Presentación' by Heraclio Bonilla and José Matos Mar but instead a shorter one by Matos Mar. It also added a new and long essay by Bonilla (Bonilla 1981). The other book that I believe radically changed our understanding of the period, is O'Phelan Godoy 1985.

Bonilla's edited volume in 1972.[6] Over fifty years later, this book, a razor-sharp critique of nationalist interpretations that whitewashed class and regional divisions, still casts an enormous shadow on independence studies in Peru and all historiographical discussions return to it.[7]

In a highly critical or even caustic 1988 review of Peruvian historiography, Flores Galindo highlighted this inability to develop new approaches to the wars of independence. He condemned conservative historians for their obsession with Spain and blindness to other cultural traditions while also critiquing 'new social history' for its inability to develop novel lines of analysis and to foster necessary debates. He criticised the interpretations of generations of scholars, with unusual bluntness, particularly for a junior scholar. I contend that this absence of innovative studies has continued in the more than three decades since Flores Galindo published it. His work suggests some promising alternative paths.[8]

Perhaps many good historians in Peru have steered clear of the Independence period due to the nationalist trap, the seeming inevitability of tired debates about 'conceded Independence', or, worse, the search for heroes and heroines. The history of the independence period can go hand in hand with patriotic history, which is inevitably bad history, and so arguably some historians stay away. We also need to consider the lack of research support. Despite the bicentennial campaign or campaigns, (seen in the existence of multiple commissions), there is no funding initiative for archival research and the situation of the archives in Lima and beyond is lamentable. The explanations for the lack of new studies and new perspectives are numerous, and require further analysis, but the bicentennial has not prompted a resurgence of rigorous work.

I argue in this essay that the work of Alberto Flores Galindo on the wars of independence deserves a much greater presence than it has now, more than three decades after his death. I am surprised to see how often he is not cited in articles and books on the independence period, including topics that he made his own. There seems to have been a near systematic discrediting of his

---

6 Bonilla 1972. For the uproar about this book, see Contreras 2007, Morán 2007, Loayza Pérez 2016.

7 For example, the entire first half of a 2015 edited volume on Independence edited by Carlos Contreras and Luis Miguel Glave dealt with the debate about the 'conceded independence' from Bonilla and Spalding 1972 and O'Phelan Godoy 1984. The other essays contribute to well-known debates ranging from the rupture with Spain to the southern Andean uprisings from 1808–1815. Contreras and Glave 2015.

8 Flores Galindo 1988b. This work, for example, is not cited in the historiographical introduction to Contreras and Glave 2015 or in Chust and Rosas 2017.

concept of an Andean utopia. Few historians have followed his leads. At this point, however, of disenchantment with the intellectual harvest of the bicentennial and pessimism about the emergence of novel approaches and serious discussions, a return to several of Flores Galindo's key ideas and methodological insights is particularly promising if not downright urgent.[9]

1   Searching for New Paths

Institutional history or studies that analyse a specific person, institution, or place in a short period predominate in the recent historiography. These are, of course, valuable. Flores Galindo himself was a master of resurrecting a highly empirical article from traditional journals such as *Histórica* or *Boletín del Instituto Riva-Agüero* to fortify one of his own arguments, often very different than that of the article's author. Nonetheless, this more descriptive and institutional approach needs to be accompanied by broader arguments about the substance and significance of the wars of independence. This has not been the case – despite numerous edited volumes and historiographical essays – as no question or polemic has caught the attention of scholars and prompted a sustained debate in the last two decades or so.[10]

Some of the best studies in recent decades have followed the culturalist insights of François-Xavier Guerra, who examined the press, rituals, and political culture.[11] But Guerra downplayed the role of insurgency in Spanish America (and social history in general), focusing instead on changes in Europe, particularly in political structures and mentalities. Many scholars have questioned this interpretation, underlining the power and diversity of lower-class politics in the Americas.[12] Other historians have taken a trans-Atlantic approach, stressing the importance of the Córtes de Cádiz or how changes in Spain affected Peru.[13] We count on valuable and accomplished studies, but none have prompted debate and a broad rethinking of the period. This is perhaps not as much

---

9   My view about the pessimism is admittedly subjective. It is based on conversations with many historians and my own perception.
10 Contreras and Glave 2015, Chust and Rosas 2017. For a strong historiographical evaluation, see Sobrevilla Perea 2015a. For another keen historiographical essay, see Drinot 2004.
11 A good starting point for Guerra's vast work is Guerra 1992. For an incisive evaluation of change and continuity in political cultures that deserves greater attention, see Peralta Ruiz 2010. On the press, see Morán 2013, Huerta Vera 2019; on rituals, Ortemberg 2014.
12 Di Meglio 2021.
13 For insightful work with trans-Atlantic approaches, see Peralta Ruiz 2002, Sobrevilla Perea 2015b, Martínez Riaza 2018.

a reflection of the scholarship but instead the absence of forums to debate. In Lima and elsewhere, fewer and fewer reviews appear, and colloquiums, conferences, and round tables rarely lead to deep discussion.

My main criticism, one linked to my understanding of the need to return to Flores Galindo, is that our vision of the war of independence in Peru remains far too teleological, with the foci and analysis shaped by the defeat of the Spanish and the implementation of a republic. In chronological terms, there is too much attention on the latter, coastal phase (1818–24), when José de San Martín and Simón Bolívar led the struggle against the Spanish. In the previous decade, southern Peru and the Andes had witnessed fascinating uprisings against Spanish control. These earlier uprisings and social movements have been cast as mere precedents, curious, perhaps even intriguing, but ultimately insignificant. I contend (along with many colleagues) that earlier uprisings in Tacna (1811), Huánuco (1812), and Cusco (1814–15), among many others, provide tantalising insights into questions that are at the heart of the fundamental arguments about the wars of independence throughout Spanish America: the reception of the whirlwind changes in Europe; the broad arsenal of counter-hegemonic ideologies; the challenging creation of fragile alliances and their breakdown because of both internal dissent and repression; and the search for ties with Río de la Plata, Chile, and beyond. The rich cases of Tacna, Cusco, and Huánuco as well as other mutinies, conspiracies, and uprisings also help understand subsequent 'regional' movements that struggled against Lima centralism and presented a different understanding of Peru and its political organisation. Furthermore, these earlier social movements constitute fascinating and often tragic stories in themselves and deserve to find a new generation of historians.[14]

It is not just a matter of chronology and geography – an exaggerated focus on the later 'coastal' and central Sierra phase – but also one of ideology or platform. Historians (and I include myself) too often fall into the assumption that republicanism was inevitable. We need to examine the Andean utopia, federalism, and the various strains of royalism that rose, declined, yet persisted from 1805–1824 and beyond. This, to me, is the great fault of teleological history – a focus on the latter period and what developed into what Basadre deemed the 'minor caudillos', the assortment of strongmen who ran the countries for decades after independence, without discussing what could have been.[15] This is

---

14 Of course, there are many but insufficient exceptions of important studies on these alternatives. On Cusco, see Najarro 2017; on the 1814 uprising, Colectivo por el Bicentenario de la Revolución del Cusco 2015 and 2016; on the Iquichanos, Méndez 2005; on Huánuco, Bazán Díaz 2017. Chust and Rosas 2017 has numerous other relevant essays.
15 Basadre 1990, p. 20.

not simply counter-factual history – all of these strains (regionalism and forms of anti-centralism as well as the alternative models such as the invocation of the Incas) continued to weigh heavily on political currents in the decades after independence. Failed or defeated projects often have a long afterlife, appearing and reappearing in phantasmagorical fashion.

I contend that while we count on valuable studies since the 1980s – and I would put the Chust and Rosas book as an example – we must go back to that decade to find new approaches and broad debates. As every historiographical essay notes, the Bonilla-Spalding bombshell in 1972, when they lambasted the Velasco Alvarado regime's nationalist interpretation of the sesquicentennial celebrations, prompted a variety of actions and responses from leading figures, including Jorge Basadre, Pablo Macera, Scarlett O'Phelan Godoy, and others.[16] Newspapers and cultural supplements such as *El Caballo Rojo* and (after 1981) *La República* published articles by historians as well as interviews.[17] I hope this is not simply nostalgia on my part, a wistful look back at a time when historians were important public intellectuals and history had a decisive role in debates. This is no longer true in Peru. So perhaps this is the central question – how can we improve the level of *debate* (not commemorations) about the wars of independence and move beyond the *bicentenario*, a somewhat anxious episode (made worse by COVID and political instability in Peru) of flag waving, infinite conferences, and unexceptional books? I believe that Flores Galindo provides important clues and suggestions in this regard.

2   Túpac Amaru

Flores Galindo lived in France from 1972 to 1974 studying for his doctorate at the École pratique des hautes études in Paris. He planned to write his thesis on the Túpac Amaru rebellion under the supervision of Pierre Vilar. On 31 January 1974, he wrote to his friend Manuel Burga that 'I'm beginning to become fond of my topic, the Túpac Amaru uprising'.[18] In numerous letters to Burga, he described his progress, noting, for example, his plan to have a 'prolonged stay in Cusco'.[19] The Velasco regime (1968–75) had prompted a boom in Túpac

---

16   For a typically pithy overview, Flores Galindo 1987c, especially pp. 13–14. For further essays, see Bonilla 2007.
17   I want to thank Ricardo Portocarrero for sharing the list he put together of conversations and interviews.
18   Burga 2010, p. 41.
19   Burga 2010, p. 89.

Amaru studies, including the publication of the invaluable *Colección Documental de la Independencia del Perú* (CDIP), whose four tomes on the rebellion appeared in 1971.[20] In 1973 and 1974, Flores Galindo conducted research in the Archivo de Indias in Sevilla and Spain's National Library, essential repositories on the uprising. In 1975, he published in a mimeographed text, *El carácter de la sublevación de Túpac Amaru: algunas aproximaciones*.[21] However, he returned to Peru and did not finish his thesis until 1984, changing topics and advisors. Instead of the 1780 rebellion with Pierre Vilar, he wrote the basis of his landmark book, *Aristocracia y plebe: Lima, 1760–1830*, with Ruggiero Romano as his advisor. This did not mean that he lost interest in Túpac Amaru. Quite the opposite.

Flores Galindo published more than twenty texts on Túpac Amaru.[22] The progression of these publications followed the pattern described by Carlos Aguirre in Chapter 3 of this book: a preliminary note often based on a talk developed in a subsequent text or a published interview and then formalised in a longer, more rigorous article. For example, his 1982 article, 'Independencia y clases sociales', was first published in *Debates en Sociología*.[23] Briefer versions would appear in *El Caballo Rojo* and *El Diario de Marka* and several years later in the valuable two-volume book that he would edit, *Independencia y revolución, 1780–1840*.[24] In 1976 he edited *Túpac Amaru II-1780. Antología* that included essays by leading scholars, Peruvian and foreign (American, Argentine, English, and Polish-Israeli), well-known (John Rowe and John Fisher) and junior (Scarlett O'Phelan Godoy, Lorenzo Huertas, and Flores Galindo himself). He opened the book with a characteristically pithy paragraph:

> After having been a relegated and uncomfortable character for official historiography, Túpac Amaru is now undeniably at the forefront. His image is repeatedly found in newspapers, magazines, posters, paintings, movies, etc. He has now apparently become a familiar character.[25]

Flores Galindo shaped our understanding of the Túpac Amaru rebellion in numerous ways. Appreciating how different periods fit together or related

---

20 On Túpac Amaru, Velasco, and the *Colección Documental de la Independencia del Perú*, see Aguirre 2017a and Walker 2017.
21 Flores Galindo 1975.
22 In her bibliographical account, Lucila Valderrama lists twenty texts. There are more. Valderrama 2004, p. 102.
23 Flores Galindo 1982f.
24 See note by editor Maruja Martínez in Flores Galindo 1997, p. 419.
25 Flores Galindo 1976a, p. 8. Other authors include Oscar Cornblit, Jan Szeminski, and Emilio Choy. The cover was by the eminent artist Jesús Ruiz Durand.

to one another was important to him, particularly in his consistent quest to challenge traditional history. He sought to assure that the uprising had a central place in national discussions about independence and the nation, debates that raged in the 1970s. He placed the rebellion within the cycle of uprisings that occurred in the eighteenth century in the Andes, studied by Scarlett O'Phelan Godoy.[26] He deemed it the 'culmination' of this long cycle.[27] At the same time, he stressed that the rebellion should be considered part of Peru's wars of independence, even though it had a radically different agenda and social base. He repeatedly objected to the interpretation of Túpac Amaru as a *precursor*, not wanting the rebellion to take a secondary role as a failed beginning or mere antecedent. Instead, he stressed that the rebellion took place in a radically different context – the world changed mightily from 1780 to 1808 – and had a different character and platforms than what emerged decades later. He firmly understood that Peru had many paths in the Age of Revolution – a period he understood well – and that mass uprisings such as Túpac Amaru brought to the fore alternatives that while not victorious in 1821 (Andean utopia, Cusco as the capital), weighed heavily on Peru for decades if not centuries. Peru's recent bicentennial has revived the question of the relationship between Túpac Amaru and the wars of independence. Flores Galindo still provides the best response.

Moreover, Flores Galindo also sought to compare Túpac Amaru with other revolutions, without falling into black and white reductionisms. He debated the Hungarian historian Adam Anderle on this point in 1981, questioning whether the Andean uprising was merely a bourgeois revolution. He noted that perhaps it should be considered an early revolution as portrayed by Federico Engels in reference to the German Peasant Wars (1525). Even here, he noted the danger of falling into anachronisms.[28] On the other hand, he no doubt despaired at the assertion by Bonilla and Matos Mar about Peru's war of independence, that 'unlike the authentic Atlantic bourgeois revolutions of the eighteenth and nineteenth centuries, Peru's independence was just a military and political act, leaving the very structures of the colonial system intact'.[29] Flores Galindo did not believe in the notion of 'authentic revolutions' (i.e. European), nor that

---

26 OPhelan Godoy 1985. In a footnote in his text in his edited volume on Túpac Amaru, Flores Galindo noted that advising O'Phelan Godoy's BA thesis rekindled his interest in the rebel leader. Flores Galindo 1976a, p. 315.
27 Flores Galindo 2010, p. 80.
28 See his conversation with the Hungarian historian Adam Anderle, in López Soria 1982. He refers to Friedrich Engels, *The Peasant War in Germany*.
29 Bonilla and Matos Mar 1972, p. 11.

independence was merely a limited military action that prompted little change beyond a political rupture with Spain. He sought to place Túpac Amaru at the centre of national discussions about the creation of modern Peru, without sacrificing it to reductionisms or simplifications.

Flores Galindo's contributions to our understanding of Túpac Amaru moved far beyond chronology or his contextualisation of it within a long arc of sedition and utopianism. His articles stressed the movement's complexities and internal tensions. In his 1976 introduction to *Túpac Amaru-II*, he called for studies on rebels' social composition and ideology as well as the regional situation or *coyuntura*. He would develop all three of these points in his two essays on Túpac Amaru included in his *In Search of an Inca*, 'The Túpac Amaru Revolution and the Andean People' and 'Govern the World, Disrupt the World'. In terms of social base, he underlined in both texts the heterogeneity of the campesinos who backed the uprising and the tensions with the leadership. For example, he explored the people of two provinces that served as the base of the rebellion, Canas y Canchis and Quispicanchi. In brief but suggestive paragraphs, he examined their identity as comuneros or members of an Andean community and their place within late colonial social and economic structures. He built off secondary literature, also mining the *Colección Documental de la Independencia del Perú* and his research at the Archivo de Indias in Sevilla. In his work on insurgency and rebellion, from Juan Santos Atahualpa to the early twentieth-century peasant movements, Flores Galindo never fell into class reductionism. He stressed the complexities of class and ethnic identities in Peru, seeking not to reduce a specific group into a proxy of an abstract social class. He used his research and writing abilities to flesh out individuals to show tendencies and contradictions.

In 'The Túpac Amaru Revolution', he never moves too far from the question of the rebellion's internal tensions: 'two coexisting forces ... ended up clashing'.[30] He underlines the growing divisions between the leadership and the masses, their divergent projects, and brings up Túpac Amaru's deep Catholicism and the potential contradiction this prompted, with the need for revolutions to confront and rupture power relations. He stressed the multiple strains of thought that Túpac Amaru, Micaela Bastidas, and other leaders wove together, their search for a platform. In a 1981 conversation with Manuel Burga and Jan Szeminski, he contended, 'There is a peculiar mix there of the Andean with the western that was definitively an impossible combination to pull off, conflictive. In the end, perhaps the explanation for the defeat of the Túpac

---

30 Flores Galindo 2010, p. 104.

Amaru movement can be found within this internal tension'.[31] His interest in the Túpac Amaru era nourished his interest in the Andean utopia. In *In Search of an Inca*, he discussed Andean apocalyptic thought and the concept of Pachacuti (the world turned upside down, after which harmony and order would be restored). He did not limit himself to the question of their arsenal of ideas but also examined the qualitative nature of the violence – who was killed, in the name of who, and how. In this essay, he addressed the essential questions within the uprising: internal divisions, its heterodox ideology or platform, and the brutal violence.

The next essay in *In Search of an Inca*, 'Govern the World', fulfils his earlier call to contextualise. Here his erudition and intellectual versatility is evident: he looks at changes over time in Cusco and the Andean south as well as within trans-Atlantic cycles and within capitalism. Not all the arguments are fully developed, and the essay maintains the tone of an exploratory talk. Nonetheless, it places the Túpac Amaru rebellion within broader currents, while also developing the question of why it spread so quickly but also failed to defeat Spanish colonialism. Although many of these ideas were more hypotheses or leads rather than fully fleshed out ideas backed by archival research, scholars of the Túpac Amaru rebellion like me owe him an immense gratitude for these clues.[32]

3   Aristocracy, the Plebe, and Historians

In 1984, Flores Galindo published what for many is his most accomplished book, *Aristocracia y plebe*.[33] Rereading it I was struck by Flores Galindo's incredible versatility and the extreme ambition of his book. The book emerged out of his PhD thesis at the École des hautes études en sciences sociales, under the Italian historian Ruggiero Romano. The influence of Romano and the *Annales* school can be seen in his attention to enduring structural processes and the material base of Peru's dominant class, Lima's aristocracy. He scrutinises the wheat economy, underlining the opportunities but also dangers of the Chilean market and production, while also exploring sugar plantations. He moved beyond export statistics and Merchant Guild (*Consulado*) politics to examine labour, particularly slavery. This is excellent economic history. Yet the book is much more than a brilliant analysis of the rise and eventual fall of the Lima merchant class, their inability to create their own project.

---

31   Szeminski, Flores Galindo, and Burga 1981, p. 11.
32   He continued this fascination with historiography and Túpac Amaru until the end. See Flores Galindo 1989c and 1989d.
33   Flores Galindo 1984a.

Flores Galindo delves into ideologies and class anxieties, probing the Lima's elite dread of lower-class insurgency. *Aristocracia y plebe* is also a cultural history of Lima, touching on topics such as architecture, public space, and municipal power. Furthermore, the author studies groups that had been largely overlooked by traditional history or Marxist-influenced studies that used conventional class categories, moving from the urban plebe, the heart of this study, to Indian fishing villages. You could apply other historiographical categories to define *Aristocracia y plebe*. For example, the analysis of the July 1821 riots (that are much more than anti-Spanish efforts) constitutes rich micro-history.[34] Furthermore, his attention to Lima's built environment and the production for its consumption approaches environmental history, a non-existent field in Peru in the 1980s. In the end, I struggle to find a type of history not employed by Flores Galindo (gender analysis is present), while he also builds on other disciplines – archaeology, anthropology, and literary criticism appear in his footnotes.

But how could a rereading of *Aristocracia y plebe* help us rethink the independence period? I will focus on two categories, resistance and the upper classes. Flores Galindo provided us a stunningly rich portrait of slaves, maroons, plebeians, and common men (and some women) who revolted against exploitative labour conditions and contested the disciplinary zeal of the late colonial period. In the words of Magdalena Chocano, 'A central concern in the work of Flores Galindo is to unravel the history of the lower classes. For him, 'el pueblo', as they were called back then, was not an abstract category but an analytical universe, a possibility for new and multifaced perspectives'.[35] In the initial paragraphs of the first chapter, he presents a sophisticated and important definition of social class, clearly built around the work of E.P. Thompson, cited at the end: 'Every class is a specific manner of expressing the social whole, where internal factors matter as much as the oppositional relations and complementarity with other groups. In other words, social class is above all else a temporal reality "defined by men as they live their own history"'.[36]

Some of the groups that made up *la plebe* would in some cases support the war of independence insurgency but not always and under their own terms; they cannot be subsumed as mere 'lower-class independence fighters'. Building

---

[34] He does not cite Carlo Ginzburg in *Aristocracia y plebe* but he was familiar with his work, particularly *The Cheese and the Worms*, which he cites in other writings.

[35] Chocano 2001, p. 8. Sinesio López deemed Flores Galindo 'the historian of the oppressed'. López 2005, p. 2.

[36] Flores Galindo 1984a, p. 16. The quote is from Thompson 1964, p. 11. On Flores Galindo and Thompson, see Aguirre 2005a and Cáceres Valdivia 1993. Several articles that discuss Thompson's influence in Latin American social history were included in a dossier to commemorate his 100th birthday. See https://lehmt.org/thompson-at-100-dossier/.

on and contributing to the rich line of work on popular classes and independence across Spanish America, Flores Galindo argued that these groups could only be understood in their own context, their material conditions and comprehension of the events of 1808–1824 and beyond. As Flores Galindo showed here and elsewhere, political coalitions required cross-class and multi-ethnic coordination, efforts which proved fraught and fragile in a viceroyalty as hierarchical and fragmented as Peru. He underlined the lack of cohesion among the 'aristocracy', as a class and as the ultimately failed creator of a political project. Therefore, he stressed the autonomy of the plebe, illuminating their range of political activities; their agendas and ideologies; and their ultimate inability to form the base of a larger social movement. In a notable synthesis of decades of work on the lower classes and politics, Gabriel Di Meglio noted how Flores Galindo underlined 'the structural impossibility of Lima's plebe, due to their heterogeneity, to move beyond their challenge to the system and propose an alternative'.[37]

Flores Galindo cautioned us that 'Independence – in Lima or outside of the city – was not a social or popular revolution, but this does not oblige us to overlook the intervention of the popular classes or, even less, to deny changes'.[38] He clearly disagreed with the assertion by Bonilla and Matos Mar in 1972 that 'furthermore, the lower classes were absent because in the independence process the interests that could incorporate them were not brought into play'. Nor did he believe that 'Indians, blacks, and mestizos fought indistinctly for the patriot and royalist armies'.[39] In *Aristocracia y plebe* and other publications, he sought to put the lower classes at the forefront of the analysis but without forcing them into politically charged anachronisms or falsehood. He was fighting here against various reductionisms, from the left and the right. He rejected Marxism that understood class as a formula rather than a relationship, or those writers who sought revolutions and not *reformas* and thus dismissed the complex world of subaltern politics.

On the other hand, Flores Galindo was very critical of traditional history, which focused on Peru's European roots and paid scant attention to its diverse multicultural and multilingual populations or to the lower classes. For example, in his 1988 historiographical essay, after lauding Guillermo Lohmann's erudition and incessant archive work, Flores Galindo notes how he 'ignored the Indigenous presence and even at times assumed the language (his prose is

---

37 Di Meglio 2021, p. 237.
38 Flores Galindo 1984b, p. 227.
39 Bonilla and Matos Mar 1972, pp. 11, 10. As noted, this short introduction was not included in the 1981 edition.

plagued with archaisms) and the attitude of colonial authorities (paragraphs disparaging Indians and even with disdain for Jews jump out of his texts)'.[40] He reviews the work of other conservative historians, summarising their project as inscribing Perú 'in the western and Christian tradition which subordinated Indians'.[41] In terms of the wars of independence, the conservative approach stressed the unity of Peruvian forces, reducing popular participation to guerrillas or montoneros that lacked any autonomous project, with only a short-term impact if any.[42]

Aristocracia y plebe as well as his essay on *montoneros y guerrillas* in *In Search of an Inca* no doubt influenced the work of many people. Without Flores Galindo's enthusiastic guidance, I would not have worked on banditry and politics on the coast and Carlos Aguirre and I would not have published *Bandoleros, abigeos y montoneros*.[43] Flores Galindo's influence can be seen in the scholarship of Carlos Aguirre and Maribel Arrelucea on slave resistance and of the former on domestic servitude and prisons.[44] Jesús Cosamalón's book on Lima's Indian population dialogued critically with *Aristocracia y plebe* while the edited volume by Aldo Panfichi and Felipe Portocarrero, *Mundos interiores, Lima 1850–1950*, although on a later period, displays Flores Galindo's influence.[45] Flores Galindo built on Eric Hobsbawm, George Rudé, and other social historians of popular protests as well as Latin American historians such as Mario Góngora (Chile) and Germán Carrera Damas (Venezuela). He also synthesised works on Peruvian guerrillas by Ella Dunbar Temple.[46]

Nonetheless, although *Aristocracia y plebe* encouraged and even shaped work on slave resistance, since its publication in 1984 we have not seen a resurgence of studies on the popular classes and independence. We have some publications but the promising lines of inquiry proposed by Flores Galindo have not been followed, a lamentable contrast with other Spanish American historiographies.[47] He proved that sources existed in Peru, working in numer-

---

40 Flores Galindo 1988b, pp. 289–90.
41 Flores Galindo 1988b, p. 290.
42 See his critique of José Agustín de la Puente, 'a follower of Riva Agüero and before him Bartolomé Herrera, part of an entire current of conservative thought that sought Peru's identification with Spain'. Flores Galindo 1988b, p. 290.
43 Aguirre and Walker 1990.
44 Aguirre 1993, Arrelucea Barrantes 2018, Aguirre 2005b.
45 Cosamalón 1999, Panfichi and Portocarrero 1995.
46 Dunbar Temple's edited volumes in the CDIP, which come with a rich and suggestive introduction, is cited in *Aristocracia y plebe*. Surprisingly, books by Gustavo Vergara Arias or Raúl Rivera Serna are not. Dunbar Temple 1971a, Rivera Serna 1958, Vergara Arias 1974.
47 One exception, Escanilla Huerta 2018. For a model study, see Rabinovich 2017.

ous national archives and libraries. Although the Archivo General de la Nación proved the most important, his bibliography lists seven Lima archives and libraries, as well as the Archivo de Indias and the Biblioteca Nacional de Madrid. It would be wonderful if historians built from his insights and published innovative work on criminality, insurgency, and politics from below.

From a very critical perspective, *Aristocracia y plebe* also explores the mentalities and economic base of the merchant elite. His pages on their 'ephemeral splendor' are among his finest writing, bringing in incisive examples and employing sharp prose to examine the rise of a rich, confident, aristocratic monopolists in Lima and the threats they faced in the late eighteenth century: the Bourbons' tampering with Lima's hegemony; economic competition; an inability to impose control on the lower classes; and their own divisions and contradictions. We count on important studies of merchants by Cristina Mazzeo and on the finances of the war of independence period, from Carlos Contreras, Ramiro Guzmán, Mazzeo, and others. This is a field that has thrived since the 1980s.[48] In addition, Claudia Rosas has contributed mightily to our understanding of fear in this period, in her own research on the shadow of the French Revolution and her work as an editor.[49]

Nonetheless, building on Flores Galindo, more could be done with mentalités, fear, and intellectual history. His audacious declaration, in reference to Hipólito Unanue, Manuel Lorenzo de Vidaurre, and José de la Riva-Agüero, leading figures during the Wars of Independence period, that 'Infected by the upper classes' fear, intellectuals did not go beyond timid reformism. Only at the last hour did they join the patriots fighting for independence', provides much food for thought.[50] He captures the fragility of political or military alliances in this period, the ease in which groups passed from one side to another. Contingency marks the years from San Martín's arrival in 1818 to Bolívar's bitter departure in 1825. Flores Galindo explores the different paths (Spanish victory; constitutional monarchy; the hegemony or loss of the southern Andes) that could have occurred but did not. Intellectual history of the period has been an abandoned field.[51] Flores Galindo provides important clues once again.[52]

In a 1980 conversation with Washington Delgado and Pablo Macera, Flores Galindo stated, 'Until about fifteen years ago, traditional historiography wrote

---

48 Mazzeo 2010, Flores Guzmán 2010, Contreras 2015.
49 Rosas Lauro 2005, Rosas Lauro 2006.
50 Flores Galindo 1987b, vol. 1, p. 138.
51 Exceptions include Ortemberg 2014, McEvoy 2015.
52 Here, Flores Galindo is often dialoging with or at least referring to Pablo Macera, particularly Macera 1955.

a great deal on independence, providing a version of the nation separated from real people. History needs to bring to life the popular classes'.[53] I believe that this refers to two separate but linked ideas that guided him as an intellectual and writer. First, the need to understand Peruvian history (all history) from the perspective of the lower classes, as active participants. As noted above, his reading of E.P. Thompson and other social Marxists deepened this perspective. But I also think it refers to his belief that human stories were the best way to transmit the complexity of history, to understand its logic and contradictions and to reach a broader readership. He abandoned an *Annales* approach that stressed long-term structures over individuals. For example, he drove home many of his major points in *In Search of an Inca* with brief portraits of, for the period discussed here, Juan Santos Atahualpa and Gabriel Aguilar. In *Aristocracia y plebe*, he quotes the Polish historian Bronislaw Geremek, 'social history needs to conciliate the collective dimension with individuals' destinies'.[54] I cannot name a strong biography written in recent decades of anyone from the wars of independence. Flores Galindo provides important guide for improving historical approaches.

4   Searching and Searching

Lower-class resistance and the paradoxical dominance and fragility of the upper classes are just two of several topics in Flores Galindo's work on the wars of independence that deserve more attention. *In Search of an Inca* offers additional rich alternatives to the current state of the historiography, radical departures from what had been done before and, in my view, what is currently being done. While *Aristocracia y plebe* covered and rethought some well-traveled ground (Lima in the independence period, particularly the final agonic years), *In Search of an Inca* takes us well outside of Lima, to Andean mentalities and little-known social movements, while exploring novel methodologies. It overcomes the focus on the coastal phase and on well-known actors as well as the premise that centralist republicanism was inevitable. Flores Galindo challenges all of these, while developing one of the topics in his work on Lima, the role of *montoneros* and guerrillas.

By definition, Flores Galindo's work on the Andean utopia examines alternatives to Spanish colonialism and republican domination. His study moves

---

53   Cisneros and Martos 1980, p. 7.
54   Flores Galindo 1984a, p. 17.

from the sixteenth to the twentieth century, demonstrating how the reimagining of the Incas, their presentation as a utopic alternative to the present, undergirded a grand variety of fantasies, conspiracies, uprisings, and rebellions. In terms of the period of independence, he includes two essays on Túpac Amaru and one on the 1805 Cusco conspiracy led by Gabriel Aguilar and Manuel Ubalde, and another on guerrillas in the wars of Independence. His chapters on Juan Santos Atahualpa, the messianic leader of a mass rebellion in the Amazon from 1742–1756, and on post-independence racism constitute bookends, as part of what could be construed as his rethinking of the 'transition from colony to republic', a long arc of anti-Spanish and anti-colonial insurgency.

The essays constituted a radical departure for Peruvian historiography. Flores Galindo abandoned most of the period's conventions, moving away from Lima and debates about national politics and capitalism to delve instead into utopian programs that had little expectation of success and often barely made it into the historical registrar. He examined episodes or stories from across the centuries with thematic ties more than chronological continuity, building on other disciplines such as psychoanalysis and his own enviably wide-ranging reading in Spanish and French. While regional history was in vogue in the period, *In Search of an Inca* is much more than a shift of focus away from Lima. In reality, he studies more than one region, covering the Amazon, the north coast, and numerous parts of the Andes. He presents Peru as multicultural or pluricultural, stressing the role of Quechua and (a term he disliked) *el mundo andino*.[55] Flores Galindo was a pioneer, exploring plural Peru well before debates and political struggles about interculturality and cultural pluralism had taken root among intellectuals in Peru.[56]

But what new paths does a rereading of *In Search of an Inca* offer in terms of the wars of independence? First, his analysis of the 1805 Aguilar and Ubalde conspiracy shows us the benefits of analyzing social movements that ultimately had no chance of victory and did not greatly affect Cusco's political configurations. The essay has been lauded for moving into the subconscious, linking microhistory with psychoanalysis in its examination of twenty-three dreams, twenty by Aguilar and three from other participants. I want to stress its importance in terms of political and intellectual history.

One characteristic that links his different work on 1780–1850 and is very present in this essay is his scrutiny of the search for platforms or ideologies.

---

55   See his introductory comments about 'the Andean'. Flores Galindo 2010, pp. 1–2.
56   Stefano Varese's memoirs have much to say about these topics. Varese 2020.

As seen, in *Aristocracia y plebe* he underlined the Lima aristocracy's inability to create a program; they could not convert their opposition to the Bourbons, the resentment over growing taxes, their fear of the lower classes, and their preeminence into a feasible political program. In 'Los sueños de Gabriel Aguilar', he writes, 'Every revolution requires an intellectual scaffolding ... Creoles such as Ubalde and Aguilar had no alternative but to invent their own traditions: the Andean utopia was one of the few instruments that they had in the confrontation with the colonial order'.[57] He explores Aguilar and Ubalde's reading of the Bible, Garcilaso de la Vega and his supposed prophecies, and other texts that contributed to messianic and utopian notions. All the Andean uprisings of the eighteenth century searched for a platform, combining a variety of ideologies and inspirations. Flores Galindo and Manuel Burga showed the importance of utopian views that looked to the Inca past, their inventive search for alternatives and the primary material for this scaffolding.[58]

The creation of the Andean utopia is not only a matter of individuals or collectives; space or place matters. Flores Galindo thus examines Cusco in the period, how creole outsiders (Aguilar was from Huánuco and Ubalde from Arequipa) fit in and how the city understood or viewed the conspiracy. It's a rich story with numerous implications about the period. As Flores Galindo notes in his introduction, Aguilar and Ubalde have barely made it into national narratives, in part because of the conspiracy's small impact. But this single chapter shows the benefits of examining obscure(d) movements that illustrate the search for alternatives, the experimentation in ideology and political practices. To improve our understanding of Peru's war of independence, we need to look at the smaller and frustrated movements. These shed light on the multiple projects, tensions, and expectations of the era.

In a lesser historian, the short chapter *Soldados y montoneros* would be disappointing. It's a brief text with little new archival research. Yet in these ten pages, Flores Galindo returns to the question of popular participation in the wars. He summarises the work on the guerrillas, building from *Aristocracia y plebe*, and develops the concept of the Andean utopia to probe the complicated and temporary alliances between the formal armies and Indigenous fighters. He suggests that the different guerrilla groups 'were fragile and lacked cohesion', unable to challenge Spanish rule, at least on their own.[59] What stands out is not the military or political analysis (he had done that elsewhere, as had

---

57   Flores Galindo 1986a, p. 174.
58   Burga 1988.
59   Flores Galindo 2010, p. 128.

Rivera Serna, Dunbar Temple, and others) but his attention to popular ideology. He examines how the patriot armies sought to make ties to Indigenous people via the Incas. Flores Galindo, of course, was never one to whitewash class or ethnic tensions and he bluntly states, 'Inca discourse, however, did not eliminate political conflict'.[60] After making passing references to the Iquichanos, an Andean community that confronted the newborn republic in the years immediately after independence, and the Uchuraccay massacre of 1983, when eight journalists were killed in a confusing chapter of the Shining Path conflict, he closes with '[p]olitical and ethnic rivalries coincided'.[61] Although *In Search of an Inca* shows how the promise of utopia could build from and fortify multiclass and multiregional alliances, his section on the wars of independence shows the deep divisions within Peru based primarily on what he deemed the 'colonial knot', the ethnic fissures that defined Spanish colonialism. He called for the study of popular participation in the wars of independence but stood clear of any celebratory nationalist discourse about a *united* us versus *them*.

5   More Than One Alternative

The work of Alberto Flores Galindo is more necessary, more suggestive than ever. He provides many alternatives for an historiography that seems rather stale. First, we need to decentralise, move away from the second phase, focused on Lima and its hinterland, and the well-known figures and battles. This does not mean that innovative work on San Martín, Monteagudo, or the central Andean guerrillas is not welcome – more needs to be done. But in general, the most promising topics lay outside the more traditional sightlines.

Second, we need to pay attention to defeated programs, impractical projects, half-baked conspiracies. The well-known uprisings of Tacna, Huánuco, Cusco, and others also merit more attention. My own work has taken me to Huánuco 1812, a fascinating brief but brutal class war that still has many mysteries. More should be written about it.[62] But it's not just the first 'Andean phase', but in general the smaller, less significant conspiracies and uprisings such as Aguilar and Ubalde that can shed light on the hopes, ideologies, and tensions of the era. *In*

---

60   Ibid.
61   Flores Galindo 2010, p. 130.
62   On Huánuco, see Dunbar Temple 1971b, an outstanding collection of documents, and Bazán Díaz 2017.

Search of an Inca gives clear directions in this regard.[63]

And finally, we need to stop assuming that republicanism and the dominance of Lima and Spanish were inevitable. We should explore federalism, monarchism, various strains of royalism, and Inca utopianism as well.[64] All of these currents emerged in the long war of independence and each cast a long shadow on the early republic and beyond. It is not just counter-factual history (although what would have happened if royalists had been detained in Charcas and not defeated the Angulo rebellion is a beguiling question, for example), but instead attention to these significant (and in some cases insignificant) plans, utopias, and conspiracies. As *In Search of an Inca* so brilliantly showed, the dreams of alternatives to Spanish colonialism, Lima centralism, and capitalism can seem distant, minor, and moribund, but, in reality, they have a fascinating and impressive ability to resurrect in strange ways and odd times. As Flores Galindo wrote, 'there is more than one alternative'.[65] These paths or clues seem more urgent than ever with the bicentennial having passed with no new historiographical renaissance.

---

63 Daily life both in regions that witnessed fighting and those that did not also constitutes a rich, overlooked point of inquiry.
64 The essays in Aljovín de Losada and Velásquez 2017 have some interesting leads, but many seem encyclopedic rather than analytical and do not develop arguments.
65 Flores Galindo 1987b, vol. 1, p. 15.

CHAPTER 3

Leftwing Political Culture and Print Culture in Contemporary Peru: The Making of a Public Intellectual

Carlos Aguirre

> Socialism was born with a
> printer's docket around its neck.
> RÉGIS DEBRAY[1]

∴

Between 1968 (the year of the military coup d'état perpetrated by Juan Velasco Alvarado) and 1990 (when Alberto Fujimori came to power), Peru's Left underwent a process that spanned its coming of age, rise, and catastrophic downfall. Various local and international factors fostered the radicalisation of broad sectors of the population in the late 1960s, with the ensuing emergence of a diverse but clearly identifiable leftwing *political culture*. These factors included the impact that the Cuban Revolution, Ernesto 'Che' Guevara, and guerrilla groups had on a generation of young people, especially from the middle class, who adopted positions advocating for radical, and even violent, social change; the reforms and promises, as well as the limitations, of the Velasco government, which tried to satisfy the aspirations of a wide range of social sectors; the peasant mobilisation in the Andes, which had been challenging the traditional landholding system for over a decade and had placed peasants and rural societies on the country's political agenda; and the consolidation of a combative and organised labour movement that, together with the radicalisation of teachers that crystallised in the SUTEP (Sindicato Unitario de Trabajadores de la Educación Peruana), formed a wide network of formidable and radical trade union organisations.[2] The national strike of July 1977 saw the radical 'clasista'

---

[1] Debray 2007, p. 7.
[2] On SUTEP and its radicalisation, see Angell 1982, Wilson 2007.

(*class-based*) Left at its most combative moment, and the elections for the 1978 constituent assembly reflected the growing resonance of such radical alternatives in Peru's political landscape. Trotskyist activist Hugo Blanco was the third most voted candidate nationwide, behind such historic political leaders as Víctor Raúl Haya de la Torre of the centre-left American Popular Revolutionary Alliance (Alianza Popular Revolucionaria Americana, or APRA) and the conservative Luis Bedoya Reyes of the Christian Popular Party (Partido Popular Cristiano), with the conglomerate of leftwing groups securing almost a third of the votes. In 1983, the election of the socialist lawyer Alfonso Barrantes Lingán as mayor of Lima seemed to cement the Left's role as a major political player in Peru's electoral scene, and not just in the labour movement and in the streets. However, by the second half of the 1980s, various factors – including acute divisiveness, the lack of critical distance from Alan García's steering of APRA, the brutal irruption of Shining Path (Sendero Luminoso), and the crisis of international socialism – triggered a gradual and thus far irreversible decline of the Peruvian Left.

This process – the full history of which is yet to be written[3] – was accompanied by the emergence of a *leftwing political culture*, that is, a way of doing politics and conceiving activism that was a common feature of the many factions into which Peru's Left was divided.[4] The precise significance of the various components of this political culture varies depending on which specific actors are analyzed (workers, party activists, intellectuals, university students, etc.). Overall, however, they shared the following characteristics: (1) a view of politics as a lifetime commitment, a *full-time endeavour* that touched all aspects of public and private life, although the degree to which an individual activist experienced that commitment varied greatly in each case; (2) a clear inclination toward thinking about the *inevitability* and *proximity* of the revolution, which led them, on the one hand, to strengthen their conviction regarding the *rightfulness* of their own political choice, and, on the other, to believe in the *exacerbation* of contradictions as a strategy that could be relied on for attaining certain objectives in the shortest time possible; (3) a constant effort to define and impose the *correct* approach or interpretation, using debate, controversy, and a recourse to theory – almost always Marxism and generally applied dog-

---

3   On the history of the Left after 1968 see, in addition to the extensive literature on the Shining Path, Lynch 1990, Gonzales 1994, Hinojosa 1998, Rénique 2007, Rénique 2019.
4   The concept of *political culture* has prompted interesting debates on its analytical usefulness. For an overview of the genealogy of the concept, see Formisano 2001. For its application to the case of the Andes, see Aljovín de Losada and Jacobsen 2007.

matically[5] – as tools; and, finally, (4) a sectarian culture that involved secrecy, the conviction of being the bearers of the *truth*, and a somewhat exacerbated proclivity to break with anyone who did not share that truth. Thus, dogmatism and divisiveness were, despite a few honest and productive efforts (such as in the 1978 and 1983 elections), two of the most distinctive features of the Peruvian Left during this period. The existence of dozens of political groups that identified themselves as leftist during these years is evidence of such internal flaws.[6]

There is an additional element, however, that has thus far not been explored in detail and which characterised this leftwing political culture during the period studied, namely, a way of doing politics in which *the written word* played a pivotal role. The Left's extensive and constant use of flyers, pamphlets, weekly magazines, cultural supplements, books, party newsletters, doctrine papers, ephemeral *denunciation* documents, posters, and other printed matters was intensified to a degree that was unprecedented and unparalleled by any other political group.[7] To a certain extent, the term *political publications* in the 1970s was virtually synonymous with *leftwing publications*. There was no party or faction in the Left that did not have its own periodical.[8] At times, newsstands in the streets of Lima seemed to be completely overrun by these publications.[9]

---

[5] Lynch writes that at the University of San Marcos, 'it was not just about replacing reality with ideology, rather, ideology ceased to be a theoretical point of view, or an analytical framework, and became "scripture" to be believed without much prior reasoning … Thus, the radical movement did not adopt just any version of Marxism; it adopted a Marxism understood as faith, a supernatural belief, which had an inherent force and imbued the organisation that professed it with that force'. Lynch 1990, pp. 64–5.

[6] On secrecy and the sectarian nature of the radical parties of the university Left, see Lynch 1990, pp. 91–3.

[7] Interestingly, while Sendero Luminoso shared the Left's obsession with printed propaganda, it combined it with an intensive use of oral means for the transmission of its ideology. According to an account documented by Rénique, 'in the 1970s the spoken word of a Sendero Luminoso leader carried more weight than that militant's written word'. Rénique 2007, p. 483. Another element that could be included in this discussion is the use of mural writing, which, in San Marcos and other universities, became widespread. Lynch 1990, p. 69.

[8] Examples of such magazines were *Amauta, Unidad, Voz Rebelde, Kausachum, Patria Roja, Bandera Roja, Trinchera Roja, Prensa Obrera,* and *Voz Campesina*. Some of these were in print for many years. The Trotskyist publication *Prensa Obrera*, for example, published 300 issues, as Maruja Martínez recalls in her memoir (Martínez 1997, p. 229). Others were more short-lived.

[9] Martínez remembers seeing as many as twenty people at a time gathered around a newsstand and reading the front pages of several numbers of *Comunismo*, the Trotskyist magazine (Martínez 1997, p. 167). In the late 1970s, a printing company – most likely ItalPerú, although it is not mentioned by name – offered its services to many leftwing publications, along with payment

It was practically unthinkable for any militant or activist not to know how to operate a mimeograph. The production of all kinds of writings, rudimentarily put together in semi-clandestine printing presses and over the course of long, exhausting nights, was a substantial part of revolutionary action, a true *rite de passage*.[10] In addition to being played out in trade union, university, and street forums, the debates and controversies within the Left and between its various factions and the other political options necessarily had to go through the printing press and the mimeograph. The circulation of Soviet and Chinese printed matter sold at extremely cheap prices (magazines such as *Pekín Informa*, or the multi-volume complete works of Karl Marx, Vladimir Lenin, Joseph Stalin, and Mao Zedong, for example) gave anyone interested in the theory and history of international communism access to writings that would later be read and disseminated through endless discussions or rehashed in articles on theory published in magazines and supplements.[11] The growing number and increas-

---

flexibility. During the campaign for the 1978 constituent assembly election, it announced: 'In addition to leftwing newspapers, we print flyers, party platforms, and propaganda for candidates of various political affiliations. We work three shifts'. (Martínez 1997, p. 227).

10   Martínez provides details on the use of printed matter by the 'Atusparia Cell' of Vanguardia Revolucionaria, a political group of which she was a member. The cell printed a pamphlet called *Horma Clasista* (literally, Class Shoetree) for distribution among shoe factory workers; an internal newsletter meant for militants only; another newsletter under the title *El Proletario*, which was sold in factories; and the magazine *Fichas*, which dealt with international issues. The party had its own printing press, and, although the visit ultimately never happened, when Martínez was given the chance to see it in operation she could not hide her excitement: 'I can't wait to see the party's printing press for myself, meet new comrades, be privy to part of the secrets that only those in the inner circle know'. (Martínez 1997, pp. 116–7). See also Martínez 1997, pp. 167–72, on the production of printed mater by Trotskyist cells, as Martínez was active in this movement in the 1970s and she recounts the debates and accusations among the various groups of the Left over such materials. She also describes how exhausted she was after serving as *press* officer ('encargada de prensa') for the movement for some time. The production and dissemination of these materials could be dangerous, and Martínez was arrested several times, accused, among other things, of running the printing press, proofreading articles, and doing the layout for the *Comunismo* newspaper (Martínez 1997, p. 182).

11   Patricia Oliart and Gonzalo Portocarrero reconstruct the link between the circulation of such materials, especially in the provinces, and the process of radicalisation of the teachers organised in SUTEP: 'After graduating, teachers had to draw on the knowledge acquired in the university to prepare their classes. Their access to specialised literature was generally very limited due to both their extremely low wages and the lack of incentives. These problems were compounded by the fact that bookstores were practically nonexistent in the provinces. The bibliographic materials available to teachers were the Chinese and Soviet magazines, the mimeographed booklets, the educational technology manuals sold by traveling salesmen or in occasional book fairs held in SUTEP headquarters or at the uni-

ing quality of what can generically be called *cultural magazines* also contributed to forge this close relationship between Leftist activism, intellectual work, and print culture. Some of these publications, including the excellent magazine *Textual*, were sponsored by the State during the Velasco administration. Most, however, were the result of efforts (at time heroic) by intellectuals, students, and workers, both in Lima and in other cities. In an important work on the relationship between intellectuals, revolution, and leftwing culture in the 1960s and 1970s in Latin America, Claudia Gilman has also emphasised the close connection that existed between the public role of the committed intellectual and the space opened up by political-cultural magazines: 'The networks formed by the various publications and their echoes were instrumental in inspiring confidence in the discursive potential of intellectuals ... In these magazines, writers found a powerful amplifier for their discourses and, at the same time, they felt called on to speak out and adopt a position on contemporary issues'.[12]

The proliferation of study groups among young leftwing activists served as a conduit and incentive for the consumption and production of printed political and cultural materials.[13] Images of young men and women walking with a book, reading while waiting in line to see a movie at a *cine-club* or to attend a concert of protest music, or while riding on a packed public bus, are paradigmatic of an era when activism, reading, book culture, and the dissemination of the printed word were inseparable. These young people were disparagingly dubbed the *sobacos ilustrados* (or 'enlightened armpits') by both the far Left, which accused them of intellectualism, and the Right, which was wary of their anti-establishment ideas. In Alfredo Pita's novel *El cazador ausente*, one of the characters recalls 'those blissful, adolescent nights in the winter of 1965, when a book or a poem mattered more than anything else, even politics, which so captivated them and which, without them realising it, was already casting and tightening its tragic net, a net that had enveloped their faces like an indelible spider's web'.[14] The combination of that passion for politics – and, more specifically, leftwing politics – and their love of books and reading was a

---

versity, where they could be purchased at affordable prices'. Oliart and Portocarrero 1989, p. 117.

12 Gilman 2003, pp. 76–7. Pablo Ponza has also defined the 1960s and early 1970s in Argentina as a time characterised by both 'a book-centered culture' and 'a feeling of change, optimism, and rebellion'. Ponza 2008, p. 76.

13 Maoist militants at the National University of San Marcos 'turn to the readings and discussions in their circles seeking what they had not been able to find as a political antecedent upon entering the university, thus furthering ... the self-taught method of learning. Studying is seen as an essential phase for attaining their future objectives'. Lynch 1990, pp. 78–9.

14 Pita 2000, p. 52.

distinctive feature of that generation. Several accounts from radical San Marcos students of that time, gathered by Nicolás Lynch, mention the importance that reading had in their development as activists. One of the slogans chanted by young university students actively involved in radical leftwing groups was 'Study/Work/Rifle'.[15] Maruja Martínez recalls all the bookstores she used to go to in downtown Lima in the early 1970s: Mejía Baca, La Familia, Época, Cosmos (which specialised in Soviet books), Horizonte, and the many that lined-up on Camaná or Azángaro streets, 'set up in the entrances of old stately homes'.[16]

This relationship between leftwing activism and print culture was, of course, far from new. There was a long tradition dating back to the time of the anarchist movement and the beginnings of socialism in Peru.[17] José Carlos Mariátegui and his heroic and multifaceted publishing activity marked a peak moment in that tradition.[18] But the years following 1968 were a particularly intense period in this association between activism and print culture, furthered, among other things, by a drop in production costs, the expansion of the universe of readers, a growing student population, and the increasing process of radicalisation and activism noted above. The Velasco administration's role as one of the elements that shaped this new stage must also be considered here: the mass publication of magazines and books (including the Biblioteca Peruana collection, for example, sponsored by the government, which included books by such authors as Mariátegui, former guerrilla fighter Héctor Béjar, sociologist Carlos Delgado, and others) fostered in its own way an introduction to politics through culture and the promotion of reading.[19]

Leftwing students and intellectuals were actively involved in forging this political culture that was underpinned by the printed word. The fact that most leftwing groups were formed and often led by students and intellectuals (in the broadest sense of the category) reinforced precisely that tendency to see books and other printed matter as powerful tools for political action and debate. The boundaries separating academic publications – monographic books on history and sociology, for example – from ideological and political publications were

---

15   Martínez 1997, p. 113.
16   Martínez 1997, p. 160.
17   Régis Debray has written a thought-provoking essay on the relationship between socialism and print culture. Interestingly, he identifies the year 1968 as the end of the stage he calls *graphosphere*, which began in 1448 with the invention of the printing press, and during which socialism flourished. According to him, this long stage was followed as of 1968 by the *videosphere*. Debray 2007. On anarchism and print culture in Peru, see Machuca Castillo 2006.
18   On Mariátegui and his incursión in the publishing industry, see Flores Galindo 1989e.
19   Aguirre 2025.

blurred. This was the case, for example, of the books by Wilfredo Kapsoli and Denis Sulmont on the history of the labour movement.[20] Moreover, numerous scholars became directly involved – to an extent that is very rare today – in a range of cultural and political magazines as promoters, contributors, and board members. For leftwing intellectuals, their participation in such publications – some extremely short-lived and often intellectually poor – was an essential part of their work. The appeal that this kind of *print activism* held for them is explained not only by the expectation of reaching a wider readership, but also by the deeply internalised idea that the printed word was a source of credibility, permanence and, ultimately, power. According to Germán Merino Vigil, 'with the large newspapers controlled by a military government in slow retreat, the small leftwing or right-wing press media – written in the heat of popular debates, put out by printing houses that generally worked on credit, and authored by highly committed journalists – concentrated the debate on political issues in a society without elections, congress, or active parties'.[21] The launching of the magazine *Marka* in 1978 and the publication of *El Diario de Marka* and its supplement *El Caballo Rojo* as of 1980 are probably the most important experiences in this process. Merino Vigil highlights the role of the weekly *Marka*, which at its peak reached a print run of 42,000 copies:

> *Marka* expressed, better than any other media, the political will of the Left that incubated in silence during the Velasco years, almost secured the majority of seats in the 1979 constituent assembly, and was extinguished two or three years later under the blows of the economic crisis, amidst the sterile debates in parliament and the bombings of Sendero Luminoso, to finally collapse under the rubble of the fallen Berlin Wall.[22]

The connection between leftwing activism, intellectual work, and print culture was not limited, however, to periodicals devoted to political struggle and cultural dissemination. According to data gathered by the *Boletín Bibliográfico Peruano* of the National Library of Peru, in the ten years from 1963 to 1973, the volume of printed matter published in Peru increased twofold, and by the mid-1970s, there were 531 publishing houses operating in Lima.[23] That growth included the consolidation of an extensive network of publishers and printing

---

20 Kapsoli 1976, Sulmont 1975.
21 Merino Vigil 2008.
22 Ibid.
23 Guevara and Gechelín 2001, p. 156.

houses interested in promoting intellectual work and culture, and their efforts were sponsored by research centres, trade unions, non-governmental organisations (NGOS), international cooperation agencies, political parties, and even private companies. Publishing houses, printing companies, and intellectual production centres such as Industrial Gráfica, Ediciones Educativas, Tarea, Editora Rikchay Perú, CEDEP (Centre for Development and Participation Studies), IEP (Institute of Peruvian Studies), DESCO (Centre for the Study and Promotion of Development), and many others also contributed in a variety of ways to consolidate the prestige of intellectual work and the publishing world.

This leftwing political culture and its connection with the printing world had a notable impact, not only because it resulted in the widespread perception that being an *intellectual* and being *leftist* were one and the same thing, but also because it boosted the consolidation of the *public intellectual*.[24] During the 1970s, a number of intellectuals who identified with the Left, including writers, sociologists, historians, artists, and journalists, gained an increasing, albeit still limited, presence in public debates. They viewed their role as intellectuals as necessarily linked to the participation in such debates and the commitment to anti-establishment and socialist positions that were emerging within labour and social movements. Among them were sociologists, theologians, writers, poets, and historians. Gradually, a significant number of them, especially after 1980, began withdrawing from such public debates, coinciding with the crisis of the Left and the irruption of Sendero Luminoso. With few exceptions – historian Pablo Macera was one of the small number of intellectuals that continued to give interviews and openly comment on almost any issue – the leftwing intelligentsia began a slow retreat into the reduced sphere of the universities and the increasingly ubiquitous NGOs.[25]

Alberto Flores Galindo was perhaps the figure that best encapsulated in his intellectual and political biography the convergence of leftwing activism, intel-

---

24 Although the term is commonly used today, some analysts note that it is redundant. What intellectual – they ask – is not a public figure or does not aspire to become one? Edward Said defines the intellectual as 'an individual endowed with a faculty for representing, embodying, articulating a message, a view, an attitude, philosophy, or opinion to, as well as for, a public' and whose role 'cannot be played without a sense of being someone whose place it is publicly to raise embarrassing questions, to confront orthodoxy and dogma (rather than to produce them), to be someone who cannot easily be co-opted by governments or corporations, and whose *raison d'être* is to represent all those people and issues that are routinely forgotten or swept under the rug'. Said 1996, p. 11. A public intellectual is necessarily an anti-establishment intellectual, according to Said's definition.

25 To reconstruct Pablo Macera's career as an intellectual oracle see the compilation of interviews with him in Macera 1983.

lectual work, and print culture, and who was most successfully able to bring together those characteristics in his activities as a public intellectual. Flores Galindo was not just a brilliant and prolific professional historian, who practiced his craft with rigour and creativity, but also an unequivocal and persistent leftwing militant, a *public* figure in the broadest sense of the word, a contributor in any and all journalistic and publishing ventures that sprang from the Left and, in general, from the intellectual world, and an aggressive (in the best sense of the word) publicist, who not only knew how to take advantage of all the possibilities that print culture offered, but became himself an inspiration for and a promoter of that culture. As we will see below, Flores Galindo was far from being a traditional scholar who conducted research, wrote books for an essentially intellectual and academic readership, and limited his activities to the realm of the university. Quite the opposite. As a speaker, he alternated between university classrooms, conference halls, and trade unions or grassroots organisations. As an author, his books were published by prestigious publishing houses and his articles were featured in specialised journals, but he also contributed book reviews and articles in newspaper op-ed pages, supplements, and cultural magazines. Rather than diminishing, his presence in the intellectual and political debates of those years grew steadily. At times, he seemed to embody a quixotic effort to keep the flame of socialism alive, when the possibility of a socialist world seemed to be undermined by various forces, and to preserve the figure of the committed and public intellectual that others were leaving behind. His writings from the late 1980s, for example, in which he polemically engaged the writings of representatives of the intellectual Right (including Mario Vargas Llosa and Hernando de Soto), can be read today as agonistic efforts to rescue radical alternative thought from its demise. His death in 1990 tragically coincided with the beginning of the electoral and political collapse of the Left in Peru and the start of the long night under Alberto Fujimori's rule.

This chapter attempts to retrace Alberto Flores Galindo's steps as a public intellectual, and, in particular, the connections between that role and the development of a leftwing political culture in which the printed word was key. The aim is to show how an intellectual such as Flores Galindo developed and matured within this culture. He carried out an intense, almost feverish activity as an intellectual and put out an impressive and sustained stream of publications. I posit that all of this was possible because of the audacious and creative use that Flores Galindo made of the possibilities afforded by the printed word, which was, in turn, guided by a conception of intellectual work and political activism in which *writing* and *publishing* were unavoidable imperatives. In the following sections, I will try to reconstruct the political and intellectual environment in which he worked, identify the core elements of his conception of intellectual work and the relationship with print culture, and describe the way in which, thanks to a clever and aggressive strategy, he was able to transform his intellectual endeavours into a veritable machinery of publications whose volume and quality continue to astonish us today.

1 The Making of an Intellectual: Flores Galindo and the Generation of 1968

From a young age, Flores Galindo had access to a well-stocked library at home, which allowed him to be in close contact with books very early in his life, developing a passion that he would continue to nurture in the library of the La Salle school he attended.[26] When he entered the PUCP in 1966 he would be drawn into the process of gradual radicalisation of a generation that accompanied the growth of the Peruvian Left.[27] Although he was initially influenced by Christian social ideas, Flores Galindo would promptly embrace socialism as a political utopia and Marxism as a theoretical framework. The intellectual atmosphere at the PUCP was taking on a reddish hue. According to Eduardo Cáceres Valdivia, a close friend of Flores Galindo since their adolescence, the reading of authors such as Jean-Paul Sartre would be key, as would be the Marxist books 'distributed by Fernando Lecaros'.[28] Sociologist Guillermo Rochabrún remembers those years as a time in which they shifted toward Marxism – in his case, from structural-functionalist positions – by way of liberation theology. Listening to Gustavo Gutiérrez, its founder, Rochabrún says, 'heightened my interest in Marx and the *Manuscripts*'.[29] During those years, according to accounts by Manuel Burga – a historian who was a very close friend and collaborator of Flores Galindo –, 'we were all emotionally or coactively Marxists'.[30] Flores Galindo joined and actively participated in the Revolutionary Front of Socialist Students (Frente Revolucionario de Estudiantes Socialistas, or FRES) and the Revolutionary Left Movement (Movimiento de Izquierda Revolucionaria, or MIR), and he engaged in 'political advocacy efforts among assembly plant

---

26   Cáceres Valdivia 1993, p. xiii.
27   Cáceres Valdivia 1993, p. xiv.
28   Cáceres Valdivia 1993, pp. xiv–xv.
29   Rochabrún 2007, p. 13.
30   Burga 2005, p. 109.

workers'.³¹ This was a stance shared by many middle- and upper-class students and intellectuals – although not as many as is usually thought – who decided to *engage with the people* during those years of dreams and illusions. Flores Galindo himself would later remember that time as one in which socialism 'was a mythification and not a proposal, much less a project, but which held enough passionate content to fuel a kind of "march toward the people" ... that drove many in the university to the peasant communities, the mining camps, the sugarcane cooperatives, the shantytown dwellings, and, especially, the factories'.³² According to historian José Luis Rénique, 'the effervescent atmosphere reached the lecture halls of the traditional Pontifical Catholic University, where parties with a strong Maoist rhetoric, such as the Revolutionary Communist Party and the Revolutionary Vanguard-Communist Proletariat Party, recruited young leaders willing to join the peasant or mining fronts in remote areas of the country's hinterland'.³³ Other students would go on to join Sendero Luminoso, which at that time was still in its formative phase. Most tried to combine their studies with a kind of mandatory revolutionary service, which included distributing propaganda and proselytising among workers, raising their (class) consciousness, and helping them strengthen their trade union efforts. This mixture of voluntarism and idealism became widespread among the members of the 'Generation of 1968', as sociologist Eduardo Arroyo later called it.³⁴ These were the years of the New Left and the class-based movement that Velasco's military coup in 1968 would help consolidate by furthering a political culture of confrontation, as Flores Galindo would later note: 'The criticism of the military regime was thus born. Every analysis began by negating. Twenty years on, this may all seem objectionable. But the truth is that had there been no negative criticism, there would have been no Generation of 1968, let alone a New Left'.³⁵

At the PUCP, Flores Galindo took classes with theologian Gustavo Gutiérrez and historian Heraclio Bonilla, among others. From the former he would absorb the idea of commitment to the poor, and from the latter, the concern – which Bonilla encouraged back then – with studying the history of the working and lower classes. His early research work reflects that concern, both intellectual and political, with writing a history from below, which would also contribute to raise class-consciousness among workers. Flores Galindo wrote his under-

---

31 Cáceres Valdivia 1993, pp. xvi–xvii. See also Martínez 1997.
32 Flores Galindo 1987a, p. 218.
33 Rénique 2007, p. 481.
34 Arroyo 1986.
35 Flores Galindo 1987a, p. 217.

graduate thesis on the mine workers of Cerro de Pasco in 1972, with Bonilla as his advisor;[36] at the same time, he worked with sociologist Denis Sulmont on several projects, including a bibliography on the labour movement and a monograph on the fishermen of Chimbote.

After spending two years in Paris between 1972 and 1974, where he studied at the École pratique des hautes études with Fernand Braudel and Pierre Vilar, among others, he returned to Lima and to the PUCP. Almost immediately, he began contributing to non-academic publications. His first journalistic pieces were featured in the op-ed pages of *La Prensa*, which had been seized by the military government, in *La Jornada*, the supplement of the same newspaper directed by César Lévano, and in the leftwing magazine *La Palabra del Pueblo*.[37] The opportunity that the Velasco government offered leftwing intellectuals allowed many of them to not only contribute to such publications, but also have a *training* of sorts, which they would later put into practice independently in other magazines and supplements. Numerous journalists and intellectuals who identified with the Left (César Hildebrandt, Mirko Lauer, César Lévano, Hugo Neira, and others) shared in those experiences. Flores Galindo wrote book reviews, published early drafts of the research he was working on, and addressed some issues that would later characterise his preoccupations as a historian, such as the debate around the *national question*. Two aspects are worth highlighting in this early period of his public trajectory: the young Flores Galindo's interest in *disseminating* the knowledge produced by academics (his own and that of others), an interest not very common among Peruvian historians then or now; and the special emphasis he placed on issues connected with what we can generically call *popular history*. A review of his published works from the early stages of his career shows the confluence of his political and ideological choices and his academic and intellectual concerns.

In the second half of the 1970s, Flores Galindo began a fertile period, researching, writing, and publishing. He ventured into an impressive range of topics, including the history of the labour movement, the Túpac Amaru rebellion, Mariátegui and the history of the Communist movement, the colonial crisis, Peruvian independence, agrarian history, the history of mentalities, messianism and the Andean utopia, Shining Path, peasant movements, the history of intellectuals (from Mariátegui and Haya de la Torre to José María Arguedas), and racism and authoritarianism. At the same time, he stepped up his involve-

---

36   Flores Galindo 1972.
37   Cáceres Valdivia 1993, p. xviii; Valderrama 2004.

ment as an active promoter of various publications: in 1978 he was a contributor in the magazine *Vaca Sagrada*, directed by poets Marco Martos and José Watanabe; directed between 1978 and 1982 the journal *Allpanchis*, published by Instituto de Pastoral Andina; contributed regularly to the cultural supplement *El Caballo Rojo* from 1981 to 1983; participated in several leftwing publications such as *El Búho*, *30 Días*, and *El Zorro de Abajo*; served on the editorial board of *Revista Andina* since its inception in 1983; and finally, in 1987, cofounded the centre for socialist studies SUR Casa de Estudios del Socialismo, and served on the editorial board of the journal *Márgenes* until his death in 1990. He was not merely a contributor, however. He was an almost obsessive promoter of such publications. In an imagined conversation with Flores Galindo after his death, Maruja Martínez, who worked with him in SUR, reminds him how 'day in and day out you pushed and pushed for the journal to come out'.[38] At the same time, Flores Galindo's presence as a public intellectual grew exponentially, and his spheres of action multiplied: he was a university professor, a lecturer, an event organiser, a visiting professor in foreign universities, a panelist in conferences and seminars, and a promoter of interdisciplinary studies. The pace in which he produced written works, including journalistic writings, was dizzying. As poet Antonio Cisneros wrote, Flores Galindo, 'unlike most in the social sciences, is a fine writer ... always ready (almost always) to write in urgent, ruthless lengths and deadlines'.[39] It was not only the quantity and quality of his production, however; he also used a wide range of genres and forms of the printed word. I will return to this.

To complete this portrait of the public intellectual, I will quote sociologist Guillermo Rochabrún here, as he has aptly summarised the different elements of Flores Galindo's intellectual and political profile. According to him, in his thinking and his actions Flores Galindo was guided by six convictions, namely: 'defining his actions and projects on the basis of the problems affecting the country, and not the other way around'; 'engaging in team work, coordinating efforts, sparking dialogue, inviting debate'; 'studying the great national historical problems, but understanding them not as issues of the "past" but as continuing problems'; 'renewing topics and points of view, without abandoning a fundamental ideological and political core'; 'training new generations, particu-

---

38   Martínez 1997, p. 286. The journal she refers to is *Márgenes*. The importance that Flores Galindo placed on journals as vehicles for thought and action is underscored by his assertion, in his study of Mariátegui, that 'a journal [*Amauta*] could be more important and necessary than the production of a treatise on Marx or a study backed by abundant statistical data'. Flores Galindo 1994b, p. 446.

39   Cisneros 1988.

larly researchers sensitive to the great national questions'; and 'combining the utmost intellectual independence with an ethically informed political commitment'.[40]

This is certainly not meant to idealise Flores Galindo, as, due to his own limitations and the challenges he faced, he did not always succeed in fully achieving his objectives. But Rochabrún is right in identifying the main lines that steered his difficult intellectual and political path. In these traits highlighted by Rochabrún lies the essence of his role as a committed and public intellectual: concern for the present and the future, not just for the past; a ceaseless theoretical and thematic renovation; the pursuit of dialogue and collaboration, instead of shutting himself off in strictly individual work; the call for a political and ethical commitment to certain fundamental principles; and, finally, the exercise of freedom, which is the foundation of any critical intellectual. The extent to which Flores Galindo was able to fulfill his role of public intellectual depended greatly on his relationship with the printed word, as we will see in the following section.

2   The Printed Word as an Intellectual Weapon

The most thorough bibliography of Flores Galindo lists 333 entries in which he features as author, coauthor, or editor.[41] Of these, 58 are 'books and booklets', but the list also includes reeditions, translations, and posthumous publications. Another 163 references are 'articles and essays', including both journalistic articles published in newspapers and cultural supplements and essays featured in academic journals. The rest are letters, interviews, and various other types of writings. It is interesting to examine the outlets in which Flores Galindo published this impressive number of works, as well as the diversity of formats and the textual and material connections between them.

Flores Galindo wrote historical monographs based on original research (*Los mineros de la Cerro de Pasco, Arequipa y el sur Andino, La agonía de Mariátegui,* and *Aristocracia y plebe*); a book of synthesis, with a combination of original research and secondary sources (*Apogeo y crisis de la república aristocrática*, written in collaboration with Manuel Burga); a volume of essays that dealt with a common theme but were relatively stand-alone (*Buscando un Inca*); a collection of published and unpublished short pieces (*Tiempo de plagas*);

---

40   Rochabrún 2007, pp. 457–8.
41   Valderrama 2004, pp. 23–71.

multi-authored compilations for which he served as editor (*Túpac Amaru II, Independencia y revolución*); and anthologies of texts by Marxist intellectuals (*El pensamiento comunista* and *Invitación a la vida heroica*). They were released by various publishing houses, including the Social Sciences Department of the PUCP;[42] the PUCP's Fondo Editorial; INIDE (National Institute for Research in and Development of Education, an agency of the Ministry of Education); the publishing house Editorial Horizonte, directed by Humberto Damonte and specialised in literary and social science topics; Ediciones Rikchay Perú, a briefly successful publishing venture founded by Fernando Lecaros in the late 1970s and closely connected with leftist circles; Mosca Azul Editores, a prestigious publishing house founded by the poet and writer Mirko Lauer and the literary critic Abelardo Oquendo; DESCO, one of the most renowned and long-standing research and promotion centres; Instituto de Apoyo Agrario, an NGO that Flores Galindo defined as 'a centre that promotes rural and peasant development but is also receptive to intellectual work;'[43] El Caballo Rojo, an imprint created by editor Luis Valera that published short books of historical essays and literary criticism; and the Instituto Nacional de Cultura, the main State agency for the promotion of culture. A couple of short pamphlets (*Violencia y campesinado, Europa y el país de los Incas*) were published by SUR Casa de Estudios del Socialismo and Instituto de Apoyo Agrario respectively. It is interesting to note that, except for the second edition of his first book, *Los mineros de la Cerro de Pasco*, none of his books was published by a university press. This clearly signals Flores Galindo's preference for non-academic publishers, which offered the possibility of reaching a larger and more diverse readership.

Flores Galindo's connections with various individuals and institutions, evidenced by the list of publishers that put out his work, reveal another feature of his intellectual practice. He maintained (with some inevitable exceptions) friendly and collaborative relationships with associations and individuals who were not part of the same groups or circles he frequented and who did not necessarily agree with his political and intellectual positions. These characteristics are also evident in the sheer number and range of collective publications to which he contributed. These included, for instance, the tribute to Jorge Basadre, coordinated by Francisco Miró Quesada, Franklin Pease, and David

---

42 Some of Flores Galindo's first publications were printed on mimeograph and distributed as workbooks or booklets for use as material in university courses, although they were also sold in bookstores and newsstands in downtown Lima and thus reached a wider readership.

43 Flores Galindo 2010, p. 255.

Sobrevilla, and which was published by the PUCP in 1978;[44] the tribute to Mariátegui's *Siete ensayos* (published in English as *Seven Interpretative Essays on Peruvian Reality*) on the occasion of the fiftieth anniversary of its first edition;[45] the compilation on research in social sciences, organised by Javier Iguíñiz and published by Tarea in 1979;[46] the very successful synthesis of Peruvian history, *Nueva historia general del Perú*, published by Mosca Azul that same year;[47] the twelve-volume collection *Historia del Perú*, edited by Juan Mejía Baca and published in 1980;[48] the compilation by Carlos Franco entitled *El Perú de Velasco*, published by CEDEP in three volumes in 1986;[49] the remarkable two-volume anthology *Estados y naciones en los Andes*, published by IFEA (French Institute of Andean Studies) and IEP in 1986;[50] the volume of essays on Peruvian political thought, *Pensamiento político peruano*, compiled by Alberto Adrianzén and published by DESCO in 1987;[51] and the book *Violencia y crisis de valores en el Perú*, coordinated by Jesuit historian Jeffrey Klaiber and published with the support of the Tinker Foundation in 1987.[52]

The range of magazines and newspapers that featured his articles also illustrates Flores Galindo's interest in and ability to reach different kinds of readers. These publications can be divided into two categories. The first includes mass circulation newspapers and supplements, such as *La Prensa, La Jornada, La Palabra del Pueblo, Marka, El Diario de Marka, El Caballo Rojo, Amauta, La Revista, 30 Días, Sí, La República, El Búho, El Zorro de Abajo*, and others. The second category includes publications with a more limited circulation, produced by NGOs, research centres, and universities, such as *Socialismo y Participación* (CEDEP), *Allpanchis* (Instituto de Pastoral Andina), *Análisis, Revista Andina* (Centro Bartolomé de las Casas), *Los Caminos del Laberinto, Cultura Popular, Márgenes* (SUR), *Apuntes* (Universidad del Pacífico), *Debates en Sociología* (Sociology Department, PUCP) and *Histórica* (History Department, PUCP). The diversity and eclecticism of these publications do not match the traditional pattern usually followed by historians and other scholars to make their work known. Flores Galindo deliberately sought to escape the restrictive disciplinary parameters of academic journals and displayed an inclination toward particip-

---

44 Miró Quesada, Pease, and Sobrevilla 1978.
45 Romero 1979.
46 Iguíñiz 1979.
47 Araníbar 1979.
48 Mejía Baca 1980.
49 Franco 1986.
50 Deler and Saint-Geours 1986.
51 Adrianzén 1987.
52 Klaiber 1987.

ating in endeavors that were not only *extra-academic* but also interdisciplinary. Some might see in this pattern a compulsive obsession to see his name associated with any and all cultural ventures that arose in those years. I am more interested in the *sociological* aspect of the matter, that is, in exploring how and why an intellectual like Flores Galindo was so determined to connect his professional work with political debates and with shaping public opinion; who did not shy away from polemic discussions and debates, but rather promoted and engaged in them; and who sought to access the greatest number of media in order to disseminate his work.

There were certainly foreseeable risks in that accelerated rush to produce and publish as fast as he could and wherever he was given the opportunity to do so. Speaking of his collaboration with Flores Galindo in the drafting of the book *Apogeo y crisis de la república aristocrática*, Burga conceded that during those years 'we lacked the calmness and the time to define and hone concepts. Our youth and the urgencies of the country pushed us to turn to history in search of answers that would help us understand the most pressing problems of the present'.[53] Several of Flores Galindo's works show a certain carelessness in the accuracy of citations and references. In others, judgments were hastily made, resulting in some arbitrariness. However, these were the exceptions. Flores Galindo was for the most part a diligent historian, although he was less concerned with the positivist rigour of an exact science than with the need to promote a problem-based historical discipline and put forward questions and hypotheses that would advance critical thinking.

I would like to focus on two aspects that have to do with that convergence of leftwing political culture and the print culture tradition that Flores Galindo fully embodied. First, his writing style, and second, his recurrent practice of revising, expanding, reproducing, reprinting, correcting, combining, and publishing texts, sometimes aimed at different audiences and always linked to each other through a series of intertextual connections and borrowings.

Several commentators have addressed Flores Galindo's narrative style. Cisneros praised the quality of his prose, placing it within a tradition of Peruvian historians such as José de la Riva-Agüero, Raúl Porras Barrenechea, and Pablo Macera, who had 'a healthy and familiar relationship with literature'.[54] Literary scholar Peter Elmore described the 'intense and dynamic rhythm of his prose' and referred to his use of 'almost epigrammatic phrases with which he sometimes caps and summarises his arguments'.[55] Poet Marco Martos called Flores

---

53   Burga 2005, p. 117.
54   Cisneros 1988.
55   Elmore 2005, p. 6.

Galindo's prose 'pleasant, brisk, and vigorous'.[56] The Italian critic Antonio Melis dedicated a whole article to this subject, highlighting, among other things, Flores Galindo's 'continuous use of questioning as a stylistic device', a recourse that Melis saw as 'encapsulating his approach to research': 'More important than the supposedly definitive answers is the ability to raise new issues, but always buoyed by hope'.[57] In addition to these features, Flores Galindo's works were characterised by an aspect that was central to his work as a historian and public intellectual but also to that period's leftwing political culture, namely, a *polemical and combative* style that runs through almost all of his production. Flores Galindo was always arguing with someone, rejecting interpretations that he found inadequate, proposing new ways of answering old questions, and pointing out clearly in his writings the differences with other interpretations, including those from other Marxist camps. By way of example, I will just mention here his exchanges with Franklin Pease on Andean myths, with Henrique Urbano on Andean utopia, with Juan José Vega on the participation of the masses in the wars of independence, with Eduardo Arroyo on the 1968 Generation, with Carlos Iván Degregori on Sendero Luminoso, and with numerous leftwing intellectuals on Mariátegui.[58]

Flores Galindo even mentioned this aspect of his personality and his work in his farewell letter, calling it 'my aggressive style', but then adding a phrase that in a way sums up the justification he offered for the polemical style of his writings: 'disagreeing is another way of coming together'.[59] As Rochabrún and Burga have stressed, Flores Galindo was above all a heterodox intellectual, so his polemical style was not a mere gimmick or a way of disparaging his opponent, but a central element of his intellectual method and his critical attitude.[60]

In this we not only see the legacy of the pamphleteering and polemicist tradition in Peru's print culture – which can be traced back to the nineteenth century or earlier and includes writers such as Manuel Atanasio Fuentes, Manuel González Prada, José Carlos Mariátegui, Alberto Hidalgo, Víctor Raúl Haya de la Torre, and Luis Alberto Sánchez, among others –, but also the stamp of the leftwing culture of the 1970s. To debate (*polemizar*) was a widely used term and

---

56 Martos 2005, p. 8.
57 Melis 2005, p. 14.
58 A dossier with a sample of these exchanges on Mariátegui and Peruvian Marxism was included in the commemorative edition of Flores Galindo's *La agonía de Mariátegui* (Flores Galindo 2021).
59 Flores Galindo 1989f, p. 390.
60 Rochabrún 2007, p. 457; Burga 2005, p. 113.

practice among leftist activists, and everyone was or aspired to be an inveterate debater. Student leaders of various left-wing groups, as well as from other parties such as APRA, would take part in polemics that were highly anticipated and commented upon, attracted huge crowds, and often ended in violent brawls.[61] The culture of ideological relativism had not yet caught on and such polemicising was generally viewed as a sort of boxing match that inevitably had to end with the opponent knocked-out. Flores Galindo was, among other things, a fierce polemicist, and he usually displayed a blunt style (described by Romano as 'harsh'[62]) that was also respectful of the ideas he was challenging, although at times he could also descend into verbal excesses and even disparaging. In a furious response to an unfair review of his book *Buscando un Inca* written by U.S. historian Eric Mayer, he called the review a case of distortion of his arguments that is 'somewhere between pathetic and ludicrous', 'an absurdity' that could only be explained – he suggested sarcastically – by the fact that Mayer did not understand Spanish.[63] Flores Galindo responded to historian Juan José Vega, who published an extensive critical commentary on *Aristocracia y plebe* in the newspaper *La República*, by accusing him of harboring 'a dark animosity' toward him, and, after rebutting his criticisms, he questioned Vega's reaction to a book that, according to its author, made some people 'uncomfortable' because it dealt with issues such as violence and racism, demolishing the idea of a unified Peruvian nation championed by Vega, 'a traditional version of history pretending to be anti-establishment'.[64] When anthropologist Luis Millones penned a piece about a work by Juan Ansión and Jan Szeminski featured in the journal *Allpanchis*, questioning it because it included an allegedly oral testimony that was actually a written and published account, Flores Galindo, then director of *Allpanchis*, saw it necessary to remind Millones that 'bitterness and acerbity are bad bedfellows of critique because they narrow horizons and cloud all intelligence'. He also suggested that Millones made no attempt to understand the overall argument of the work in question and in his commentary could 'only resort to a small-minded criticism of the origin of one source'.[65] An equally aggressive, although less personal, tone can be perceived in a long commentary on economist Hernando de Soto and the contributors of the book *El otro sendero*, including Mario Vargas Llosa,

---

61 On the university polemics of those years, see Martínez 1997, p. 239.
62 Romano 1991a, p. 11.
63 Flores Galindo 1989b, pp. 336–7.
64 Flores Galindo 1985b, p. 148.
65 Flores Galindo 1982b, p. 355.

who wrote the prologue.[66] He accused them of having produced 'an ideological book ... in which the facts are only there to support pre-established assumptions and ideas'.[67] Referring to what he considered the true purpose behind their alleged defence of popular capitalism, he argued that this 'new Right', which held up capitalism as a project for the future, 'intends to detach itself from any involvement with the past'.[68] In that sense, he sarcastically added, 'they have not been the 'owners of Peru' ... There is no connection between abject poverty and capitalism, as capitalism does not yet exist. Capitalism represents the new, while socialism, with its supposedly 'statist' ambitions, would be a continuation of the previous history'.[69] The project, in sum, revealed 'questionable ethics, a lack of rigorous research, and a completely unoriginal version of things'.[70]

It is not my intention to rehearse old polemics, much less settle them by declaring that Flores Galindo was in the right in every one of them. Nor do I mean to suggest that this *aggressive* style was always as acerbic and incensed as the examples cited above. In most cases, the tone was much less emphatic, although that did not make it less polemic. However, his rhetoric regained its sharp aggressive edge when it came to denunciations of human rights violations and other issues involving injustice, abuse, and repression. His writings on torture, the June 1986 prison massacre, or the existence of mass graves show, as Romano noted,[71] a capacity for denunciation 'fueled by hate, anger, rage' toward the object of his denunciation and which, I add, could prove very effective in sparking outrage in readers.

The second trait of Flores Galindo as a public intellectual that is worth highlighting is the unique way in which he intertwined the production of different kinds of texts with the formats, opportunities, and media he used to publish them. This, again, clearly reflects his formation during his student years and his growth as an intellectual, both of which took place within the leftwing political culture described above. As an author, he used a strategy that had much in common with communist *agitprop*, with the aim of maximising the impact of his ideas, maintaining a sustained presence in public debates, and causing the greatest stir possible among readers. We have already seen how he used

---

66 De Soto 1986. The book became a bestseller in multiple languages and enjoyed wide acclaim among defenders of free market and State deregulation.
67 Flores Galindo 1988d, p. 177.
68 Flores Galindo 1988d, p. 184.
69 Ibid.
70 Ibid.
71 Romano 1991a, p. 11.

a wide range of media to publish his work. Let us now look at the strategies implemented to achieve the results he sought. The process was more or less as follows: once he began reflecting on, researching, and writing about a given topic (Túpac Amaru, Mariátegui, or the Andean utopia, for instance), the initial formulations of his ideas would appear in the form of articles in the op-ed pages of newspapers or in cultural magazines and supplements. Some of those ideas – sometimes whole paragraphs or even the entire texts – would eventually be incorporated into an article or an essay that was featured in an academic journal or as a contribution to a multi-authored book. Finally, with some revisions and adjustments, the text would end up as part of one of the many books that Flores Galindo wrote and published. Along the way, he also addressed the same topics in public conferences and seminars, in reviews and prologues of books written by other authors, and in the compilations he prepared. One of the advantages of this strategy was the possibility it gave him of building his readers' expectation for the upcoming publication of a larger work. Another one was that he could test out his ideas with others, which allowed him to refine them in future and usually more extensive versions of those texts. A third advantage was that it satisfied the constant demand for his contributions. In this way, his name and style, in addition to his way of thinking and discussing, became increasingly familiar to readers, and thus ended up exerting an influence that, without exaggeration, surpassed that of most Peruvian intellectuals of his time.

Writing for a mass and non-academic audience was as important to Flores Galindo as writing for his academic peers and university students. In this, he undoubtedly shared the utilitarian and instrumental view of the printed word that characterised the leftwing political culture of his generation. To say that for him writing and publishing were also a way of doing *propaganda* does not in any way diminish his merits or the quality of his works. On the contrary, it underscores his commitment to certain intellectual and political practices in which he deeply believed: the need to connect intellectual work and cultural production with the everyday political action of the lower classes.

The strategy outlined above can be illustrated with the numerous works he published on Mariátegui. Flores Galindo's interest in Mariátegui and his time is already visible in his early research on the labour movement, published in 1972. This was the beginning of a period of rediscovery of Mariátegui by the Peruvian Left, to which Flores Galindo contributed greatly. Around 1976, he began publishing brief pieces on Communism, the labour movement, and the 1930 crisis, all of them related to Mariátegui's work and legacy. In 1978, coinciding with the celebration of the fiftieth anniversary of *Siete ensayos*, Flores Galindo published two articles on Mariátegui in *Amauta*, a magazine linked to the radical left. After that, and over the course of almost two years, he published a series of articles on Mariátegui, socialism, the Peruvian nation, and the Communist movement. Flores Galindo engaged in polemics with other scholars (Ricardo Luna Vegas, César Lévano, César Germaná) and with publications such as *Unidad*, the official mouthpiece of the Peruvian Communist Party. In his articles, Flores Galindo discussed the links between Mariátegui and *indigenismo*, Aprista reformism, and the Komintern. In an article published in Amauta in April 1980, under the title 'Uses and Abuses of Mariátegui', he condensed his view, which he would later expand on in his book *La agonía de Mariátegui*: 'Mariátegui's thinking must be understood in connection with his biography, and both his life and his works must be understood within the context of his time as part of the history of socialism, on the one hand, and as part of the history of Peru, on the other'.[72] In other words, he saw the need to historicise Mariátegui, his works, and his contributions.

The articles he published during those two years would inform, and sometimes would be incorporated in, *La agonía de Mariátegui*, his seminal study of Mariátegui's final years, published by DESCO in 1980, but Flores Galindo's reflection and publications on the founder of Peruvian Marxism did not end there. The second edition, which came out in 1982 and was also published by DESCO, saw a few changes in content – including the addition of some chapters that had appeared in other media –; and the third edition, published by Instituto de Apoyo Agrario in 1989, featured additional chapters, but it also went through some changes in tone. Manuel Burga noted that 'in the 1980 edition there is a subtle desacralising and even destructive tone that shifts to a humanising and constructive one in the 1989 edition'.[73]

The book *Aristocracia y plebe* offers a different version of the same strategy. It was first presented as his doctoral dissertation at Nanterre University in 1983, and the first edition was published in Lima by Mosca Azul Editores in 1984.[74] But sections and even entire chapters of the text had already been published in different outlets at least since 1981. These articles included 'Independencia y clases populares: el mundo al revés', that presented information and arguments from various chapters;[75] 'La pesca y los pescadores en la costa central (siglo XVIII)', a section of chapter 6;[76] 'La aristocracia mercantil limeña', a section

---

72 Flores Galindo 1980j, p. 138.
73 Burga 2005, p. 117.
74 Flores Galindo 1984a.
75 Flores Galindo 1982c.
76 Flores Galindo 1981b.

of chapter 3;[77] 'Vida de esclavos: un suicidio en Lima colonial', a short section of chapter 4;[78] 'Un motín: 5 de julio de 1821. El ocaso de la aristocracia colonial', part of chapter 3;[79] and 'Los rostros de la plebe', which corresponded to chapter 5 of the book.[80] As soon as the first edition sold out, Flores Galindo began preparing a second edition, which according to his wife Cecilia Rivera would include a new section 'where he would address the different worlds that Lima hides, including the Andean world'. This section was to be called 'The Submerged City', the same title Flores Galindo had chosen for the new edition of the book. The posthumous edition published by Editorial Horizonte in 1991 was in fact entitled *La ciudad sumergida. Aristocracia y plebe en Lima, 1760–1830.*[81] While it was essentially the same book, the different title and his plan to write a new section – cut short by his death – reflect both the author's constant concern with updating and revising his own writings and, regarding the dissemination of his works, the desire to convey a certain sense of novelty to his readers.

His most ambitious book, *In Search of an Inca*, which originated in a project on the Andean utopia ('La utopía andina') that he undertook with Manuel Burga, has a complicated and fascinating biography that further illustrates Flores Galindo's publishing strategies. While the idea for a joint research project appears to have matured around 1982 and the concrete proposal was drawn up in early 1983, when they coincided in Paris, their interest on the topic had begun several years earlier. In 1977, Flores Galindo published the article 'La nación como utopía. Túpac Amaru 1780',[82] and, in 1980, the two historians released *Apogeo y crisis de la república aristocrática*,[83] which featured some of the themes that would later be taken up in the Andean utopia project. Accord-

---

77   Flores Galindo 1983b.
78   Flores Galindo 1983c.
79   Flores Galindo 1984c.
80   Flores Galindo 1983d. The next issue of *Revista Andina*, where this essay was published, included extensive commentaries on it by half a dozen scholars (Julio Cotler, Luis Pásara, Steve Stern, Christine Hünefeldt, Paul Gootenberg, and Miguel Izard) and a response by Flores Galindo. *Revista Andina* 1984. Once again, this interesting exchange generated anticipation for the book's release, as did the many articles – both journalistic and academic – that the author had published and would later be incorporated in the book.
81   Cecilia Rivera, untitled note, in Flores Galindo 1991. Silvia Spitta compared Flores Galindo's book with Ángel Rama's *La ciudad letrada* (*The Lettered City*), also published originally in 1984, and stressed the former's concern for shedding light – in contrast to Rama – on that other (submerged) city of commoners, slaves, indigenous people, and castes. Spitta 2003.
82   Flores Galindo 1977b.
83   Burga and Flores Galindo 1980.

FIGURE 1   First Peruvian edition of *Buscando un Inca* (1987).
© INSTITUTO DE APOYO AGRARIO

ing to my sources, the notion of *Andean utopia* was used for the first time in a 1981 article by Flores Galindo entitled 'Utopía andina y socialismo'.[84] The first joint reflections with Burga regarding their ambitious project were published in 1982 in three different texts of varying lengths and titles: a mimeographed booklet printed by the Department of Social Sciences of the PUCP;[85] an article published in two issues of the supplement *El Caballo Rojo*;[86] and an article in the journal *Allpanchis*.[87] From 1982 to 1986, Flores Galindo presented several essays connected with this project in conferences, workshops, and seminars, and preliminary versions of those essays would later appear in various journals and compilations.[88]

In late 1985, Flores Galindo organised them into a book manuscript titled *Buscando un Inca. Identidad y utopía en los Andes*, which he submitted to Cuba's prestigious Casa de las Américas competition in the essay category. The book was awarded the prize in 1986. The first edition, published in Havana in November of that year by Casa de las Américas, consisted of six chapters, an introduction and an epilogue. That edition had only a limited circulation in Peru, but, as noted above, the book's first chapter, 'Europe and the Land of the Incas: The Andean Utopia', was published that same year in Lima in a small book format by Instituto de Apoyo Agrario, in an attractive edition by Luis Valera.[89] But even before the Cuban edition was released, Flores Galindo was already planning to expand the book for the Peruvian edition to be published by Instituto de Apoyo Agrario. A table of contents dated 28 October 1986, included three more chapters.[90] One of them (tentatively titled 'El discurso racista') did not make

---

84   Flores Galindo 1981a.
85   Burga and Flores Galindo 1982b.
86   Burga and Flores Galindo 1982c.
87   Burga and Flores Galindo 1982d.
88   Chapter 1 ('Europe and the Land of the Incas: The Andean Utopia') was published as a stand-alone booklet in March 1986 by Instituto de Apoyo Agrario (Flores Galindo 1986b); part of chapter 2 ('The Túpac Amaru Revolution and the Andean People') was featured in the journal *Allpanchis* (Flores Galindo 1981c), and an extended version was presented at the Permanent Seminar on Agrarian Research (SEPIA) in October 1985 and published the following year (Flores Galindo 1986c); chapter 4 ('Soldiers and Montoneros') was published in the journal *Los Caminos del Laberinto* (Flores Galindo 1986d); and chapter 5 ('The Utopian Horizon') was presented at the Andean history colloquium organised by IFEA in August 1984 and published in the resulting volume (Flores Galindo 1986e).
89   I would like to highlight the role played by Luis Valera as promoter, editor, proofreader, and designer of many of Flores Galindo's publications.
90   Letter from Alberto Flores Galindo to Juan Mendoza, director of Instituto de Apoyo Agrario, Lima, 28 October 1986. I thank Juan Mendoza for sharing with us copies of his correspondence with Flores Galindo.

it, and thus the second edition of *Buscando un Inca*, published in June 1987, had grown to eight chapters plus the introduction and epilogue.[91] The changes, however, were not limited to adding chapters. The epilogue to the 1986 Cuban edition was expanded and became chapter 8, 'The Silent War'.[92] A new epilogue, entitled 'Dreams and Nightmares', was written, according to the author, 'to avoid misunderstandings', and it was based on the article '¿Es posible la utopía?' originally featured in *El Caballo Rojo*.[93] The title of the new epilogue was drawn from a letter that appeared in a May 1986 issue of *Amauta*, under the title 'The Andean Utopia: Dreams and Nightmares'. The second edition sold out within a few months, and Flores Galindo began to prepare a new and enlarged edition. It was published by Editorial Horizonte and Instituto de Apoyo Agrario in 1988 and featured three new chapters, bringing the total to eleven, in addition to the introduction and the epilogue. Two of these new chapters originated in papers delivered at conferences. This was the definitive edition that would later be posthumously reprinted in Peru and Mexico and translated into Italian and English (minus one chapter in the latter case).[94]

One more compilation of Flores Galindo's texts is worth a brief mention in the context of reconstructing his publishing strategies. In 1988, he compiled seventeen articles and essays under the title *Tiempo de plagas*.[95] The idea, shared with Juan Mendoza in October 1986, was to bring together 'diverse and scattered' materials under the provisional title 'Authoritarianism and Utopia. Essays on Marxism and Peruvian Society'.[96] His trips to Havana and Barcelona in the first half of 1987 delayed the project. The selection of texts was made with his collaborators in SUR Maruja Martínez and Goni Evans. Luis

---

91 From Barcelona, where he spent a semester teaching, Flores Galindo wrote to Mendoza on 5 March and 12 May 1987, insisting that they should wait until he returned to Lima to send the book to print, since he wanted to include the new materials.

92 The text, originally presented at the Second Encounter of Intellectuals for the Sovereignty of the Peoples of Our America (Havana, 1985) was also included, along with an essay by Nelson Manrique, in a pamphlet titled *Violencia y campesinado* (Flores Galindo and Manrique 1986). In chapter 5 of this book, Charles Walker offers valuable observations on this text and highlights the differences between both versions.

93 Flores Galindo 1986f.

94 The Mexican edition was published by CONACULTA and Grijalbo in 1993. In Peru, there have been seven editions: Instituto de Apoyo Agrario 1987; Horizonte 1988; Horizonte, 1994; SUR, 2005 (as part of Flores Galindo's *Obras Completas*); El Comercio, 2010; Horizonte, 2021; and Horizonte and Universidad Nacional San Antonio Abad del Cusco, 2021. The Italian translation, *Perú: identitá e utopia. Cercando un Inca*, was published by Ponte Alle Grazie (Florence, 1991). The English edition, as noted before, was published in 2010.

95 Flores Galindo 1988c.

96 Letter from Alberto Flores Galindo to Juan Mendoza, Lima, 28 October 1986.

Valera was, again, in charge of the edition. The texts, two of them unpublished, were divided into three sections: 'Exiliados y militantes' ('Exiled and militants') included essays on intellectuals, socialism, and the left; 'Contra la corriente' ('Against the Current') consisted of a series of polemic texts that dealt with political violence, human rights violations, and other contemporary topics; and 'Fin' ('The End'), the shortest section, offered a bleak portrait of Peru's political and social crisis and stressed the pervasiveness of authoritarian traditions, but also reiterated his conviction, in the last chapter, that socialism offered a solution to Peru's social maladies. While the book title, *Time of Plagues* (Flores Galindo had a talent for sharp and unforgettable titles) reflected the sense of despair that was only deepening by the time it was released (July 1988), that of its last section ('The End') was sadly prophetic, as it anticipated the (soon to be discovered) illness that caused Flores Galindo's untimely death. This was, indeed, the last book authored by him published during his lifetime. The decision to print it in small format and font reveals his goal of reaching a wide audience. Using an independent imprint with a clear association with the left underlines his interest in connecting his intellectual output to a political tradition.

As the above accounts document, Flores Galindo had an ongoing, intense, and almost obsessive relationship with the world of printing and publishing. Through different formats and with topics that were often novel, his presence in the intellectual and public sphere was highly visible. He built his career as a historian, but especially as a public intellectual, drawing on an inexhaustible energy, an indisputable talent for thinking and writing, and a great passion for intellectual debate, but also thanks to his close and astute relationship with the world of books, magazines, newspapers, cultural supplements, and other printed media. His influence would not have been the same if he had not tapped so deeply into those publication strategies, and the quality of his works would probably not have reached the same levels. But, above all, his role as a public intellectual and his ability to make his voice heard in the debates of his time would have been severely limited had it not been for that determined, energetic, and passionate connection with the printed word.

3   Conclusion: The Public Intellectual and Print Culture

Flores Galindo was not only part of a leftwing culture that valued the printed word as an effective vehicle of communication, propaganda, denunciation, and debate, but also shared with it a conception of the intellectual as someone morally obliged to participate in public debates at every opportunity and in whatever platform was available to him. These two factors are behind both his astonishing productivity – his complete works comprise seven volumes with 400 to 600 pages each – and his aggressive, varied, and creative publication strategy. This constant presence in intellectual and political debates and in a multiplicity of media (ranging from modest, short-lived magazines to mass circulation newspapers and supplements, as well as prestigious academic journals and solid publishing houses) enabled him to wield an influence as a public intellectual that other contemporaries of his, both less and more talented than him, never could.

Flores Galindo was a professional historian, a brilliant and creative one, but he was never interested in merely producing, every ten years, a solid and definitive monographic work on some topic of the Peruvian past that was likely to be read by only a handful of colleagues and students. His commitment was above all to the passions and stirrings of his time. It was from there that his intellectual and academic concerns sprang, and they were the source of the urgencies that led him to an almost uninterrupted production of texts aimed at the general public. His optimism for the future must have also contributed to that desire to publish as much as his energies allowed him to. His activism in the Left did not go through a phase of disenchantment and skepticism: his conviction of the importance of intellectual work and the link between that work and the social struggles of the disadvantaged classes accompanied him to the end, and his faith in the power of the written word never waned, judging by his tenacious and constant dedication to preparing texts to be sent to the printing press.

Acknowledgements

This chapter is a revised and updated version of Aguirre 2007. I thank José Ragas for his careful reading of the original manuscript, as well as for his suggestions and help in obtaining some materials, and Pedro Guibovich, with whom I prepared the dossier that included this text. Laura Pérez Carrara translated it into English.

CHAPTER 4

'Theres Is No Happy Island': Flores Galindo, Cuba, and the Socialist Utopia

Carlos Aguirre

In 1986, Alberto Flores Galindo was awarded the Casa de las Américas prize in the essay category for his book *Buscando un Inca. Identidad y utopía en los Andes*. The Cuban edition was released in November of that year, and in June 1987, the first Peruvian edition was published by Instituto de Apoyo Agrario with a memorable cover design by Luis Valera. In the acknowledgments page Flores Galindo wrote:

> The original version of this book was awarded the Casa de las Américas prize in Havana, Cuba, which was a source of happiness for me for two reasons. First, because of the institution and the country that awarded me the prize. Second, because a committee comprising intellectuals from different Latin American countries demonstrated that they did not share the misgivings and attacks that supposedly orthodox Marxist critics had launched against my previous works.[1]

The joy he felt at being awarded the prize in 1986 reflected, among other things, the important place that Cuba occupied in Flores Galindo's intellectual and political horizon. He identified with the Left and socialism very early in life and belonged to a generation that came of age in politics amidst the illusions created by the Cuban Revolution. As a young student, he became an active member of the Revolutionary Front of Socialist Students (Frente Revolucionario de Estudiantes Socialistas, or FRES), which he later abandoned to engage more directly with the working classes. With other young students such as Alberto Adrianzén, he would hand out flyers to factory workers near Plaza de Acho or Plaza Unión. They also visited detained Trotskyist leader Hugo Blanco at El Frontón penal colony, 'to explain our views'.[2] Flores Galindo was for some time a member of Peru's Revolutionary Left Movement (Movimiento

---

1 Flores Galindo 2010, p. 256.
2 Adrianzén 1990.

de Izquierda Revolucionaria, or MIR), but he ultimately left the party and would not be involved since in any partisan activity.[3] While Cuba was very important to his generation, Flores Galindo maintained a critical distance with respect to the Fidel Castro regime. His relatively cold attitude toward Cuban socialism responded to his adherence to a form of Marxism that was more open and less dogmatic than the Soviet version of it, which had become entrenched in Cuba, and by his rejection of any form of State authoritarianism.[4] His critical stance insulated him from any unconditional affiliation. Adrianzén suggests that Flores Galindo was always a 'dissident', even when it came to leftwing movements or regimes.[5] While his affinity to Cuba was undeniable, so was his skepticism about the island's political model.[6]

In fact, a comprehensive review of his extensive journalistic and essayist production yields very few references to the Cuban Revolution.[7] In his numerous texts on Marxism and the Left there are hardly any references to Cuba and Fidel Castro. After his first two visits to Cuba, in 1981 and 1985, when he participated in the first and second Encounter of Intellectuals for the Sovereignty of the Peoples of Our America (Encuentro de intelectuales por la soberanía de los pueblos de nuestra América), Flores Galindo did not write about his experiences in socialist Cuba. In his 1982 article on the Peruvian New Left – which was actually an account of the history of the Vanguardia Revolucionaria

---

3 See Nelson Manrique's account in a 22 March 2015 interview by Ricardo Portocarrero (https://bit.ly/39P7nUA). According to Manrique, Flores Galindo described his experience in the MIR as 'a disaster'. Later, during his time in Paris, he was close to Vanguardia Revolucionaria, but he was never actively involved in any of the many parties of the Peruvian Left.

4 In his overview of the development of the New Left in Peru, Adrianzén points to 'the abandonment of Cuban Castrism' as one of the features that characterised it in the early 1970s (Adrianzén 2011, p. 52). In general, history books and articles on the Peruvian Left and the accounts of its militants cite Cuba as a major influence and inspiration, but there is no systematic study on the complex and changing relations between the various groups and intellectuals of the Peruvian Left and the Cuban Revolution.

5 Author's personal communication with Alberto Adrianzén, 29 February 2020.

6 According to Augusto Ruiz Zevallos, Flores Galindo criticised real socialism and condemned the Soviet invasion of Czechoslovakia, but 'seemed very tolerant of Castro's regime'. This last assertion refers to an opinion given by Gonzalo Portocarrero in 1991, in which he stated that Flores Galindo 'harbored an illusion about Fidel Castro's Cuba that I have long ago abandoned'. Ruiz Zevallos 2011, pp. 15–16.

7 Eduardo Cáceres Valdivia's excellent introduction to the complete works of Flores Galindo is highly indicative of that relative silence: neither Cuba nor the Cuban Revolution are mentioned. What defined Flores Galindo's generation, Cáceres argues, was Velasquismo (the nationalist military regime project led by General Juan Velasco Alvarado between 1968 and 1975), because it posed a great dilemma for the Peruvian Left, torn between viewing it as 'a socialist revolution or a caricature of a revolution'. Cáceres Valdivia 1993, p. xiv.

(Revolutionary Vanguard) party – he stressed the importance that 'the feats of the twelve Granma survivors' and, after 1967, the image of Che Guevara, had in the new recruits' motivation for joining the party.[8] In 1984, he reviewed *La historia como arma*, by prominent Cuban historian Manuel Moreno Fraginals, in which he credited the Revolution with having 'broadened [the historian's] horizons' and stimulating the practice of 'a new history, thought in terms of a future that was under construction, rather than from the present'.[9] He did not add any further comments about the revolutionary process, most likely because he felt uncomfortable given the relative isolation that Moreno Fraginals was subjected to in Cuba.[10] In his much-commented article on the 'Generation of 1968',[11] published in March 1987 but written sometime late in 1986, the Revolution is only mentioned a couple of times, as a distant reference. After visiting Cuba for the third time in January 1987, when he served on the committee that awarded the Ernesto Che Guevara Extraordinary Prize of Casa de las Américas, Flores Galindo wrote 'El socialismo a la vuelta de la esquina', his only substantial text on Cuba and which is crucial for understanding his relationship with the Revolution.[12]

Although Cuba had been an important reference for Flores Galindo since his youth, it was not until the mid-1980s that he forged a closer relationship with the Revolution as a result of his visits to the island and his interactions with Cuban intellectuals. Consequently, while he did not entirely shed his reservations about the form of socialism implemented in Cuba – Flores Galindo was never an 'unconditional' supporter –, he did gain a deeper understanding of the difficulties faced by the Cuban Revolution, which led him to explain, and even justify, some of the measures with which he disagreed, especially with respect to the role of the State and the suppression of criticism. At the same time, he witnessed firsthand and celebrated the changes that the Revolution had brought to the Cuban people's everyday lives.

---

8   Flores Galindo 1982d, p. 119.
9   Flores Galindo 1984d, p. 84.
10 In the prologue to Moreno Fraginals's book, Catalan historian Josep Fontana does mention the fact that the Cuban historian 'was unsettling for those who understand Marxism as a simple intellectual school or a party affiliation', and whose master work, *El ingenio*, 'met with reticence and incomprehension in Cuba itself, not from authentic revolutionaries, but from a cultural bureaucracy ... with the self-appointed role of deciding who is or is not a "Marxist"'. Fontana 1983.
11 Flores Galindo 1987a.
12 Flores Galindo 1987d. The article was originally published under the title 'Caminar por La Habana. El socialismo a la vuelta de la esquina', in *Sí* (Lima), 12 October 1987. An expanded version was published with the shorter and definitive title in Flores Galindo 1988c.

1 Latin American Intellectuals Respond to Reagan

In November 1980, Republican candidate Ronald Reagan was elected president of the United States, having gained the support of a large share of U.S. voters, thanks in part to his aggressive stance against Cuba, Nicaragua, and the Central American revolutionary movements. His victory ushered in an extremely troubling scenario for the future of the region, to which neither Cuba nor Latin American intellectuals close to the Revolution remained indifferent. On 4–5 February 1981, shortly after Reagan's inauguration, Havana hosted an 'Encounter of Latin American and Caribbean Writers'. Participants at that event issued a final statement highlighting the 'new global political state of affairs' marked by, among other things, an 'intimidation and disinformation campaign' launched by the Reagan administration.[13]

A few months later, Casa de las Américas organised the first Encounter of Intellectuals for the Sovereignty of the Peoples of Our America, held in Havana on 4–7 September 1981. Nearly three hundred intellectuals accepted the invitation to attend.[14] At the inauguration ceremony, Fidel Castro was accompanied by renown writers and artists such as Gabriel García Márquez, Mario Benedetti, Oswaldo Guayasamín, and Juan Bosch, all seated on the main stage under a huge banner displaying a quote by José Martí: 'Trenches of ideas are worth more than trenches of stone'. In his opening address, the Cuban minister of culture, Armando Hart, vigorously condemned 'the imperialist domination of our America' and 'the genocide and violence suffered by most countries in the continent'. Hart then focused on the cultural aspects of U.S. penetration and denounced 'the system of imperialist exploitation [that] imposes a vicious tyranny over the creative capacity of the popular masses and the best talents of Latin America and the Caribbean'.[15] In an article published a few days later in the Spanish newspaper *El País*, García Márquez also warned of the 'dangers that threaten the cultural identity and sovereignty of our nations, at a time when a movie cowboy has galloped his way into the White House'.[16]

Participants were organised into three working groups, each of them dealing, respectively, with economic and social factors affecting sovereignty, cultural factors, and the 'current situations and problems' in the struggle for sover-

---

13   'Llamamiento por los derechos soberanos y democráticos de los pueblos de nuestra América', Archivo Vertical, Casa de las Américas.
14   Individual files for 295 participants are kept in Archivo Vertical, Casa de las Américas.
15   *Granma* (Havana), 5 September 1981.
16   García Márquez 1981.

eignty.[17] The event closed with a final statement that included a categorical condemnation of the interventionism of the Reagan administration: 'Now, as the government of the United States not only threatens to reinstate the anachronistic policy of the bludgeon in our continent, but is arming up to wage a new war of global devastation, we intellectuals of Our America must redouble our commitment to our peoples, and especially to those who are going up against age-old oppression with more bravery than resources'. Participants also issued a 'Letter to the People and Intellectuals of the United States' in which they spoke of 'the danger of an armed intervention that threatens the peace of our peoples, their cultural heritage, their territorial integrity, and even their very survival'. They also agreed to create a 'Permanent Committee of Intellectuals for the Sovereignty of the Peoples of Our America', formed by Mario Benedetti, Juan Bosch, Chico Buarque, Ernesto Cardenal, Suzy Castor, Julio Cortázar, Gabriel García Márquez, Pablo González Casanova, George Lamming, Roberto Matta, Miguel Otero Silva, and the president of Casa de las Américas, Mariano Rodríguez, the only Cuban representative in the committee.[18]

In an article published a few days after the event, Benedetti described it as a 'miracle of harmony and fraternal discussion', and stressed that 'the key factor behind this exceptional unity has a name: Ronald Reagan'. The gravity of the situation, he concluded, 'imbued the sessions with a dramatic, rigorous, and determined tone, something not often seen in conferences of intellectuals. Nobody digressed or got caught up in interminable debates, nor did anyone voice pamphletary statements or give free rein to their vanity'.[19] While it was undoubtedly a major event that exuded an atmosphere of solidarity and commitment, Benedetti's account seems somewhat idealised.

Flores Galindo traveled to Cuba for the first time as part of the group of Peruvian intellectuals who participated in this conference. Also attending were the writer Alfredo Bryce Echenique, the sociologist Sinesio López (at that time director of the leftist daily *El Diario de Marka*), the journalists Juan Larco and Francisco Moncloa, the literary critic Antonio Cornejo Polar, the poets Washington Delgado, Antonio Cisneros, and Reynaldo Naranjo, the musicians Cesar Bolaños and Celso Garrido Lecca, the theater director Luis Peirano, and the filmmaker Alberto Durant.[20] Revealingly, Flores Galindo signed-up for the

---

17 *Granma* (Havana), 1 September 1981.
18 The speeches, messages of support, declarations, and other documents pertaining to the meeting were published in *Casa de las Américas* 1981.
19 Benedetti 1981.
20 They all left for Havana together on 3 September, boarding a Cubana de Aviación aircraft that also transported participants such as Chico Buarque and Roberto Drummond

second discussion group, chaired by Mario Benedetti and Roberto Fernández Retamar, which dealt with 'cultural factors that limit the sovereignty of our peoples'. This group heard presentations by, among others, Néstor García Canclini from Argentina, Cintio Vitier from Cuba, Luis Britto García from Venezuela, and Eduardo Galeano from Uruguay.

Unlike other Peruvian participants such as Francisco Moncloa or Juan Larco, Flores Galindo traveled to Habana with more curiosity and even skepticism than strong enthusiasm for the Revolution. Flores Galindo, like Luis Peirano, with whom he shared a hotel room, felt warmly toward Cuba, but could not disguise his unease with certain aspects of the Cuban regime. Peirano recalls how, upon first entering their room, Flores Galindo said jokingly, 'Let's find where the bugs are planted'.[21] After the event ended, participants were invited to visit Pinar del Río, a municipality famous for its tobacco and the Viñales valley, but Flores Galindo declined the invitation. When Peirano insisted that he had to go see with his own eyes how Cuban socialism worked, Flores Galindo tried to dissuade him instead, arguing that 'they are going to tell you the story they want you to hear' and suggesting that it was all arranged to convey the official version of the Revolution.[22] During one of their walks around Havana, Peirano, who acted as photographer for the group, took the well-known snapshot of Flores Galindo, Sinesio López, Antonio Cisneros, and Alberto Durant, which seems to betray the historian's mood: while his three companions look amused and laughing, Flores Galindo projects a more somber image, even in the way he is dressed; he appears to be taking things more seriously and looks more con-

---

from Brazil and Héctor Agosti and Osvaldo Pugliese from Argentina. Undated document, Archivo Vertical, Casa de las Américas. In the first volume of his memoirs, Bryce Echenique wrote his impressions on the 1981 conference, characteristically combining humor and exaggerations, sprinkled with a bit of fantasy. During the event, he says, 'I feel somewhat lost amidst a pro-Soviet or Maoist Marxist Left that is starting to seem somewhat anachronistic to me ... in the crowded lobby of the Riviera hotel, surrounded by people arriving, eager and beaming, at the mecca of Latin American revolution, centuries of contradictions and doubts weigh down on me as united revolutionaries from around the world embrace in fraternal reunions'. On the day of the inauguration, 'the large organising committee, which would preside over the ceremony from the stage, made its entrance. Fidel came in, filling the room with his presence ... Gabriel García Márquez had already appeared, dressed impeccably in white ... I swear I had never seen someone as solemn as a solemn Gabo', he writes referring to the Colombian writer by his nickname. And on the day the event closed, 'the united revolutionaries of the world debate over lobster, various delicacies, superb aged rum, and an opportunity to come really up close to Fidel Castro and exchange a few friendly words'. Bryce Echenique 1993, pp. 349–81.

21   Author's personal communication with Luis Peirano, 3 March 2020.
22   Ibid.

cerned with his surroundings than with gazing into the camera and joining in his friends' merriment.²³

This unease with respect to Cuba explains in part why he did not write any reflections about this visit and what he had seen and heard in Havana. He most likely wished to keep his criticisms to himself at such a delicate moment in Cuba-U.S. relations.²⁴ At the same time, there is an aspect of his trajectory as historian and intellectual that has seldom been stressed and that could also help explain, at least in part, his 'silence' about Cuba: international affairs never occupied a prominent place in his abundant written production. That is not to say that he was not interested in international topics or that he was uninformed about them – quite the opposite.²⁵ But when it came to choosing the topics to be addressed in his essays or opinion pieces, Peruvian history and contemporary events were an absolute priority. Flores Galindo wrote several articles on foreign writers and intellectuals – Pierre Vilar, Lev Tolstoi, Bronislaw Geremek, E.P. Thompson, Isaac Deutscher, Leon Trotsky, Fernand Braudel, and Ruggiero Romano – and, in some, he referenced historical events such as the Russian Revolution, but it is hard to find any writings by him that focus on international current events. He never wrote, for example, about the military dictatorships in the Southern Cone, the Sandinista victory in Nicaragua, or Reagan's aggressive interventionist policy.²⁶ In light of this, it becomes somewhat less surprising that neither the 1981 conference nor his experiences in the Cuban capital would motivate him to commit his impressions to paper.

In 1985, Flores Galindo traveled again to Cuba to participate in the Second Encounter of Intellectuals, which was held in Havana from 29 November to 2 December. At the time, the bloody 'Contras' war was being waged in Nicaragua, supported and financed by the CIA and the Reagan administration. The call issued to potential participants stressed the sense of urgency created by 'a

---

23 The photograph was printed in Portocarrero 2005, p. 19, although it was incorrectly dated 1987. Other photographs taken by Peirano capture different moments of the event as well as leisure activities. In one of them, members of the Peruvian delegation, including Flores Galindo, can be seen enjoying drinks at a Havana bar.
24 It should also be noted that Cuba was still dealing with the repercussions of the January 1980 incident at the Peruvian embassy in Havana that sparked a diplomatic crisis, followed by the exodus of thousands of Cubans through the port of Mariel.
25 Flores Galindo added his signature on various manifestos and open letters regarding foreign affairs, such as one supporting the holding of an international conference in solidarity with Nicaragua (*Expreso*, Lima, 7 June 1979) or another one condemning U.S. 'military threats against Cuba and Central America' (*El Diario de Marka*, Lima, 22 November 1981).
26 An exception is a public letter he wrote on terrorism in the Basque Country. See Flores Galindo 1987e.

difficult international state of affairs, in which the economic crisis and foreign debt, political blackmail, and threats of direct military intervention on the part of U.S. imperialism, and its unbridled arms race cast a shadow on the present and future of the countries in the region and of humanity'. The opening address was delivered by Nobel Prize writer Gabriel García Márquez.[27] Besides Flores Galindo, the Peruvian delegation included the cartoonist Juan Acevedo, the philosopher José Ignacio López Soria, the historians Alberto Tauro and Nelson Manrique, the anthropologist Rodrigo Montoya, the poets Carmen Ollé, Arturo Corcuera, and Roger Santiváñez, the journalist Carlos Urrutia, and the psychoanalyst Cesar Rodríguez Rabanal.

Flores Galindo joined Working Group 1 on 'Culture, Democracy, Sovereignty, and Peace in Our America', which was chaired by the Cuban literary historian and critic José Antonio Portuondo. His presentation was entitled 'Violence and Authoritarianism in Peru', and in the official publication of Casa de las Américas it was described as 'a detailed analysis, with abundant information and data, of the violence that occurred in Peru between 1980 and 1984, which left a death toll of more than 5000 people, mostly peasants. Flores Galindo offers an account of the strategy implemented by the government at the time, which even involved pitting communities against each other, in what he called the 'silent war'.[28]

As Nelson Manrique would recall years later, Flores Galindo took the opportunity afforded by his visit to the island to see for himself what Cuban socialism was like. The full passage where Manrique describes this trip is worth quoting here:

> In December 1985, as part of a large delegation, we traveled to Havana to participate as guests in a conference of Latin American intellectuals. We were particularly interested in seeing Cuban society unmediated, and, throughout the week of the event, we visited every place we could: factories, schools, trade unions, hospitals, universities, parks, etc.
>
> Once the official stay was over, and despite the fact that Tito did not like to be away from home for long, I managed to persuade him to stay

---

27 The speech by *'compañero* Gabo', the presentations, the summaries of the working groups, and other documents of the meeting were published in *Casa de las Américas* 1986.

28 Casa de las Américas, 'Memoria periodística del Segundo Encuentro de Intelectuales por la Soberanía de los Pueblos de Nuestra América', 4 December 1985, 4. Archivo Vertical, Casa de las Américas. See also *Granma* (Havana), 2 December 1985. As mentioned in chapter 3, the text of this presentation would be included as the epilogue to the first edition of *Buscando un Inca* and, later, will be expanded and turned into the book's final chapter.

FIGURE 2 Nelson Manrique and Alberto Flores Galindo in Cuba (1985)
SOURCE: NELSON MANRIQUE'S PERSONAL ARCHIVE

one more week, so we could have a better idea of what went on in the socialist island. That was *the beginning of a deep relationship with Cuba and its people* [...] He was not oblivious to the problems that Cuba faced. *Neither did he keep his criticism of the Cuban model to himself.*

Tito found a formidable interlocutor in Fernando Martínez, the former editor of *Pensamiento Crítico*, the Cuban journal on theoretical issues that ran during the first decade of the Revolution. While it was an exceptional journal in terms of quality and openness, it was ultimately shut down in the late 1960s due to pressure from the Soviets, who were concerned over the heterodoxy of the Cubans.[29]

---

29 Manrique 2005.

Flores Galindo's friendship with Fernando Martínez Heredia (1939–2017), the prominent Marxist intellectual who had been the editor of *Pensamiento Crítico* from 1967 to 1971, that Manrique mentioned, is very important to understand the Peruvian historian's relationship with Cuba in the second half of the 1980s. I have been unable to identify the exact times and places in which they met over the years. It is likely that they first met in Lima, in 1984 or 1985, when Martínez Heredia was touring several Latin American countries as part of his work for the Centro de Estudios sobre América (CEA). In an interview, years later, Martínez Heredia would recall that during a trip to Peru, for which he provides no date, 'I met and began a beautiful friendship with Alberto Flores Galindo, who was one of the best historians in the continent … Alberto was a notable Marxist'.[30]

Martínez Heredia fought consistently against the temptation of dogmatism, disseminated works by heterodox Marxists and by non-Marxist thinkers, and turned *Pensamiento Crítico* into a leftwing platform open to debate and dissent. The core group of contributors to the magazine were associated with the Department of Philosophy of the University of Havana and were known as the 'K Street Group', in reference to the location of the house where they met. Its members were committed supporters of the Revolution, but they also hoped to disseminate opposing viewpoints and lesser-known authors; in particular, they wished to resist the rigidity of the Soviet model of socialism.[31] During the first few years, they were not only tolerated but also supported by the revolutionary regime. A quantitative study of the magazine's content reveals that the most featured authors were Fidel Castro and Che Guevara.[32] Encouraged by Castro, they created Edición Revolucionaria, a publishing project that aimed to 'produce quality books in Cuba, drawn from any sources, which could help [the country] take the giant leap that needed to be taken in education and knowledge'.[33] However, as the Cuban regime became increasingly sovietised, the magazine, which sold 15,000 copies a month and was very popular among Cuban and international readers, began to be perceived as a threat to the Revolution. In 1971, the same year of the famous Padilla case, the magazine was shut down by the government and its staff was laid off from their positions in the university. It was even proposed that they be stripped of their Communist

---

30   Suárez and Kruijt 2012.
31   See Martínez Heredia 2008. The magazine's editorial board was formed by Martínez Heredia, Aurelio Alonso, Jesús Díaz, Ricardo J. Machado, Thalía Fung, José Bell Lara, and Mireya Crespo.
32   Information drawn from Ponce Suárez 2014.
33   Martínez Heredia 2008, p. 242.

Party membership.³⁴ The order to shut down *Pensamiento Crítico* came at the beginning of the so-called 'gray quinquennium', a period of intellectual obscurantism that characterised the 1970s in Cuba.³⁵ What Flores Galindo wrote in 1987 (that his work had been met with 'skepticism and disparagements' from 'supposedly-orthodox Marxists') could also describe the situation that Martínez Heredia himself faced in revolutionary Cuba in the 1970s. After working for some years in Nicaragua, Martínez Heredia joined in 1984 the Centro de Estudios sobre América (CEA), created within the Cuban Communist Party in 1976 and tasked with promoting intellectual thinking on Latin American issues.

In a 2007 essay, Martínez Heredia would say, with respect to the shutdown of *Pensamiento Crítico*, that it had occurred at a time in which 'social thinking was subjected to changes that led to the stunting of its development, and to a great impoverishment and dogmatisation'.³⁶ This hardening of the intellectual field gave way to 'painful witch hunts or infamous practices in the treatment among colleagues'. But these tensions were not new; they had emerged with the dawning of the Revolution: 'From the beginning, the obsession with classifying, disciplining, enforcing orders, and attributing ulterior motives clashed with the *healthy combination of liberal spirit and power* that the revolution achieved'. (Emphasis added). He then provided a first-hand account of the experience of the group of intellectuals involved in the magazine:

> First, young members, like me, *agreed that the revolution had to protect itself from its enemies with whatever means it deemed necessary. We thought that the requirement of not acting against the revolution was very valid*. Second, it seemed very natural to us that intellectuals with ideas different from our own should work as such, and we admired the work of [Fernando] Ortiz, [José] Lezama [Lima], Ramiro Guerra, and others already deceased, such as [Enrique] Varona, [Jorge] Mañach, or [Carlos] Loveira. Third, *we were against sectarianism, dogmatism, authoritarianism, and so-called socialist realism*. Fourth, we did not think that the political authorities were conceding anything to us, because we felt *we shared the same ideals*; and at the same time we believed that anyone who tried to gain something for themselves through the intellectual work they did in favor of the revolution was an opportunist …

---

34 On the closing down of the magazine, see Díaz 2000, Grenier 2017, pp. 108–12, and Rodríguez Rivera 2017.
35 The term was coined by Ambrosio Fornet. Others refer to this period as the 'the black decade', suggesting it was longer and darker. See Fornet 2007.
36 Martínez Heredia 2007.

In that dialectic of freedom and activism, how are the scope and protection of thinking and its subjection to rules and discipline determined? Who determines all this? What mechanism and guarantees are put in place to avoid mistakes or abuses? (Emphases added).

Martínez Heredia's questions go to the very heart of the complicated relationship that has existed between the Cuban Revolution and intellectuals (freedom versus activism, to put it in his terms), but also the more general problem of the type of relationship between the state and its citizens that a socialist society must forge. In other words, the model of political organisation of socialism.

Did Martínez Heredia and Flores Galindo discuss this during those days in Havana in 1985? There is no doubt that they did. These were two socialist intellectuals interested in fostering doctrinal and political debate, open to non-Marxist currents of thought, opposed to dogmatism and monolithic thinking, and supporters of a version of socialism that was both revolutionary and democratic. The confluence of interests and positions with respect to socialism proved very fertile. Martínez Heredia included Flores Galindo among the 'brothers' who accompanied him in 'researching the major contemporary problems affecting the continent and the paths, strategies, and tactics for liberation'.[37] Martínez Heredia is said to have recommended Flores Galindo's books to young people who reached out to him.[38] In the interview conducted by Suárez and Kruijt, Martínez Heredia said of Flores Galindo that 'his book *Aristocracia y plebe. Lima, 1760–1830* should be a classic'.[39] In another text on Mariátegui he included several references to works by Flores Galindo.[40] The problems of Marxism, Mariátegui's ideas, and the reality of Cuban socialism were major topics of conversation between Flores Galindo and Martínez Heredia.

Martínez Heredia's reservations towards certain aspects of the Revolution did not turn him into a dissident. Despite the hostility he suffered from time to time from the government, he was able to continue with his intellectual work and he never wavered in his defence of the cause of socialism.[41] Moreover, he

---

37 Martínez Heredia 2005.
38 Alonso 2017.
39 Suárez and Kruijt 2012. Martínez Heredia added: '*Buscando un Inca* and *La agonía de Mariátegui* are also among his major works'.
40 Martínez Heredia 2000.
41 In 1989 he was awarded the Casa de las Américas prize for a book on Che Guevara. In 1996, CEA was effectively disbanded by the leadership of the Cuban Communist Party 'after issuing a devastating public critique', as Martínez Heredia mentioned in the interview cited above, that included an accusation by Raúl Castro of being complicit with foreign

accepted the idea that the Revolution had the right to defend itself and maintained, as seen above, that taking action against its enemies was 'very valid'. Flores Galindo would also adopt this stance, as we will see below.

2   The 1986 Casa De Las Américas Prize

Casa de las Américas, the most important cultural institution of the Cuban Revolution, was established in April 1959, a few months after the revolutionary victory. The following year, it launched its annual literary contest, awarding prizes in several categories: poetry, short story, novel, drama, and essay. Years later, other categories were added, including testimony and Caribbean literature in French and Creole. One of the main goals of these competitions was to break the cultural isolation the island suffered as a result of the U.S. embargo and the hostility from most Latin American governments. The prizes also served to showcase intellectuals from around the region, both the awardees and those who were jury members.

Several Peruvian authors had been awarded the prize or obtained an honorable mention, and their books had been published by Casa de las Américas, including César Calvo (honorable mention in poetry, 1966); Antonio Cisneros (first prize in poetry, 1968); Alfredo Bryce Echenique (honorary mention in the short story category, 1968); Edmundo de los Ríos (honorary mention in the novel category, 1968); Héctor Béjar (first prize in the essay category, 1969); Hugo Neira (first prize in the testimony category, 1974); and Oswaldo [Jorge] Salazar (first prize in the novel category, 1980). In 1971, Manuel Espinoza García, a Peruvian author that is barely remembered today, won first prize in the essay category with his book *La política económica de los Estados Unidos hacia América Latina entre 1945 y 1961*, beating Eduardo Galeano's *Las venas abiertas de América Latina* (*The Open Veins of Latin America*), which would become one of Latin America's most influential books but only merited a honorable mention.[42]

The call for the 1986 contest announced that each winner would receive 3,000 dollars in addition to the publication of the manuscript. Writers competing for the prize in the essay category were expected to 'address Latin American and Caribbean issues, and, in addition to conceptual value, submissions [would

---

enemies. Martínez Heredia relocated in the Instituto Cubano de Investigación Cultural Juan Marinello. See Suárez Salazar 2022. In 2006 Martínez Heredia received the National Social Sciences Prize and in 2015 the National Prize for Cultural Research.

42   Aguirre 2022.

have to] possess literary quality'. The deadline for submissions was 30 November 1985, and jury members were scheduled to meet in January 1986, but these dates were later changed.[43]

As discussed in Chapter 3, Flores Galindo had been writing and publishing several essays connected to his and Manuel Burga's project on the Andean utopia. At what point he thought of compiling them into a single book is unknown, but it is clear that the call for submissions for the 1986 Casa de las Américas prize triggered a sense of urgency to complete the book that would later become *Buscando un Inca*. Flores Galindo finished the manuscript on 15 November 1985, according to the date he wrote on the acknowledgments page. Typing it up, which was done by Sofía Jiménez at the Instituto de Apoyo Agrario in Lima, may have taken a few more days, and it is not hard to imagine that it was done, as the author noted, 'under extreme pressure'. Since he had to be in Havana to attend the second Encounter of Intellectuals, which opened on 29 November, it is likely that Flores Galindo took the manuscript with him and delivered it in person.

A total of 840 entries were submitted that year in the various categories of the competition, a figure that was described as 'an unprecedented number'.[44] More than half (430) were poetry entries. Sixty-five manuscripts competed in the essay category. The awarding committee gathered on 8 March in Havana and then moved to Sancti Spíritus, a beautiful colonial city in the centre of the island, where it conducted its deliberations. In the essay category, the jury was formed by Bolivian historian René Arze (b. 1947), a participant, along with Flores Galindo, in the second Encounter of Intellectuals in Havana;[45] Sergio Benvenuto (b. 1930), a Uruguayan essayist and historian living in Havana; Mexican sociologist and economist Sergio de la Peña (1930–98); and Cuban journalist, diplomat, and historian Oscar Pino Santos (1928–2004), author of *El asalto a Cuba por la oligarquía financiera yanqui*, which had been awarded the Casa de las Américas essay prize in 1973. It was an interdisciplinary panel with a marked leftwing intellectual and political profile. In an interview in a Cuban

---

43 The deadline for submission of manuscripts was extended to 30 January 1986, and the deliberation period was postponed until March. The reason for the postponement was the celebration of the third congress of the Cuban Communist Party, which was to be held on 4–7 February 1986. The postponement was announced on 11 January 1986 on several Havana newspapers.
44 *Granma* (Havana), 24 February 1986.
45 Arze had attended in 1984 the conference on 'States and Nations in the Andes', organised in Lima by the French Institute of Andean Studies, where Flores Galindo had presented his essay 'El horizonte utópico', included in *Buscando un Inca*. Arze therefore knew Flores Galindo and was familiar with his work.

newspaper before deliberations, René Arze declared that he 'would like to give the award to an essay that discusses a difficult problem affecting Latin America's current sociopolitical situation and offers solutions'.[46] Strictly speaking, Flores Galindo's book would not fit that mold.

The award was announced on 25 March. That same day, the newspaper *Juventud Rebelde* had featured statements by Sergio de la Peña highlighting the fact that among the manuscripts competing for the prize 'there are repeated references to the foreign debt issue and the crisis faced by Latin America'. And he added: 'On a second level, there is a predominance of socio-historical essays, generally dealing with national or regional aspects and seeking to prove the hypotheses formulated in a previous long period of global assessment essays'.[47] While De la Peña's description might be confusing, *Buscando un Inca* falls in the second category he identifies. It was de la Peña who announced the award and read the jury's decision:

> The author reveals the historically persistent role played by traditions and mythological elements in the social struggles that – with underlying economic forces – have characterised the centuries-long history of the Andean peoples, in particular, Peru's Andean peoples. In doing so, he uniquely introduces interpretative approaches that contribute to the understanding of the historical process of the Andean area, from the beginning of colonisation to the present day. In addition to the research effort and analytical rigor behind it, *Buscando un Inca* has the literary quality of an essay written in an elegant and brilliant style.[48]

According to Alfredo Bryce Echenique, who was a member of the short-story award jury that year, 'everyone coincided ... in recognising the extraordinary quality of a book like *Buscando un Inca. Identidad y utopía en los Andes*, presented in the essay genre by the young Peruvian historian Alberto Flores Galindo'. For the members of the jury, he added, 'Flores Galindo's work would mark a milestone in the historiography of Peru and the other Andean countries, because of the ambitious scope of his initial project and the unquestionable mastery with which he carried it out'.[49]

---

46   *Escambray* (Sancti Spíritus), 11 March 1986.
47   'Frecuentes referencias en los ensayos a la crisis económica de América Latina', *Juventud Rebelde* (Havana), 25 March 1986.
48   *Granma* 1986. See also Casañas and Fornet 1999, pp. 164–5. This text was reproduced, with slight changes, in the front flap of the Cuban edition of *Buscando un Inca*.
49   Bryce Echenique, c. 1986. Bryce Echenique also gave an account of that visit to Cuba in his memoirs. See Bryce Echenique 1993, pp. 382–408.

From Lima, an AFP news agency cable reported that 'Humberto [sic] Flores Galindo' had welcomed the prize, 'first, because it comes from such a prestigious and important institution in Latin American culture as is Cuba's Casa de las Américas, and, second, because it represents, in a way, an acknowledgment of the work that a group of social scientists and researchers has been conducting in Peru'.[50] The newspaper *Granma* also featured statements by the winner, who said that this was a prize 'for all those in Peru engaged in studying history and our national identity'. In addition, the report noted, somewhat inaccurately, that the author recalled that 'the work began with a journalistic article published some three years earlier in a now defunct Lima newspaper, and he later expanded it'.[51]

On 14 July, Flores Galindo sent Casa de las Américas a list of errors that he had identified in the manuscript and that needed to be corrected. The Casa de las Américas edition came out in November 1986. The (rather unimaginative) cover design was done by Cuban illustrator César Mazola (b. 1939), who used an image by Brazilian photographer Walter Firmo (b. 1937).[52] Very few copies of this edition circulated in Peru. According to Flores Galindo, most of the copies he was given in Havana when he returned in 1987 were distributed among his many Cuban friends. In March 1987, from Barcelona, he requested that 25 copies be sent to him 'urgently' to meet the demand from friends and colleagues who were eager to read it.[53] Most Peruvian readers were only able to access the book when the expanded edition by Instituto de Apoyo Agrario was published in June 1987.

50 AFP cable, Archivo Vertical, Casa de las Américas. Friends and colleagues celebrated the prize with Flores Galindo at the home of sociologist María Teresa Oré. A photograph held in the Alberto Flores Galindo Digital Collection at the Catholic University provides an image of the celebration (https://bit.ly/33mu1Cv).

51 *Granma* (Havana), 28 March 1986. Although the reference clearly simplifies things, the article that Flores Galindo alluded to is most certainly '¿Qué es la utopía andina?', written in collaboration with Manuel Burga and published in two parts in *El Caballo Rojo*, a supplement of *El Diario de Marka* (Lima), on 27 June and 11 July 1982.

52 César Mazola designed many covers for Casa de las Américas, including those for the award-winning books from 1984 to 1986 and from 1988 to 1991. The tradition was to have a consistent design for every annual series but use different illustrations for each book. The four books that were awarded in 1986 featured photographs by Firmo, who had exhibited his work in Casa de las Américas in December 1985. See, on this, *Granma* (Havana), 21 December 1985, and *Casa de las Américas* (Havana) 26, 155–156 (March–June 1986), 220.

53 Letter from Alberto Flores Galindo to Roberto Fernández Retamar, Barcelona, 17 March 1987, Archivo Casa de las Américas.

3 Return Visit to Cuba

On the same day the 1986 prizes were announced, Casa de las Américas issued the call for submissions to the Ernesto Che Guevara Extraordinary Essay Prize to commemorate the twentieth anniversary of his death. The prize would be awarded along with the other categories of the 1987 contest. The Extraordinary Prize was sponsored by the Centro de Estudios sobre América (CEA), the institution where Martínez Heredia worked.[54] Flores Galindo was invited to be part of the awarding panel and, after taking care of some complications with his calendar, he accepted the invitation. 'I am looking forward to returning to Havana and participating as a member of the jury of the Casa de las Américas Prize', he wrote in a letter to Roberto Fernández Retamar. 'It will be an opportunity to learn more about Cuban life and see old friends again'.[55] Flores Galindo's third and final visit to Cuba took place in January 1987.

The awards' opening ceremony was attended by the minister of culture, Armando Hart, and intellectuals such as Roberto Fernández Retamar, Gabriel García Márquez, Mario Benedetti, and Frei Betto. Jury members then traveled to Sancti Spíritus, checking into the Zaza Hotel outside the city, where they stayed from 25 January 25 to 4 February reading manuscripts. A total of 419 entries were submitted in the various categories – half the number of the previous year – and only 17 manuscripts competed for the extraordinary essay prize.

In addition to Flores Galindo, the awarding panel of the Extraordinary Prize was formed by William Gálvez, a Cuban journalist and military veteran of the 26th of July Movement, Álvaro Ramírez, a Nicaraguan socialist lawyer who had fought against the Anastasio Somoza dictatorship and became undersecretary of foreign affairs of the Sandinista government, and Horacio Verbitsky, a well-known Argentine journalist and former Montonero guerrilla member. In a statement to the press, Flores Galindo highlighted the importance of the prize for providing a deeper understanding of the life and work of Che Guevara, 'not as an isolated character, but as part of the history of the continent'.[56] The jury unanimously awarded the prize to two essays: *El pensamiento económico de Ernesto Che Guevara*, by the Cuban Carlos Tablada Pérez, and *Che Guevara en*

---

54 *Casa de las Américas* (Havana) 27, 157 (July–August 1986), 138; *Granma* (Havana), 26 January 1987.

55 Letter from Alberto Flores Galindo to Roberto Fernández Retamar, 21 October 1986, Archivo Casa de las Américas. Flores Galindo had initially declined the invitation because of his obligations at the University of Barcelona, where he was scheduled to teach in the first semester of 1987. Some weeks later, however, he managed to rearrange his schedule and notified Casa de las Américas that he would be participating as a member of the jury.

56 Undated document, Archivo Vertical, Casa de las Américas.

FIGURE 3   Flores Galindo (first from the left), with the other members of the jury of the Ernesto Che Guevara Extraordinary Essay Prize (1987)
© ARCHIVO FOTOGRÁFICO, CASA DE LAS AMÉRICAS

el presente de América Latina, by Pedro Vuskovic and Belarmino Elgueta, both from Chile. According to the jury, the first 'shows the integrity of the concept of development in socialism', while the second 'reveals the continuing validity of socialism as a possible and necessary utopia for our peoples, twenty years after Che's death'.[57]

Flores Galindo participated along with his fellow jury members in several gatherings and visits, some of which would leave a positive impression on him and he would later mention them in an article discussed below. They visited the Institute of Biotechnology and Genetic Engineering; the International Film and Television School, recently opened in San Antonio de los Baños thanks to García Márquez's sponsorship, where they spoke with its director, Fernando Birri, and met with García Márquez himself; a clinic operated under the Family Doctor program; the colonial old town of Sancti Spíritus; the music centre Casa de la Trova 'Miguel Companioni', also in Sancti Spíritus, where one of the groups sang 'Hasta siempre, Comandante', the song written by Carlos Puebla as a tribute to Che Guevara; and the UNEAC headquarters, where they met with local writers. They also participated in a dialogue with Sancti

---

57   Casañas and Fornet 1999, p. 169.

Spíritus journalists, much commented in the Cuban press. The newspaper *Trabajadores* reported that the discussion 'addressed the issue of exercising discretion', that is, the thorny question of the limits of criticism in Cuban society. Jury members 'inquired about the forms of expressing criticism, which media published such criticism, and the responses it received', and they were told that the Communist Party supported 'journalists who were critical', but also encouraged 'the raising of awareness regarding the need to promote actions in response to the publication of a negative fact'. The journalists provided examples of the problems that were reported and criticised and of the sanctions imposed on 'those responsible for the deficiencies denounced'.[58] These criticisms, of course, referred to very specific matters affecting people's everyday life, and did not involve any questioning of the major aspects of State policies. Nonetheless, according to the account by the newspaper *Escambray*, the debate was 'intense because of the fraternal polemic prompted by the problems regarding the social role of journalists in our society'.[59] Echoes of the issues addressed in that debate will reverberate in the article by Flores Galindo discussed below.

During a visit to the city of Trinidad, Flores Galindo had a discussion with Esther Pérez, who worked at Casa de las Américas at the time. In a conversation that Esther and I had in March 2020, she recalled in great detail that exchange and she revealed to me that it had to do with Fidel Castro and his role in the Revolution. Flores Galindo, she said, found the constant references to Castro and his overwhelming presence as the leader of the revolutionary process disturbing. Although she did not explicitly say it, it seems that Flores Galindo likened that feature to Latin American caudillismo and the tradition of official cult of political leaders, and this caused certain resistance in him. His feelings towards Cuba were also shaped by the sense that Cuban socialism had become too orthodox and rigid.

On 5 February, back in Havana, Flores Galindo gave a talk on 'The Current Situation in Peru', at the Centro de Estudios sobre América. A few days later, *Juventud Rebelde* published a profile of him.[60] As was customary in every edition of the prize, on 9 February there was a presentation of the books that had won the previous year, including *Buscando un Inca*. Casa de las Américas issued a press release, penned by César Ramos (who is named in the book as the editor) and published later by *Granma*, summarising the contents of the book

---

58   *Trabajadores* 1987.
59   Rey Yero 1987a. An interview with Flores Galindo on the legacy of Che Guevara was published in the same issue of this newspaper. See Rey Yero 1987b.
60   Evora 1987.

FIGURE 4 Alberto Flores Galindo in front of the Lenin monument in Havana (1987)
SOURCE: PONTIFICIA UNIVERSIDAD CATÓLICA DEL PERÚ, ALBERTO FLORES GALINDO DIGITAL COLLECTION

somewhat confusingly: 'It is a serious attempt to bring us an interpretation of the Andean phenomenon with an objective and peculiar approach … The way in which the different topics are addressed is novel and they bear a close relationship with respect to the apparently known "Andean world" without detriment to the historical validity and the thematic unity'.[61]

Near the end of the visit to the island, all the members of the jury issued a statement thanking the Cuban people 'for the warm affection they surrounded us with while we carried out our task'. And they added: 'We have been able to see the different quality of life enjoyed here, from the central aspects of existence to small everyday things. We take with us the feeling that, twenty years after Che's death, the cause of a more noble and generous humanity to which he gave his time has prevailed, despite all the difficulties, in this land that made him universal'. They were also able to observe 'how the surplus produced by social work is given a humanist use, and compare it with the implacable draining of resources that in our countries are channeled toward the payment of

61   Ramos 1987.

interests for financial loans and squandered in the manufacture and purchase of weapons'.[62]

During the 1987 visit to Cuba, Flores Galindo came into contact again with Martínez Heredia and was surprised to discover that he was married to Esther Pérez. This is how he described it: 'It was only after a certain heated – but friendly – discussion with a friend from Casa de las Américas that someone in Havana invited me to her house. It was only then that I found out that she was the wife of another friend. To continue with this clandestine game, I will not disclose their names. They are an intellectual couple: she works at the most important cultural centre created by the Revolution and he at a research centre focusing on Latin America'.[63] The discussion about Fidel Castro that began in Trinidad seems to have continued later in Esther and Fernando's house. In a 1991 essay in which he praised Castro's revolutionary leadership (describing him as 'an extraordinary and very experienced political leader, with immense and unquestionable moral authority, a globally renowned personality, Fidel expresses the popular political unity behind the revolutionary principles and patriotism, the whole history of the process'), Martínez Heredia added in a footnote: 'On the last day of a visit to Cuba, Alberto Flores Galindo said to me: "Fidel is a collective pseudonym"'.[64]

The following month, Sergio Benvenuto, one of the members of the jury that had awarded the prize to Flores Galindo, wrote a long review of *Buscando un Inca*. The Uruguayan author was not short on compliments. According to him, Flores Galindo 'teaches us – brutally, one could say – that identity is not unity, homogeneity, simple repetition of common features or of the most widespread, sacralised features. Identity is contradiction'.[65] About the book, he said that it reflected,

---

62 'Agradecimiento del Jurado al pueblo de Cuba', 10 February 1987, Archivo Vertical, Casa de las Américas.
63 Flores Galindo 1987d, p. 190.
64 Martínez Heredia 1991, p. 846. In my conversation with her, Esther also remembered that Flores Galindo had uttered that phrase. In June 1988, Martínez Heredia joined the team of contributors of *Márgenes*, the magazine promoted by Flores Galindo, and he continued collaborating with the magazine until it closed in 2000. He returned at least three more times to Peru. In 1998 he wrote, 'ten years ago I wandered through Calcutta in downtown Lima', which would mean he was there in 1988 (Martínez Heredia 1998, p. 647). After Flores Galindo's death, he went back in 1992 and 1994, participating on both occasions in roundtables at SUR Casa de Estudios del Socialismo, the centre for reflection and debate that Flores Galindo had helped found in 1986. The theme of the first roundtable, held in February 1992, was 'Cuban Socialism', and the theme of the second one, held in September 1994 was 'Cuba in Latin America'.
65 Benvenuto 1987, p. 143.

an exemplary way of writing history. And a careful and thorough erudition that is, nevertheless, so well processed and presented to readers that they almost do not perceive its magnitude and read the book as if it were a novel, gliding through its simple and clear prose, a precise prose that is unadorned and without adjectives and yet captivates them.[66]

4 (Re)Thinking the Revolution

After his January 1987 visit to Cuba Flores Galindo spent a semester teaching at the Autonomous University of Barcelona in Spain. While he was there, he had time to process his Cuban experience and compare what he had seen there with what he experienced in Barcelona and other Spanish cities. He wrote Fernández Retamar from Barcelona to thank him for 'those exceptional days I spent in Havana. Returning to Cuba and participating as a jury in the Casa Prize – and in particular in the special Che Guevara prize – has been for me an experience as important as it was enriching. I did not want to let more days go by without telling you that. I hope to be able to write something more about that experience'.[67] Retamar replied with equally warm words: 'We greatly enjoyed having you here again. I hope you can repeat the visit. And please send us any unpublished work you have for the *Casa de las Américas* journal'.[68] It is obvious that the 1987 visit had left a warmer and more enduring mark on Flores Galindo than the previous ones. And he made good on his promise to write something about 'that experience'.

In August 1987, Flores Galindo returned to Lima. Maruja Martínez, a close collaborator in SUR and *Márgenes* recalls that, at that time, 'Che, Nicaragua, Cuba, the Intifada came up again and again in our conversations'.[69] He wrote two texts inspired by his trip to Cuba. One of them was just two pages long and it dealt with the popularity of Che Guevara images in Peru, where, he observed, it was not a phenomenon promoted by the State, as was the case in Cuba, but a genuine and spontaneous show of admiration. Flores Galindo interpreted this as an indication that 'in Peru, in contrast to other countries

---

66   Benvenuto 1987, p. 144.
67   Letter from Alberto Flores Galindo to Roberto Fernández Retamar, Barcelona, 17 March 1987, Archivo Casa de las Américas.
68   Letter from Roberto Fernández Retamar to Alberto Flores Galindo, 22 May 1987, Archivo Casa de las Américas.
69   Martínez 1997, p. 310. Flores Galindo and several colleagues had founded SUR Casa de Estudios del Socialismo in 1986, and sometime later Martínez began collaborating in the project.

in Latin America, the myths and traditions of the 1960s Left persist: they have not been forgotten or razed by repressive waves'.[70] It is interesting that Flores Galindo makes no mention of the connection between Che and the Revolutionary Túpac Amaru Movement (Movimiento Revolucionario Túpac Amaru, or MRTA), the armed guerrilla group that at that time was attempting to seize power through a strategy inspired by Guevara. The photograph taken at one of the first public appearances of the group's masked leaders shows a banner with the emblematic photo of Che alongside the MRTA's flag. While the movement's predominant icon was Túpac Amaru, Che Guevara was frequently invoked, and his image was often displayed by the MRTA.

Flores Galindo would say more about Che Guevara in Cuba in the long article discussed below. He was clearly influenced by the conversations he had during his visit and the many ways in which Cuba was commemorating the 20th anniversary of Che's death, including the prize for which Flores Galindo served as jury:

> In 1987, twenty years after the ambush in Ñancahuazú, Cuba is revisiting his works. It is not that he had been forgotten. But Guevara had become a mere image: the wind-swept hair, the clear gaze, the goodbye letter to Fidel ... But this man who described himself merely as a 'twentieth century *condottiero*' is responsible for some of the truly original reflections and ideas of Latin American socialism. For Guevara, socialism was not a shortcut to catch up with the developed world; it was something altogether different. Which is why it was a moral problem rather than a theoretical one. However, the starting point was not categorical imperatives but immediate needs.[71]

It is interesting to note the emphasis Flores Galindo places, first, on the abandonment of Che's message (presumably due to the Cuban regime's sovietisation and dogmatism) and his transformation into a popular icon emptied of content, and, second, on his recovery, twenty years after his death, coinciding with the launching in mid-1986 of the 'rectification' campaign that placed renewed stress on moral incentives, as Che had proposed in the 1960s.[72] Flores

---

70   Flores Galindo 1987f. The *Márgenes* issue in which this article was originally published featured numerous photographs and illustrations of Che Guevara and a quote by him on the back cover.
71   Flores Galindo 1987d, p. 195.
72   In this, Flores Galindo also agreed with Martínez Heredia, who in 1989 argued that 'Che's legacy had been largely abandoned' and stressed that, in the rectification process then

Galindo's takes on Che somehow condense both his critical attitude towards Cuba (Che 'had become a mere image') and his more positive view of the rectification process, the recovery of Che, and the impact of both on the everyday life of Cubans.

These observations on Che Guevara are taken from the second 1987 article, 'El socialismo a la vuelta de la esquina', which is the longest and most important text on Cuba written by Flores Galindo. The title of the article (which translates as 'Socialism Around the Corner') is very revealing: what Flores Galindo found to be the most admirable feature of the socialist model was not its central planning, the single party system, the ideology guiding all transformations, or the State's control over the means of production, but the changes in people's everyday life and the more horizontal and less hierarchical nature of human relations.

He begins with an observation that, although commonsensical, is quite relevant when analyzing Cuban affairs, namely, that the perception a visitor had (and has) of a city like Havana (or any other, for that matter) depends to a large extent on that visitor's place of origin. 'Someone coming from the north could have the impression that it is a city where time has stood still', he wrote, whereas for him, who was coming from Lima, 'what impressed me most was the fact that one could actually walk around Havana'.[73] The contrast was remarkable. He saw no street hawkers, nobody 'poorly dressed', and realised that 'a barefoot child is unimaginable in Havana. More inconceivable yet is a beggar or a person with mental disabilities wandering the streets. At most, you may run into *palomillas*' [kids in the street] asking for '*chicles*' [chewing gum]. There is nobody begging. Everyone's access to school, health, and food is guaranteed'.[74] He observes (and implicitly condemns) people operating a black market of dollars, but, in contrast to the official stance in Cuba, he believed it was 'disproportionate to consider them criminals'. In fact, Flores Galindo portrays an image of a city devoid of any crime: 'there are no burglaries or muggings. You can walk around late at night in the semi-dark streets of the port without feeling the least bit wary'. Havana, in contrast to Lima, is not a 'city behind bars', there

---

underway, 'it was even more necessary to assume Che in his entirety'. Martínez Heredia 1989, p. 20.

73   Flores Galindo 1987d, p. 187.
74   Flores Galindo 1987d, p. 188. A view similar to Flores Galindo's can be found in a 1975 text by García Márquez about the achievements of Cuban socialism: 'in today's Cuba there is not a single unemployed person, no child goes without schooling, no human being is shoeless, homeless, or lacking their three daily meals, there are no beggars and no illiterates ...'. And he continues listing the gains secured by socialism for several more lines. See García Márquez 1975, p. 59.

were no policemen on the streets, and there was no 'riot police'. All of this could be attributed, he stated, to the absence of unemployment, which is of course a plausible but clearly partial (and surprisingly economistic) explanation, as it does not take into account, on the one hand, the changes in education and the forms of socialisation among young Cubans, and, on the other, the mechanisms of social control implemented by the State: the Committees for the Defense of the Revolution, an effective police system, and an extensive prison network. Another difference with Lima that Flores Galindo observed was the absence of 'sexual aggressiveness' in Havana,[75] although he said nothing about the persistence of sexist attitudes and forms of socialisation that surely did not escape his keen eye.

Flores Galindo then went on to address the thorny issue of democracy in Cuba: one has to look for it, he said, in 'the everyday',[76] not just in the official sphere of elections and the political structure of the People's Power (Poder Popular). He voiced his admiration for the democratic practices resulting from universal access to education and from the supposed absence of hierarchies among the different professions and occupations. Students, he said, 'can learn this or that trade, practice sports, engage in manual and intellectual activities, without putting one above the other, giving equal value to an airplane pilot, a restaurant waiter, a surgeon, and a worker in a sugar mill. This explains why the son of the Cuban ambassador to Moscow is thinking about studying to work in the hotel business. It is a kind of democracy of which we are very far from achieving here [in Peru]. Only authentic revolutions can change everyday social values'.[77]

While Flores Galindo's enthusiasm for the revolution is undeniable, he also noted some of the problems that afflicted Cuban society. 'There is no happy island', he wrote, invoking the title of a play by Peruvian writer Sebastián Salazar Bondy, and he even mocked the visitors who only sang praises, 'a rhetoric that I imagine must bore Cubans themselves, in the style of "What a beautiful socialist blue sky!"'.[78] He mentioned, for example, the shortage of housing, the young unofficial currency exchangers who swarmed hotels and took advantage of the presence of tourists,[79] the businesses that catered exclusively

---

[75] Flores Galindo 1987d, p. 189.
[76] Flores Galindo 1987d, p. 192.
[77] Ibid.
[78] Ibid.
[79] In addition to this, visitors to the island were more or less regularly pestered by mostly young locals, both men and woman, offering favors (sex, company, information) in exchange for material goods. Flores Galindo experienced this personally during his 1985 visit.

to foreigners ('the existence of these shops is not very democratic'),[80] and the lack of spaces where one could openly debate.[81] In Cuba, he said, 'it is not easy to process differences, conflicts, or dissident opinions. Critical thinking [note here the nod to Martínez Heredia's magazine *Pensamiento Crítico*] is incompatible with unanimity'.[82]

Flores Galindo concluded that the root problem 'is the antinomy between equality and freedom',[83] that ages-old and apparently unsolvable dilemma that has marked the history of socialism since its origins. The pursuit of the former 'leads to the minimisation of private property [which] results in *a disproportionate growth of the State and an excessive centralisation of economic life*', he wrote.[84] The defence of the latter tends to require 'the need to preserve private forms of surplus appropriation'.[85] According to him, the solution to that dilemma is not to be found in combining socialism and liberalism, as socialism, since its origins, 'harbors the hope of a democracy that is radically different from parliamentary democracy',[86] and, therefore, a genuine socialism should be able to reconcile equality with freedom. Flores Galindo concludes by invoking Marx, for whom 'the problem consisted in doing away not only with private property, but also with the State, turning it from an oppressive apparatus into "a body subordinated" to society'.[87] The discussion had shifted from Cuban reality and everyday life to Marxist doctrine and ideology. The utopian idea of the

---

        On one occasion, when he was entering his hotel room, he was accosted by a young Cuban woman who tried to make her way into his room to 'keep him company', in what was clearly an offer of sexual favors in exchange for money or a gift. When she was rejected by a surprised Flores Galindo, the young woman tried to convince him to give her some article of clothing as a gift or some money or to help her buy something in the shop for foreigners. Flores Galindo refused to comply with her requests and the woman left. This anecdote was told by the historian himself to the group of Peruvians who attended the meeting of intellectuals. One of them, Juan Acevedo, shared it with me.

80   Flores Galindo 1987d, p. 192.
81   An anecdote from the Second Encounter of Intellectuals in 1985 illustrates just how much Flores Galindo acknowledged that there were limits to criticism in Cuba. The Chilean historian Luis Vitale participated in one of the debates and criticised a Cuban speaker, who did not take those comments well. Flores Galindo then remarked to his Peruvian colleagues, in reference to Vitale: 'He won't be invited back again'. Author's personal communication with Roger Santiváñez, 5 June 2020.
82   Flores Galindo 1987d, p. 192.
83   Flores Galindo 1987d, p. 193.
84   Ibid., emphasis added.
85   Ibid.
86   Ibid.
87   Ibid.

withering away of the State would be the key that led to the full enjoyment of equality and freedom. Cuba was certainly very far from that.

Near the end of the article, Flores Galindo turned back to Cuba and the current situation there to underline the changing nature of the revolutionary experience, question the official story of an 'unblemished continuity since the distant times of the war against Spain',[88] and offer what can be read as a justification of those elements that he had actually questioned. Given the U.S. embargo and other obstacles, he says, 'keeping the revolution afloat was hard enough. *One could not demand too much room for dissent.* The motto that was imposed, *that the circumstances imposed,* was "within the revolution everything and outside the revolution nothing"'.[89] The pragmatic option of defending 'actually existing socialism' ultimately prevailed, uncomfortably but decidedly, in Flores Galindo. In that, too, his position resembled that of Martínez Heredia, but arriving at it responded also to other considerations.

The situation of the Left in Peru, and the debates Flores Galindo was engaged in, helped shaped his stances toward Cuba. The Peruvian Left, which had seen a significant surge in voters between 1978 and 1985, was now threatened by a series of challenges: the exacerbation of internal divisions; the rise of Sendero Luminoso; the emergence of a populist leader such as Alan García, who not only managed to garner enormous popular support early in his term, but also reached out to and seduced, at least initially, a sector of the Left;[90] the abandonment of Marxism by important intellectuals and political leaders, some of them close to Flores Galindo; and the global crisis of socialism. On a more personal level, the Peruvian edition of *Buscando un Inca* received some unfair criticism, with the author being accused of holding pro-Sendero Luminoso views, as

---

88 Ibid.
89 Flores Galindo 1987d, p. 194, emphasis added. Flores Galindo seems to have wanted to quote Fidel Castro's famous dictum in his 1961 'Words to Intellectuals' speech: 'Within the Revolution everything; against the Revolution nothing'.
90 As part of its efforts to 'open up' to the Left, in April 1986 the Alan García government held a 'Week of Latin American Cultural Integration' (Semana de Integración Cultural Latinoamericana, or SICLA) that brought together in Lima a large contingent of representatives of the region's progressive culture, including many Cuban musicians such as Silvio Rodríguez, Pablo Milanés, Santiago Feliú, Sara González, the band Irakere, and others. Silvio Rodríguez and Pablo Milanés performed at a concert held in the courtyard of the Government Palace, with Alan García and Alfonso Barrantes, the leader of the Left and then mayor of Lima, as front row spectators. Just two months later, in June, a prison massacre that killed 240 Shining Path inmates was perpetrated by the García administration, doing away with the possibility of furthering ties between leftwing sectors and the APRA government.

Charles Walker recalls in chapter 5 of this book.[91] Lima was becoming a difficult place to live, work, and foster his political and intellectual projects. Upon his return from Barcelona, Flores Galindo began seriously considering the possibility of moving to Cusco, a project that, in its motivation and ultimate frustration, can be likened to Mariátegui's projected trip to Buenos Aires, which was cut short by his death. It is in this context that Flores Galindo wrote his article on Cuba. What he had seen in the island was processed against the backdrop of what was happening within the Peruvian Left. Unlike many, Flores Galindo refused to renounce his socialist convictions and his Marxist affiliation, but the situation in Peru was conducive to disillusionment. Cuba, in contrast, offered the possibility, however imperfect and uncomfortable, of a socialism that at least worked, and that at that time – and here the conversations with Martínez Heredia appear to have been decisive – was seeking through the 'rectification' process and the return to Che Guevara's ideals a path removed from dogmatisms. 'The Cubans I have met – Flores Galindo wrote – are very tolerant to criticism, and some, like William Gálvez, even demand it'.[92] What is more, he believed he had discovered that there was now 'an intense intellectual openness in Cuba'.[93] His reservations about the Cuban Revolution seemed to fade or, at least, he now processed them differently. What existed in Cuba was imperfect but improvable, and it was certainly better than the disillusionment, desertion, and pessimism that was ravaging the Peruvian Left at that time.

5 Friendship and Solidarity

On 2 February 1989, Flores Galindo was 'suddenly struck by an ailment', as he would later write in his farewell letter. The news reached Cuba and Casa de las Américas. Esther Pérez wrote to him on 13 March: 'Dear Tito, I have learned from Hildebrando Pérez[94] of your illness. What's with that *flojera*, brother?[95] Fernando and I, and all the *compañeros* at Casa send you loads of love and solid-

---

91 The founding of SUR Casa de Estudios del Socialismo in 1986 and the launching of the journal *Márgenes* in March 1987 were attempts to overcome pessimism and move forward against the tide.

92 Flores Galindo 1987d, p. 192.

93 Flores Galindo 1987d, p. 194.

94 Hildebrando Pérez Grande (not to be confused with Hildebrando Pérez Huarancca, mentioned in chapter 6), was a Peruvian writer who won the Casa de las Américas prize in poetry in 1978.

95 *'Flojera'* is a colloquial Cuban expression that translates literally as 'laziness', but is used in the manner of a playful scolding when someone is sick or feeling ill.

arity. Get well soon. We really need you. Give our love to your wife and children. Send us good news, which are the ones that matter. Big, big hug to you'.[96] Along with the letter he wrote back to her, which was not saved, Flores Galindo sent Esther a copy of *El zorro de arriba y el zorro de abajo*, a novel by Peruvian writer José María Arguedas. In that book, or perhaps in one of his own books that he sent in the same package, he wrote a dedication where he announced that he was 'back in the neighborhood', that is, that he had returned from New York, where he had gone for treatment. Esther replied asking for more information: '**We need to** hear from you, because everyone here at Casa keeps pestering us for news from you'. She gave him the news that Fernando Martínez Heredia had won the 1989 Casa de las Américas Prize. 'Now you're almost blood brothers', she noted with obvious satisfaction.[97]

On 13 June, Flores Galindo wrote a long letter to Esther Pérez from Lima.[98] This was, he told her, the first letter he had written since his return from his second trip to New York. In addition to some details about his illness, he shared with her reflections and concerns that he would later expand on in his farewell letter:

> Amidst all the obvious ordeals, it has been very gratifying to discover or reconnect with so many friends. Without friends, I would have sunk in one form or another of despair. Also, thanks to my friends I have been able to start a very expensive treatment ... Solidarity and friendship do exist. I've had very convincing proof of that.

He also expressed his joy at Martínez Heredia's prize: 'Send Fernando a big hug for me. Congratulate him for me on the Prize. I hope to receive his book soon; meanwhile, I'll read *Desafíos del socialismo cubano*'.[99] And true to his insatiable curiosity, he asked Esther to send him Nadine Gordimer's novel *The Conservationist*, which had been published in Cuba in Spanish the year before, 'and if there is anything else by her published in Havana', he would be grateful if they

---

96   Letter from Esther Pérez to Alberto Flores Galindo, 13 March 1989, Archivo Casa de las Américas.
97   Underlined in the original. Letter from Esther Pérez to Alberto Flores Galindo, 24 May 1989, Archivo Casa de las Américas. Martínez Heredia was awarded the Thirtieth Anniversary of the Revolution Extraordinary Prize in the essay category for his book *Che, el socialismo y el comunismo*, cited above.
98   Letter from Alberto Flores Galindo to Esther Pérez, 13 June 1989, Archivo Casa de las Américas.
99   Martínez Heredia 1988.

could send it to him, he said.[100] By way of goodbye, he ended his letter by saying, 'I hope we can continue with this exchange of letters, although they seem more like telegrams. Big hug to you both. You are always in my thoughts. Tito'.

Esther's response, dated 1 September 1989, is the last letter exchanged between them that I have been able to find: 'Needless to say, everyone here is at your disposal for whatever you may need'. She also sent him two books: 'One to entertain you, and the other to make you suffer your friends; we are all duty bound to read what our friends publish'. The first book was, perhaps, the Gordimer novel he had asked for; the second was, no doubt, Martínez Heredia's book about Che Guevara that had just been released in September. 'Everyone here at Casa sends you their love', Esther tells him at the end of the letter.[101]

On 14 December, Flores Galindo finished writing his farewell letter. He died on 26 March 1990. A few days later, Fernández Retamar sent a telegram to Cecilia Rivera, Flores Galindo's widow, on behalf of Casa de las Américas: 'dismayed to hear of our dear brother alberto's death, we learned of his political testament. will review it in casa magazine. his words and his memory encourage us in moments he knew how to characterise and for which he urged us to continue creatively in the struggle for liberation and socialism'.[102] Flores Galindo's farewell letter was reproduced in *Casa de las Américas*, preceded by a heartfelt note: 'The highly esteemed Alberto Flores Galindo, one of the most important historians of his generation', had become in recent years a 'frequent presence at Casa de las Américas'. These words were followed by the transcription of his 'deep and remarkable political testimony'.[103] In this way, the brief but intense period of political and human relations between Flores Galindo and Cuba – at times uncomfortable, but always close – came to an end.

6   Conclusion

In 2005, a special issue of the Cuban journal *Temas* published the transcription of a roundtable on 'The debate of ideas in culture and thought in Cuba'.[104] The moderator, Rafael Hernández, posed the questions to be discussed: 'What does

---

100   Gordimer 1988.
101   Letter from Esther Pérez to Alberto Flores Galindo, 1 September 1989, Archivo Casa de las Américas.
102   Telegram from Roberto Fernández Retamar to Cecilia Rivera, 30 March 1990, Archivo Casa de las Américas. The telegram is translated maintaining the original summarised style.
103   *Casa de las Américas* 1990.
104   Altshuler 2005. Participants included Ernesto Altshuler, Reinerio Arce, Mayra Espina Prieto, Pedro Pablo Rodríguez, and Rafael Hernández.

debating ideas mean? What does fostering or constructing a culture of debate mean? What does such a debate culture consist in?'[105] After some presentations, one of the participants, the physicist Ernesto Altshuler, expressed his discomfort with what he called 'the debate about debating', that is, the fact that, so far, 'there has been no debate yet'.[106] The tongue twister accurately illustrates the unease that this kind of discussion generated. One of the panelists, Mayra Espino Prieto, put it more directly: 'It is an eminently political issue', she said, and in Cuba 'there is not enough space for that debate, that confrontation, that contrasting of views, because the political design of our society is *excessively authoritarian, vertical, centralist*, and strategic ideas are pre-determined, so that *debating is left for minor issues*'. And then added: 'So long as it is assumed that the country's unity and diversity depend on unanimity defined as a premise, there will be no progress, because that unanimity is predicated on *issues not being discussed with the necessary depth*, but rather with a degree of generality where everyone can agree, or where divergence is otherwise not made visible'.[107] Instead of directly addressing Espino Prieto's remarks, the moderator opened the floor for comments and, thus, the 'debate on debating' continued without much consequence.

I want to take up that expression ('the debate on debating') because I believe it illustrates quite well some of the dilemmas that intellectuals such as Martínez Heredia and Flores Galindo faced, but did not resolve, in formulating their vision of the socialism they wanted to help forge. Both thought that socialism should not be at odds with a broad and democratic debate of ideas, and both were able to verify – the former as victim and the latter as observer – the limits that existed in Cuba for the full exercise of debate and criticism. Their questioning of the Cuban model, however, as in 'the debate on debating', did not touch the heart of the matter, namely: how far should a socialist regime stretch its tolerance of dissent and criticism, that which Ambrosio Fornet called 'the noble exercise of ideological coexistence?'[108] In Martínez Heredia's case, while it is true that he was ostracised because of his heterodox approach and his stance against monolithic thinking, it is also true that during the years in which he was able to teach, write, and publish quite freely, there were other intellectuals (and also non-intellectuals, of course) who suffered persecution, exile, and imprisonment.[109] In Flores Galindo's case, as we saw, although he did not fail to point

---

105 Altshuler 2005, p. 132.
106 Altshuler 2005, p. 138.
107 Altshuler 2005, p. 141, emphasis added.
108 Fornet 2004, p. 11.
109 A member of the *Pensamiento Crítico* team, Jesús Díaz, who would later leave Cuba and

out that in Cuba 'it is not easy to process differences, conflicts, dissident opinions', he ultimately offered a justification of the mechanisms of suppression of those 'dissident opinions', based on the need to preserve the Revolution.

'Within the Revolution, everything; against the Revolution, nothing', Fidel Castro had proclaimed in his 1961 'Words to intellectuals', and Flores Galindo alluded to that maxim in his evaluation of the Cuban process. According to the Cuban writer Guillermo Rodríguez Rivera, Fidel's statement was rather 'inclusive', as 'it did not demand explicit support for the Revolution, only that it not be attacked'.[110] But the question that follows is obvious: who decides what constitutes an 'attack' against the Revolution? Ambrosio Fornet expressed it in similar terms in 2004. 'What was now at stake', he said, 'was a question of power: in the event of doubt, who drew the dividing line between *within* and *against*?'[111] Experience shows that, at certain times, the 'within' became too restricted for Cuban intellectuals and other sectors of the population, while in other periods it expanded, allowing for greater tolerance toward heterodox or critical opinions. In any case, the limits separating the 'within' from the 'against' are always set by the State, whose 'excessive growth' Flores Galindo had criticised.

Was that the model of socialism that Flores Galindo wanted for Peru? Actually, that is a wrongly stated question. Flores Galindo never stopped stressing the need to look for recipes in the country's own national reality, instead of importing them from other societies. In a 1988 interview he said that 'those who strive for socialism [in Latin America] are not thinking of reproducing in their countries a society like the one that exists now in Cuba'.[112] For that reason, because the implementation of socialism in Cuba raised uncomfortable questions, and because it was consistent with his way of seeing life and conceiving history, Flores Galindo opted for focusing more on the everyday life and interpersonal relations of ordinary men and women, where he believed he found a source of optimism and inspiration. His trips in 1985 and 1987, during which he

---

become a harsh critic of the Revolution, wrote in 2000 that the magazine did not live up to its name, because 'neither within the magazine nor in the Philosophy Department was there any critical analysis of the turbulent national reality'. And he added: 'Castro could allow us to be free with respect to the Soviets, but never with respect to him'. Díaz 2000, pp. 115–6.

110 Rodríguez Rivera 2017, p. 53.
111 Fornet 2004, p. 10.
112 Flórez-Estrada 1988. I thank Ricardo Portocarrero for sharing a copy of this interview with me. In 'El socialismo a la vuelta de la esquina', evoking Arguedas, Flores Galindo wrote that in its path to socialism Peru had to take 'a different road for a country with different dimensions and with a different historical tradition. Society models are not transplanted'. Flores Galindo 1987d, p. 196.

came into contact with people from different walks of life, strengthened ties of friendship, and consolidated a close relationship with Casa de las Américas, left a profound mark on his views on Cuba, so that, despite his known and persistent reservations with respect to the island's political model, he offered a very optimistic conclusion: 'The conviction that can be drawn walking around Havana is that socialism is an alternative'.[113]

Acknowledgements

Juan Acevedo, Eduardo Cáceres, Nelson Manrique, Luis Peirano, and Guillermo Rochabrún in Lima, Esther Pérez in Havana, and Roger Santiváñez in Collinswood, New Jersey, answered my queries to clarify some events mentioned in this chapter. Ana Cecilia Ruiz, at the Casa de las Américas archive, kindly complied with my requests for documents and photographs. Jorge Fornet was, once again, generous with his time and assistance in Havana. Ricardo Portocarrero and Charles Walker read and provided feedback on the finished manuscript for this chapter. Laura Pérez Carrara translated it into English. My sincere appreciation to them all.

---

113   Flores Galindo 1987d, 195. Again, Flores Galindo's view is very similar to García Márquez's in 1975. In a section entitled 'A socialism you can touch with your hands' (the resemblance with the title of Flores Galindo's article is obvious), the Colombian writer noted: 'A human and visible socialism is being built there, one that you can touch with your hands ... it runs freely through the streets and makes its way into people's homes, blending in with everyday life'. García Márquez 1975, p. 61.

CHAPTER 5

'Historians Cannot Overlook the Present': Alberto Flores Galindo on the Shining Path, Violence, and the 1980's Crisis

Charles Walker

Alberto Flores Galindo made his mark on a shockingly broad number of topics.[1] Perhaps the easiest way to list his contributions is to review the themes of the books that he wrote, co-wrote, or edited: Lima in the transition from colony to republic; José Carlos Mariátegui; Andean utopianism; the Aristocratic Republic (the latter two in collaboration with Manuel Burga); Túpac Amaru II; Arequipa and regional history; labour history; and more. Other topics run through and link many of his publications, including his work as an editor of anthologies and journals such as *Allpanchis* and *Márgenes*: violence, memory, racism, history from below, and the history of Communism and the left.

His writing on the emergence of the Shining Path, the violence of the era, human rights, and the multiple crises that beset Peru in the 1980s is less known and discussed than those other topics. He addressed these issues in the final two chapters of *In Search of an Inca*, in his prodigious journalistic contributions, and in round tables, debates, and interviews. He did not produce a monograph on these topics and when one thinks about *Senderólogos*, his name does not necessarily come to mind. Nonetheless, these publications display his best characteristics: his sharp pen, his creative use of sources, the ability to combine a long-durée vision with a journalistic touch to capture human stories, his willingness to disagree and debate, and his incessant effort to rethink Peru, its historical legacies, and its potential paths (always plural). Returning to these texts can shed light on the Shining Path and the violence that engulfed Peru. They can also help us understand Alberto Flores Galindo as historian and observer of his time, his methods, contributions, and perhaps even deficiencies, as well as the context when he wrote these texts: Peru's deep crisis in the 1980s.

I begin this essay with a brief review of Flores Galindo's vision and methodology regarding contemporary history – he was writing about the Shining Path

---

[1] The quote in the title comes from Flores Galindo 2010, p. 231.

during the conflict. I examine his final essays in *In Search of an Inca* that probed Peru in the 1980s, including the Shining Path itself and the broader themes of violence and authoritarianism, and consider some of the reactions and reviews of this work. I then turn to his journalistic work, specifically his articles on torture and a series of massacres in Lima in 1986, when the state targeted Shining Path prisoners. Finally, I take stock of his vision of human rights, an important issue for him. The underlying question in these different sections is what Flores Galindo contributed to our understanding of the violence of the 1980s and whether they deserve renewed attention. Furthermore, I examine at length his polemics and disagreements with another leading public intellectual of the 1980s, Carlos Iván Degregori, who had very different views on the Shining Path and Ayacucho, where the Maoist group launched its insurrection.

1 The Art of Doing Research and Writing Essays

Flores Galindo began one of the essays examined below, 'The Authoritarian Tradition: Violence and Democracy in Peru', with the following: 'This text is an essay, a genre in which the critical apparatus is put to side in order to present directly the interpretation'.[2] This *ensayista* style would characterise all his work but especially in the second half of the 1980s, the last five or six years of his life. A sense of urgency and even haste pulsates in these texts on and from Peru in the 1980s.

While always agile, his texts often included small mistakes or incomplete or unsatisfactory sections or argumentation. He had seemingly lost patience with the slow process of in-depth monograph research and writing, instead rapidly presenting and publishing his ideas and findings and then, in some cases, further elaborating them. Flores Galindo noted the cost of his tackling so many themes and writing so much, often against deadline. In a 1988 interview, he observed, 'I think that dispersion is one limitation of my work. I have dedicated myself to very different topics ... which has led to me to neglect precision in the data and has not allowed me to deepen my analysis of the specific topic or event. It's here where in the future I'd like to develop a book that does not have topics so diverse and different as those of *In Search of an Inca*, but instead take on a more circumscribed research topic where I can count on a clearly demarcated and abundant source base and where I can discuss the problems with greater depth, returning to the kind of artisan nature of histor-

---

2 Flores Galindo 1986g, p. 429.

ical work'.[3] Nonetheless, he wrote stirring and deep essays that, unlike much political journalism, hold up well over time. He himself wanted to focus more on specific projects, particularly his study of José María Arguedas, but his death prevented it.

For his writing on the Shining Path, he built from his long interest in the history of the left and debates within Marxism. In Paris in 1973 and 1974 he immersed himself in these topics. His discovery of Antonio Gramsci influenced his vision of the left and his rethinking of José Carlos Mariátegui. *La agonía de Mariátegui* (1980) would not have been possible without this deep understanding of the rich and divisive history of Marxism and its intellectuals.[4] It appeared the same year as the Shining Path (whose name came from a slogan related to Mariátegui) began its insurrection. In his production as a journalist, Flores Galindo often came back to the roots of Peruvian socialism. In these texts, he developed his ideas about Mariátegui and his generation while also discussing more recent debates within Marxism regarding the nation, the construction of class, and other topics.[5] The emergence of the Shining Path and its unique and authoritarian form of Maoism fascinated and deeply troubled him.

The Shining Path challenged progressive intellectuals such as Flores Galindo. They had little respect for other parties of the left, which included pro-Soviet communists, an emerging New Left, and a variety of other groups and factions. Since their emergence in the 1960s as an offshoot of the main Maoist party, the Shining Path had battled these groups on the left, primarily in universities. These confrontations continued after they launched their armed insurrection in May 1980. Their rhetoric and actions displayed their authoritarianism, and they showed no inclination to negotiate or accept criticism. *El Pensamiento Gonzalo* or Gonzalo's thought, the vision of their leader, Abimael Guzmán, built from the Chinese Cultural Revolution with notable carryovers from Leninism, particularly regarding the centrality of the party. For a student and man of the left such as Flores Galindo who had always sought out the utopian and even humanist nature of socialism and criticized Stalinism (particularly through his analysis of José Carlos Mariátegui's rocky relationship with the Komintern and Stalinism in the late 1920s), their use and even fetishisation of violence, rejection of the concept of human rights, and unwillingness to dialogue struck him as profoundly unethical and detrimental to the prospects of

---

3 Manco 1990, p. 41. The interview took place in June 1988, but the second part was only published in August 1990.
4 See chapter 1 of this book for the context and impact of *La agonía de Mariátegui*.
5 In 1982 he edited and wrote an introduction to an anthology of Communist thought in Peru (Flores Galindo 1982e).

the left at large. Nonetheless, their eruption onto the scene in 1980 and their expansion intrigued him. He proceeded to study, discuss, and write about them.

2   The Boiling Point

The structure and argumentation of the penultimate chapter of *In Search of an Inca*, differ from earlier chapters. Rather than exploring diverse invocations of the Incas, his focus is negative, asking why wasn't the Tahuantinsuyo present in the peasant uprisings of the 1960s into the 1980s? But to answer this question he does not survey and probe key moments such as land occupations in the 1950s and 1960s, the guerrillas in the 1960s, the impact of Velasco's 1969 agrarian reform, or the resurgence of the Confederación Campesina del Perú (CCP, Peruvian Peasant Confederation) in the 1970s.[6] Instead, in what could be considered part of the cultural turn, he examines the work of novelist and ethnographer José María Arguedas to explore power relations in the countryside, changing forms of servitude and domination, and the endurance of inequalities and campesinos' deep, almost subterranean hatreds and resentments.[7] He maps out changes in politics, mentalities, and subjectivities through the work and life of Arguedas. The prose is brilliant and the analysis penetrating. The focus moves from Arguedas to the political left to peasants themselves, in that restless and at times slightly scattered style of his. In his final years he envisioned a broad study of Arguedas, a biography, which his illness cruelly did not allow him to develop. The first part of this chapter constitutes a dazzling draft of that frustrated project.[8]

The second half of the chapter moves into the late 1970s and the Shining Path. He mentions the surprising share of the vote that the left earned in the 1978 Constitutional Assembly, 28%. Arguing that he no did not intend 'to write a history of the Peruvian left, and even less the development of Marxism in Peru', he summarises the different parties (reproducing a 1929–1975 flow chart by Peruvian leftwing leader Ricardo Letts) and the strong presence of Maoism in Peru. Flores Galindo makes a clear separation between José Carlos Mariátegui and Shining Path, 'Mariátegui did not accept the idea of an authoritarian project'.[9]

---

6 This was not out of the lack of interest or knowledge. He knew these topics well and wrote and taught about them. See, for example, Flores Galindo 1978b.
7 On Arguedas, see pp. 143–5 of this book.
8 Two brief texts on Arguedas, Flores Galindo 1986h and 1988f, were published posthumously.
9 Flores Galindo 2010, p. 218.

To explore why Sendero Luminoso emerged in Ayacucho, he stresses the role of the Universidad Nacional San Cristóbal de Huamanga, a university with distinguished professors, Peruvian and foreign, who linked the students with the rural and urban reality. A contrast developed between 'the expansion of the intellectual horizon and economic backwardness'.[10] He closes this long, incisive paragraph with a citation from the distinguished anthropologist and former rector of the Universidad San Cristóbal, Efraín Morote Best, who explained the violence of the 1980s by the ire prompted by corruption, hunger, and social inequalities.[11] Flores Galindo did not mention that Morote Best was the father of Osmán Morote Barrionuevo, part of Shining Path's 'Sacred Family'.[12]

Flores Galindo then moves to the life and work of Antonio Díaz Martínez, a Shining Path cadre who was killed in the 1986 Lurigancho prison uprising.[13] Díaz Martínez had published in 1969 *Ayacucho: hambre y esperanza*, a combination of field notes and analysis that depicted the author's political education as he and his students conducted research and visited the countryside.[14] For much of his writing on Ayacucho and the Shining Path, Flores Galindo relied on newspaper articles and interviews (the Morote Best quote came from a 1983 interview with Gustavo Gorriti in *Caretas*), academic texts old and new, and human rights reports. In the case of Díaz Martínez, however, Flores Galindo had a book to dissect. He used Díaz Martínez to underline the importance of the university and its dedication to field work (rare in Peru) and to pose a larger and puzzling quandary: '[F]rom one of the most backward spaces in Peru emerged the possibility of changing world history'.[15]

This question makes more sense if we remember that Flores Galindo had been in Ayacucho in 1979, to present a paper on Mariátegui at a Sociology conference. According to Maruja Martínez, 'he debated at length with some Ayacucho professors who belonged to what would become known as the Shin-

---

10   Ibid.
11   Ibid.
12   Morote Best 1988. Osmán's siblings, Arturo and Katia, were also involved in the Shining Path. The actual importance of Osmán Morote and perhaps Morote Best himself within the Shining Path is still open to debate.
13   On 18–19 June 1986, prisoners revolted in the Santa Mónica jail for women and the Lurigancho (San Pedro) and El Frontón male prisons. They sought to disrupt a meeting in Lima of the Socialist International, an event which President Alan García hosted to showcase his achievements. The military reacted brutally, leading to the death of approximately 224 prisoners. See Aguirre 2013.
14   Díaz Martínez 1969. A second edition was published in 1985 by Mosca Azul Editores.
15   Flores Galindo 2010, p. 219.

ing Path'.[16] This was a time of 'frequent polemics about Mariátegui, who was used to back different political positions'.[17] According to Martínez, this experience led Flores Galindo to write *La agonía de Mariátegui*.

Flores Galindo approaches this question from a variety of angles. Like all great historians, Flores Galindo had the ability to change the analytical lens, to move back and forth from the macro or longue-durée to precise events and individuals. In fact, this would be perhaps the primary characteristic of his work on the 1980s and Peru's multiple crises: the long-term analysis (the historicisation of contemporary problems), combined with the focus on individuals, particular events, or discourses. He repeatedly voiced the need to see the historic roots of contemporary Peru, referring back to the pre-Hispanic, colonial, and republican periods, while also avoiding euphemisms and abstractions by spotlighting specific people and events.

He alludes briefly to the Huari and the area's successive domination by the Chancas and the Incas. This reflected efforts by historians of Flores Galindo's generation to include the pre-Hispanic into historical analysis and provided potential grounds for comparison with Cusco and the long shadow and veneration of the Incas. From there, he outlines Ayacucho's role (in the colonial period, when the name Huamanga was used), as a religious centre and stopping point in the 'traditional longitudinal route that crossed the Andes from the Mantaro Valley towards Cusco and Upper Peru'.[18] He cites the work of anthropologist Carlos Iván Degregori about Shining Path's roots in Ayacucho,[19] and also builds off his own writing on Cusco and his collaboration with *Revista Andina*, *Allpanchis* and historians such as Scarlett O'Phelan Godoy, María Isabel Remy, and Luis Miguel Glave. His long-standing interest in regional history shines in this brief section. He describes the decline of these Andean trade routes after independence in the 1820s, with commerce shifting to coastal routes, via shipping and then trucks and other motor vehicles down Peru's long coastline. He affirms that Shining Path is seen by many as a regional movement 'and a defensive reaction to capitalist modernity'.[20]

Flores Galindo describes Shining Path's growth in the early 1980s, deeming it 'a lightning bolt across a clear sky'.[21] Flores Galindo recognises that the term was

---

16 Flores Galindo 1994a, p. 605. Martínez offered this testimony in one her notes as editor of Flores Galindo's *Obras Completas*.
17 Flores Galindo 1994a, p. 605.
18 Flores Galindo 2010, p. 220.
19 Degregori 1985. An important selection of Degregori's works on the Shining Path was published in English (Degregori 2012).
20 Flores Galindo 2010, p. 221.
21 Flores Galindo 2010, p. 222.

a cliché but it captured how Shining Path seemed to move against Peru's gravitational forces: in 1980, most of the left was adapting to democracy and electoral politics after twelve years of military rule. Social scientists and other analysts forecasted years of economic growth, development, and 'depeasantisation'. For those well versed on the literature of the period, the term recalls Degregori's lovely metaphor of a dwarf star to describe the Shining Path, one that accumulates great weight 'disproportionate to its size'.[22]

In the following pages, Flores Galindo reviews Maoist iconography; Juan Ansión's findings about Andean apocalyptic thought; Manuel Jesús Granados' important 1981 thesis; the Shining Path's use of coercion; and the State's rapid employment of the loaded concept of terrorism, searching for explanations for the group's emergence and expansion. He ultimately returns to José María Arguedas and his views about the rage against racism and injustice. Flores Galindo defines the leadership and urban base of the Shining Path as being constituted by Ayacucho's 'impoverished aristocracy' and frustrated mestizos, a suggestive but undeveloped hypothesis.

He then addresses what is ultimately the most important question, the one that analysts could not or did not satisfactorily answer in those years: which campesinos supported the Shining Path, to what extent, and why? Did this backing emerge from Sendero Luminoso's coercion or respond to a true commitment to and belief in their project? These are questions which only now, more than three decades later, are receiving sophisticated and satisfying answers.[23] These were daunting questions in the midst of the war because, simply put, there was insufficient information. Fieldwork by social scientists was inadequate before 1980 and halted abruptly with the outbreak of the war. Not only scholars but also journalists, NGO workers, and human rights activists faced great peril moving beyond Ayacucho, and the city itself was not safe.[24] The January 1983 massacre of eight journalists, a guide, and one *comunero* in Uchuraccay demonstrated the hazards of journalistic work in the warzone.[25] Unfortunately, hundreds of other incidents further highlighted these dangers from both the Shining Path and the military. To learn more, those interested depended on the courageous work of Gustavo Gorriti (which he converted

---

22   Degregori 2007.
23   Del Pino 2017, Aroni 2020. One key work in English is Gorriti 1999. For a valuable set of recent texts in Spanish, see Aroni and Del Pino 2023. The Truth Comission's *Informe Final* is also essential (Comisión de la Verdad y Reconciliación 2003).
24   On violence against journalists, see Comisión de la Verdad y Reconciliación 2003, III, pp. 522–36. The list of martyrs is long.
25   On Uchuruccay, see Del Pino 2017.

into essential analyses of the Shining Path) and other journalists such as Raúl González and the photographers Vera Lentz and Oscar Medrano. They could also consult the database on violence organised by the think-tank DESCO and the summaries and denunciations by human rights groups, overseen by the Coordinadora Nacional de Derechos Humanos after its creation in 1985.[26]

On the other hand, the thirst for knowledge about this 'distant' war among the powers that be and the broader public in Lima should not be exaggerated. As the Peruvian Truth and Reconciliation Commission's Final Report denounced with clarity and aplomb, the death of 70,000 people can only be understood in light of 'the apathy, ineptitude, and indifference of those who could have stopped this human catastrophe but did not'.[27] Any rereading of texts from the 1980s about the Shining Path needs to take into account the restricted amount of information circulating in Lima at the time, the mix of rumors, fearmongering, exoticisation, and politicised declarations alongside indifference among much of the capital.

In one long paragraph, Flores Galindo describes the first years of the war: the Shining Path's coercive impositions on the peasantry and the *leva* or forced recruitment by the army. He notes that, 'from the beginning, Shining Path was a vertical and authoritarian organisation convinced it was delivering a message that all should follow. Messianism is authoritarian: you take it or leave it'.[28] He hypothesises that some peasants joined voluntarily, particularly those from the more marginalised communities:

> But in the majority of cases, especially early in their struggle, recruitment appeared voluntary. To those enlisted, Shining Path did not offer highways, food, and schools but rather something more ethereal that paradoxically justified the greatest sacrifices: all power. To the poorest (the favorite recruits) and most disenfranchised belonged a shining future.[29]

He then develops apocalyptic metaphors: a series of earthquakes had devastated the Ayacucho region. 'Some peasants believed that Pachamama refused to tolerate any more earthly suffering and that the world had to change'.[30] He continues in this paragraph describing how the Catholic Church had abandoned the area and the fear due to the increasing power of the Shining Path in rural

---

26 DESCO 1989.
27 Truth and Reconciliation Commission 2014, p. 5.
28 Flores Galindo 2010, p. 225.
29 Ibid.
30 Ibid.

Ayacucho (he never specifies in which provinces), and their imposition that peasants withdraw from the market economy to starve out the cities.

Flores Galindo presents two hypotheses here. First, that Shining Path initially counted on some support in certain peasant communities and towns. He is not wrong. Shining Path had worked diligently to gain a foothold, often through teachers.[31] Some people embraced the idea of a new, more egalitarian society while others liked the establishment of order and the punishment of exploiters or abusers. Of course, the Shining Path imposed their vision with brutality and threats, so differentiating between full acceptance and coerced resignation is nearly impossible. But the best studies of rural Ayacucho find some initial support, which would wane as the cost of backing the Shining Path (in terms of breaking with the market economy, joining the armed struggle, putting up with the authoritarianism of the Shining Path, and facing brutal repression from the state while the guerrillas themselves fled) became painfully evident. In this regard, Flores Galindo is correct.[32]

His second hypothesis, that the poorer towns, those farther from the inroads of modernisation via roads and schools, were more amenable to the Shining Path message does not hold up. He develops this in the penultimate paragraph:

> Backward towns where llama herders (*wamani*) and folk healers (*curanderos*) ruled and reciprocity persisted might reject western civilisation and progress. But comuneros such as those from Huayopampa (Chancay), Muquiyauyo (Jauja), and Puquio (Lucanas) had access to modernity and opted for western schools, electric lights, highways, and trucks. For them progress was a palpable reality; power, only an illusion. They had something worth preserving.[33]

This passage, which, it is important to remember, refers not only to Ayacucho but elsewhere in Peru, would earn the scorn of some critics, particularly Carlos Iván Degregori, as will be seen below.

Other scholars in the 1980s and 1990s sought to find patterns in the expansion of the Shining Path in certain areas.[34] But no single model – geographical (higher or lower altitudes for example) or socio-economic – proved convin-

---

31 Comisión de la Verdad y Reconciliación 2003, II, pp. 27–8 and V, pp. 29–47. See also Degregori 2014a.
32 Del Pino 2017, Aroni 2023. Also valuable is Gavilán Sánchez 2015.
33 Flores Galindo 2010, p. 227.
34 See Favre 1984 for an intriguing early exploration of geography and the support of the Shining Path. See also Degregori 2012, pp. 159–171.

cing. In general, the Shining Path could expand and take root when peasants were less organised, where the CCP or other organisations were not as strong. They never gained a presence in peasant unions and federations, which helps explain their failures to launch in well-organised areas such as Cusco and parts of Puno.[35] Flores Galindo's idea that peasants in poorer areas, those that had not been accepted into the world of modernity or had rejected the rather dismal invitation, were more likely to join the Shining Path, did not prove to be true.

He is on more solid ground when he moves to the cost of the war, its brutality, and the exponential growth of traumas and hatreds. He outlines the fierce increase in disappearances and deaths with the declaration of the state of emergency in 1982 and the growing authoritarianism of Sendero, who 'sought to maintain an iron grip on territories it liberated, and it tolerated no dissent'.[36] He notes that the September 1982 funeral procession of Edith Lagos, a young Shining Path leader who came from a prominent Huamanga family, congregated tens of thousands. Yet that very year Shining Path attacked the Ayacucho mayor and assassinated the director of the National Institute of Culture (INC), 'acts that found no approval in the city'.[37] He is emphatic in his denunciation of the Shining Path and in other texts would develop his analysis of the terrible repercussions (personal, political, economic, and ethical) of the violence. We ought to keep this in mind given later accusations against him for being soft on the Maoists or even pro-Shining Path.

He returns to Arguedas but in the end there is not much on the Andean utopia in this chapter.[38] Flores Galindo understood well that the Shining Path did not invoke the Incas as a model and the people of Ayacucho, past and present, romanticised the Huari more than the Incas and, in general, did not look to the Pre-Columbian past for their utopias or projects. 'The Boiling Point' is above all else an approximation to the rise of the Shining Path and the nature and impact of its violence. Flores Galindo provides a lucid historical background and seeks to explain why some rural people supported the movement. He is not naive regarding the Shining Path's violence and authoritarianism – he under-

---

35 On this, the work of José Luis Rénique has been particularly influential. See Rénique 2016.
36 Flores Galindo 2010, p. 226.
37 Flores Galindo 2010, p. 227.
38 The title, 'The Boiling Point', is from Arguedas's letter to John Murra, 10 February 1967, included in the Anexo of Flores Galindo's chapter. 'If I manage to get better, I can write something on Chimbote and Supe that would end up like a strong liquor made of the substance of Peru's present boiling over, its ebullition, and the burning materials with which liquor is made'. Flores Galindo 2010, p. 230. Flores Galindo first published the letter, with the permission of Sybila Arguedas, the writer's widow, in *Allpanchis*. See Arguedas 1981.

lines their misappropriation of Mariátegui, their verticality, and reliance on threats and coercion. This would prove to be their undoing in the Ayacucho and Huancavelica countryside. His interpretation, however, of less affluent and less modern towns and communities supporting the guerrillas proved less successful.

3 The Silent War

The next chapter, 'The Silent War', opens with an illuminating epigraph, worth citing in full:

> Historians cannot and should not disregard the present. How can we write about Andean utopia without addressing the violence that today rocks the region of Huamanga, an area that once served as the stage for Taqui Onqoy? As in the eighteenth century, violence again attempts to shroud itself in incomprehension. Therefore, you must turn to critical method, the central element of historical reasoning: compare sources, consider their veracity, reconstruct events, establish a chronology, and finally, do not avoid moral judgment.[39]

It is a moving manifesto for historians to examine the present. It also richly compares the sixteenth-century millenarian movement Taqui Onqoy and the 1980s (with a passing nod to eighteenth-century Túpac Amaru and the Kataristas). In this chapter, Flores Galindo compares and ponders a variety of sources, reconstructs events, establishes a timeline, and does not eschew a moral judgement. The writing has the characteristic rapid-fire feel, as the sense of urgency pushes his argument. Not surprisingly, its content changed in each new edition.

He begins with data. Building from the DESCO political violence database, Amnesty International reports, APRODEH, and articles in newspapers press, he charts the intensification of violence from 1980 to 1984.[40] He was among the

---

39 Flores Galindo 2010, p. 231.
40 DESCO maintained a valuable database on violence, included in their weekly *Resumen Semanal* and later published in *Violencia política en el Perú: (1980–1988)*, 2 vol. Lima: DESCO, 1989. http://biblioteca.clacso.edu.ar/Peru/desco/20170222033006/pdf_77.pdf Aldo Panfichi, acknowledged by Flores Galindo, recalls gathering information for him in the DESCO files in 1984 and 1985. (Interview, 28 March 2020). Colleagues remember Flores Galindo distributing graphs and info on the violence from DESCO's database during the 1984 National Congress of History in Lima, more evidence of the importance that political violence and human rights had for Flores Galindo.

first attempting to do that kind of analysis, to offer a more realistic (not sensationalist) account of the spread of violence. Noting the military's frustration with the Shining Path's fish in water tactics, he outlines the changes within the government's counter-subversive strategy, particularly after the December 1982 decrees that put the military in charge of the fight against the Shining Path and increased the area under a state of emergency. Flores Galindo contends that because the military could not easily differentiate who was a guerrilla and who was a peasant, they increasingly relied on peasants themselves, under the firm control of the military. These were not the more autonomous peasant patrols (*rondas campesinas*) or self-defence committees (*comités de autodefensa*) that emerged elsewhere in later years but more along the lines of the 'strategic hamlet program' in Vietnam. Flores Galindo is apprehensive about this tactic: 'to recruit peasants, bring them into formation, make them celebrate the flag and army, protect them, promise to satisfy some immediate necessities, and then throw them against Shining Path'.[41] He understands that coercion was at the root of this policy to put peasants on the frontlines – that those dragooned presumably did not have a choice in the matter – but also understands that perhaps some sought this opportunity to defend themselves, their families, or communities or saw it as an honor.[42] He compares this with the guerrillas in the wars of independence, who were also poorly armed and viewed with hesitation and disdain by some military commanders.[43]

Flores Galindo notes that 'protection and handouts were not enough to compel men to fight'.[44] This is a sophisticated point, one that no doubt built on his broad reading on rural uprisings and insurgency, the literature that developed the notion of 'peasant agency'. He stresses two factors that motivated the military to support arming campesinos. On the one hand, the army understood that 'the comunero world was hardly homogenous; on the contrary, multiple internal conflicts separated wealthy communities from poorer ones, shepherds from farmers, men from the higher reaches from those in warm valleys'. He listed these different divisions (geographic and historic), explaining how the military sought to find Sendero's 'natural rivals'.[45] These are important and perhaps surprising sentences, highlighting the military's understanding of the coun-

---

41 Flores Galindo 2010, p. 233.
42 On the *rondas campesinas*, Degregori 2012, especially chapter 6; Starn 1999; Degregori et al. 1996.
43 For more on his examination of the guerrillas and montoneros in the wars of independence, see Chapter 2 of this book.
44 Flores Galindo 2010, p. 234.
45 Ibid.

tryside, in a text that otherwise laments and denounces their abuses. Flores Galindo realised that many officers understood the Andes – many of them had roots from there and some had studied about them in officer training school. For Flores Galindo, not all members of the military were ignorant thugs.

But the argument immediately becomes more critical. In the same paragraph, he explains how counter-insurgency tactics sought to dichotomise, to produce binaries: terrorists against *montoneros*, subversives against the civil defence, red flags against white flags.[46] He notes the danger for campesinos who could not prove their loyalty, who did not trap Senderistas, but also hints of the threats to others on the left, caught between Sendero and the military. Flores Galindo uses the much-publicised issue 730 (10 January 1983) of the Lima weekly *Caretas*, with the cover of the officer with a knife in his mouth, dripping with blood, to illuminate the us vs. them militaristic discourse. From there he moves to other elements of the military's counter-insurgency tactics: the broad use of torture and the intimidation of journalists.

He developed his thoughts on torture in a subsequent essay discussed below. In 'The Silent War', he noted that it was nothing new, that '"prisoner" in Peru was practically synonymous with "tortured"'.[47] He then moves to the event that drew great attention to the Andes and the war: the murder of eight journalists and a guide in Uchuraccay on 26 January 1983. He begins by noting journalists' protest on 7 January in Ayacucho about restrictions on their work. He does not develop his analysis of Uchuraccay, stressing, however, that the report by the Vargas Llosa Commission had become an official history, blaming the massacre on a misunderstanding, as local comuneros mistook the journalists for Shining Path members.[48] In a footnote, he decries their 'role in a cover up'.[49] Flores Galindo joined in both the chorus of lamentations for the massacre itself and the strong criticism of the language and vision of the investigating commission.

Flores Galindo moves to the response by the Shining Path to the military's changing tactics of relying on campesinos. Here he is spot on. He shows how Shining Path violence shifted towards peasants:

---

46   Ibid.
47   Flores Galindo 2010, p. 235.
48   After the massacre, under intense pressure from Human Rights organisations and the media, the Peruvian government created a commission to investigate the episode, made up by journalist Mario Castro Arenas, jurist Abraham Figueroa, and the renowned novelist Mario Vargas Llosa, who by virtue of his public exposure tended to be depicted as the head of the commission. Their controversial report was issued in March 1983. Comisión Investigadora de los sucesos de Uchuraccay 1983.
49   Flores Galindo 2010, p. 237.

The 'terrucos'[50] responded not against the armed forces, who generally remained barricaded in their garrisons, but against those who, by choice or force, fought on the front lines. Shining Path's war against the state became an atrocious civil war in which communities faced off against each other, in which the dividing line was not rich against poor or white against Indian, but Manzanayocc against Ocros. In this way, water turned into a swamp.[51]

Subsequent studies of the era showed the importance of peasant resistance to the Shining Path, including towns and communities that had been amenable in the first years. These comuneros, however, tired of the demands and authoritarianism of the Shining Path, and fought back, not only at the call of the military. Shining Path reacted brutally. Through his reading in Lima and conversations, Flores Galindo captured a fundamental shift in the nature of the violence in Ayacucho, one that had consequences that few foresaw in the 1980s – the defeat of the Shining Path.

He closes the article censuring those who remained silent. He lamented that he was working with numbers rather than specific individuals and that 'at best we learned the name of the victim but not the victimizer'.[52] He explains, 'Shining Path silence, the military siege, the absence of journalists and social scientists from areas where not even the Red Cross would go – all conspired to create a silent war'.[53] He decries this ignorance, this silence, in prose that recalls the denunciations of the Final Report of the CVR released fifteen years later, in 2003. Flores Galindo understood that statistics did not tell the human stories of the conflicts and that they underestimated the extent of the violence, its brutality and impact, the imposition of silence over truth, of euphemisms and falsehoods over the clear, honest language that he so appreciated. Here, he was prescient.

The essays that made up *In Search of an Inca* changed from edition to edition. Flores Galindo added new ones but also edited those already published. But in the case of 'The Silent War', he actually reduced it, cutting three paragraphs from the beginning and sixteen from the end of the original essay, published in a booklet with another essay by Nelson Manrique under the common

---

50 'Terruco' was a colloquial and usually pejorative term, a euphemism for *terrorista* or terrorist, used to refer to Shining Path members but also to stigmatise people of Indigenous or Ayacuchano background. See Aguirre 2011.
51 Flores Galindo 2010, pp. 238–40.
52 Flores Galindo 2010, p. 240.
53 Ibid.

title *Violencia y campesinado*.⁵⁴ In a sense, he replaced the three introductory paragraphs with the epigraph cited above as well as a quote from Emil Cioran, 'We must side with the oppressed on every occasion, even when they are in the wrong, though without losing sight of the fact that they are molded of the same clay as their oppressors'.⁵⁵ The edits at the end, however, were more substantial, in both length and significance.

These paragraphs not included in *In Search of an Inca*, dealt with topics that he would develop in the late 1980s: authoritarianism, racism, ethics, and, as seen below, human rights. In fact, these final two essays in *In Search of an Inca* can be seen as a bridge between his work on the Andean utopia and that on the long history of authoritarianism.⁵⁶ He never understands authoritarianism as merely a top-down elite project. Flores Galindo condemns those who remained silent about the terrible situation in Peru. He decries that 'human rights do not constitute a fundamental concern in the left', although citing prominent leaders such as Javier Diez Canseco and Jorge del Prado as notable exceptions.⁵⁷ He is clearly furious and indignant about the prison massacres of July 1986 and the muted response, including by some on the left. He also asks, in the case of Uchuraccay, 'what have Max Hernández or Juan Ossio, to name close friends, written about the deaths in Ayacucho?'⁵⁸ He hypothesises that the silencing of the truth, the justification of brutal methods by both the guerrillas and the military, and the extension of violence in Huamanga constituted an authoritarian threat to all of Peru.

He returns to his argument based on his reading of Arguedas, contending that in Peru 'classes have been confronting one another silently for centuries (as Arguedas and Alberto Escobar note); a massive abyss separates people both in terms of their income as well as their ethnicity. In these conditions, violence can appear as the only way to break a situation of total domination. On the other side, no alternative can be envisioned for an insurrection other than extermination'.⁵⁹ He scolds social scientists for exaggerating the predominance

---

54   Flores Galindo and Manrique 1986.
55   Cioran 1976, p. 127.
56   These paragraphs were not reproduced or elaborated elsewhere. They jump more than usual even for his frenetic prose from topic to topic. They outline the long history of authoritarianism in Peru and the need for compliancy and collaboration among the popular classes for it to take root.
57   Flores Galindo and Manrique 1986, p. 35.
58   Flores Galindo and Manrique 1986, p. 34. Psychoanalyst Max Hernández and Anthropologist Juan Ossio were well known scholars and both worked as consultants for the Uchuraccay commission.
59   Flores Galindo and Manrique 1986, p. 36. Here he cites his essay, 'El Perú hirviente', that would subsequently appear in *In Search of an Inca*.

FIGURE 5   Cover of *Violencia y campesinado* (1986)
© INSTITUTO DE APOYO AGRARIO

of consensus in Peru and notes that in contrast to Germany and Argentina, no one in Peru can subsequently claim that they did not know of the human rights horrors. Yet he stresses that nothing is predetermined; 'there are always options'.[60] As Italian literary critic Antonio Melis argued in his tribute to Flores

---

60   Flores Galindo and Manrique 1986, pp. 35–6.

Galindo, 'There are no absolute truths; the capacity to propose new problems, always animated by hope, is more important than the presumably definitive answers. This is the deep lesson Alberto Flores Galindo offers us, in his work as well as in his life'.[61]

Flores Galindo closes with an ominous note about the spread of censorship and the strengthening of silence and complicity, to the point that 'the fence that surrounds these tragic Andean towns is getting thicker'.[62] This is the conclusion of an intense and even bleak text, that moved rapidly from one aspect of authoritarianism to another. I do not know why Flores Galindo cut these final eight pages from the version included in *In Search of an Inca* (pp. 32–39). It may be that he found them too fragmented, too preliminary, and perhaps too personal. They reflected his despair after the July 1986 prison uprisings and the murder of hundreds of prisoners. He probably received feedback and criticism from colleagues and friends that made him rethink some of those issues: those were years of intense, passionate, and frank exchanges and debates, and Flores Galindo never shied away from them or from revising his positions.

4 Debates, Controversies, and Polemics

In the 1980s in Peru, public figures debated about the Shining Path passionately. In a recent interview, Nelson Manrique, a close friend and colleague of Flores Galindo, and a member of SUR, recalled how their positions vis-à-vis the Shining Path were not received very favorably by other sectors of the left, and that there were also real threats from both the armed forces and the Shining Path.[63] Not surprisingly, Flores Galindo's views, particularly those included in *In Search of an Inca*, generated controversy and even accusations of being pro-Shining Path, an insinuation that infuriated him. In 2001, Magdalena Chocano decried that 'some intellectuals have even accused Flores Galindo publicly and privately of being in favor of the Shining Path'.[64] Flores Galindo called out historian José Tamayo Herrera for this, noting that this view was disseminated primarily through 'the old mechanisms of Lima gossip'.[65]

---

61 Melis 2005, p. 14.
62 Flores Galindo and Manrique 1986, p. 39.
63 Drinot 2023, p. 193.
64 Chocano 2001, p. 12.
65 Flores Galindo 1989b, p. 345. Tamayo Herrera was more critical of Manuel Burga than of Flores Galindo, associating his ideas with the Shining Path in tangential and unconvincing ways. Tamayo Herrera 1988, pp. 148–62, esp. 154–5.

On the other side of the political spectrum, *Asalto al Cielo*, the Sunday supplement of *El Nuevo Diario*, published an interview with him on May 25, 1986, before the publication of *In Search of an Inca*. At that point, *El Nuevo Diario* was pro-Shining Path. Flores Galindo asked to review the interview before its publication, but they did not allow him to do so. In the words of the interview's author, César Ángeles Loayza, '[Flores Galindo] had asked to not include his final answer as it had equivocal interpretations (it was a rough period politically). However, given the interest in his answer and the intensity of the moment, it was decided during the editing phase to publish a synthesised version of his long answer'. This was clearly a questionable, even unethical decision. Flores Galindo sent a rapidly written letter to clarify 'his alleged words', expressing his rejection of the pro-Shining Path insinuation of the sentence 'since 1980 the panorama begins to change'. In another questionable decision, *Asalto al Cielo* published the 1 June 1986 letter verbatim, with Flores Galindo's cross-outs and corrections.[66] This incident revealed, among other things, that Flores Galindo was conscious of the need to be careful with language and that he did not want to be manipulated by an outlet with ties to the Shining Path.

These reviews and the ones I will refer to below need to be understood in the context of the moment, the escalating crisis and tensions among intellectuals. President Alan García's social democratic caudillismo had failed miserably by 1988, landing Peru into an abysmal economic crisis. Shining Path expanded, empowering authoritarian projects that sought to defeat it and muzzle civil society; Lima witnessed growing violence. Neo-Liberalism and its ideologues rapidly increased their presence. The left entered crisis, with the Izquierda Unida dividing once again in 1989. In a 1988 essay that appeared in *Tiempo de plagas*, Flores Galindo notes that terms used in the past to describe Peru's dire situation had taken new life: 'disintegrated country', 'bordering the abyss', and 'a country in decline'. He updated these with some contemporary terms: 'alluvial' and 'abortive'.[67] To return to the debates about Flores Galindo is a reminder of the depth of the crisis, the despair, and the sharpening rhetoric. One of his major opponents, Carlos Iván Degregori, refers to 'the demoralisation of the

---

66 Ángeles Loayza 2015, pp. 113–117. In this book, Ángeles Loayza ultimately did not include the sentence that Flores Galindo sought to edit, making the letter unintelligible. Furthermore, he published only parts of the letter, omitting sections such as this one: 'Millenarianism and even more so its close variant messianism have an evident authoritarian bent. The revolution overseen and decided by a group of visionaries who see themselves as the interpreters of "the word"; prophecy readers who do not seek those with a conscious will but instead rigidly disciplined followers'. The reference to the Shining Path could not be clearer.

67 Flores Galindo 1988a, p. 215.

80s, which made an apocalypse seem imminent and above all inevitable'.⁶⁸ Flores Galindo's work illustrates these trends as his rhetoric sharpens year by year in the late 1980s and his cautionary, almost alarmist tone builds with the crisis.

Flores Galindo criticised both the left and right. He questioned those on the left for getting too comfortable with the status quo. In a 1987 round table, Flores Galindo stated, 'I observe something among the intellectual left: they now think based on how things are, giving up thinking about how we would like them to be, what alternatives we can propose, how to make radical transformations, how to construct a new society. Politics needs to rediscover utopias'.⁶⁹ This was one foray in a complex and often bitter debate within the left discussed below. The rhetoric and tone were harshening. For example, Flores Galindo's 1988 historiographical review, 'La imagen y el espejo', is brilliant but has a severe frankness and sharp edges that did not characterise his earlier work.⁷⁰ Years before some critics, in turn, had deemed Alberto Flores Galindo a sniper or *francotirador*, noting that he was very critical of the left but was not a member of a party.⁷¹

Flores Galindo was equally harsh with the right. The liberal economist Hernando de Soto established the Instituto Libertad y Democracia (ILD) in Lima in 1981 to organise Peru's business class and to question 'statist' and Marxist approaches. Flores Galindo wrote a brilliant review of Hernando de Soto's *The Other Path*, a searing critique of the intellectual foundations of nascent neo-Liberalism.⁷² He also crossed swords with Fernando Iwasaki, a young, much-promoted conservative historian who pushed the ILD vision of the market and modernisation as panacea.⁷³ Flores Galindo reiterated this concern with the rise of the right in many of his publications and interviews. Later, in his moving, posthumously published farewell letter, 'Reencontremos la dimensión utópica. Carta a los amigos', he stated bluntly, 'The right advances on all fronts' and decried the shift to the right of many former leftist militants.⁷⁴

---

68   Degregori 2014b, p. 305.
69   *El Zorro de Abajo* 1987, p. 14. The round table included Carlos Franco, Alberto Flores Galindo, and Sinesio López.
70   Flores Galindo 1988b.
71   De Cárdenas and Elmore 1983. Flores Galindo was close to the PUM (Partido Unificado Mariateguista, a coalition of radical Marxist groups) but not a member.
72   Flores Galindo 1988d.
73   Flores Galindo 1989c.
74   Flores Galindo 1989f. pp. 386, 389. For an English translation, see https://nacla.org/article/peru-self-critical-farewell.

It was the anthropologist Carlos Iván Degregori who wrote the most damning critique of the final chapters of *In Search of an Inca*, those treated here. Their lives had fascinating parallels and intersections as they collaborated, debated, clashed, and created analogous institutions and rival publications. They studied at the same high school, La Salle, and both died tragically young, Flores Galindo at 40 and Degregori at 65. Both were spectacular writers and indefatigable editors and organisers. They both sought to invigorate the Peruvian left, to break down the rigid orthodoxies and halt its atomisation and fragmentation.[75]

Degregori was an anthropologist and Flores Galindo an historian who taught in a Social Sciences department; Degregori taught at San Marcos University and was a researcher at the Instituto de Estudios Peruanos, serving as Director for two periods while Flores Galindo taught at the PUCP and helped create SUR as a second home. In terms of magazines and journals, Degregori directed *El Zorro de Abajo* (1985–1987) and Flores Galindo, along with others, created *Márgenes* in 1987 (which would survive after his death and would continue to be published until 2000). Degregori was born in Lima but had studied and taught in Ayacucho for much of the 1970s, more focused in that decade on politics, *la militancia*, and journalism than research and teaching.[76] Flores Galindo, born in Callao, lived in Lima most of his life, counting on the PUCP as his base for almost all his career. By the late 1970s, Flores Galindo was a much-respected intellectual who was just turning 30. They were close in age, Degregori four year older. The history of their relationship, the connections between the intellectual, political, and personal, constitutes a fascinating chapter in Peruvian intellectual history.

Their battles in the press escalated after 1987, the rhetoric or tone hardening. Issue 7 of *El Zorro de Abajo* reviewed the first issue of *Márgenes*, the journal of the newly founded SUR. It lauded other texts but panned Flores Galindo's article on the 'generation of 1968': 'A vision of intellectuals practically trapped with no alternative between two ghosts that become more and more real, repression or assimilation'. Among other critiques, the author, presumably Degregori, believes the article was overly critical of those on the left who had become

---

75 Some summaries of the era and these two scholars' work underline the supposed rupture around 1987 between 'zorros' and the more radical 'libios', the former identified with the 1985–87 magazine founded by Degregori, *El Zorro de Abajo*, and the latter implicitly and pejoratively accused of sympathies with Libyan leader Muammar Gaddafi. I do not see this as a turning point, and I cannot imagine Flores Galindo seeing Gaddafi in positive light. Moreover, Flores Galindo collaborated in *El Zorro de Abajo*.

76 On Degregori, see Sandoval and Agüero 2015.

part of the democratic system, who sought to fight within the system.[77] In 1989, Flores Galindo criticised Degregori for being 'against the Andean' and harshly summarised his 1986 book with Cecilia Blondet and Nicolas Lynch, *Conquistadores de un nuevo mundo*.[78] Numerous other examples could be cited, as two of Peru's sharpest minds and pens went to battle.[79] These formed part of a broader universe of strident discussions among the left, about paths to socialism, the place of intellectuals, and the solutions to Peru's problems. Neither of them would have necessarily seen it as a personal rivalry or insurmountable conflict.

Degregori wrote an extensive essay, 34 pages single-spaced, after the 1987 publication of the Peruvian edition of *In Search of an Inca*. At just about the time Degregori finished it, Flores Galindo became ill and died on 26 March 1990. Out of respect, Degregori asked that his text only circulate among students. Upon Degregori's death, it was published (with some edits) as part of a multi-volume selected works of his. It's a classic Degregori text, with brilliant reading of a variety of sources and deft, clever prose. In this regard, rereading Degregori brings to mind rereading Flores Galindo – one is reminded of the creativity, the suggestive interpretation, the apt metaphor and similes, and the overflow of ideas.

The critique is broad and fierce. Degregori notes in the first footnote that his text 'has a polemic tone'.[80] In terms of *In Search of an Inca*, it centres on four allegations: Flores Galindo's misrepresentation of 1970s' peasant mobilisations and political history (which led him to fatalism and pessimism); a misunderstanding of modernity in the Andes; a misapplication of the concept of the Andean utopia; and an overly abstract and at times forced understanding of the Shining Path. I review these, briefly, to answer a broader question – does this critique invalidate or refute Flores Galindo's writing on the 1980s and the Shining Path?

The criticism of the lack of depth in Flores Galindo's evaluations of the 1970s echoes that of historian José Luis Rénique.[81] As noted above, Flores Galindo uses the work and life of Arguedas to examine changes in the struggle over

---

77   *El Zorro de Abajo*, 5 (Julio 1986). This refers to his essay 'Generación del 68: Ilusión y realidad' (Flores Galindo 1987a).
78   Flores Galindo 1989b, esp. 339–343.
79   Anthropologist Javier Torres, a former student at the Catholic University, recalls a public debate between the two on that campus in 1988. Alas, there is no recording. 'Presentación de las obras completas de Carlos Iván Degregori, Parte III', https://youtu.be/41WG1Vg5Knk.
80   Degregori 2014b, p. 301. Degregori toned down the rhetoric from draft to draft.
81   Rénique 1988 questioned Flores Galindo's inattention to the complexity and dynamism of twentieth-century peasant movements.

power in the Andes from the 1950s to the 1980s. I think his response would have been that to fulfill this demand, the history of rural politics over multiple decades, would have required years of research and hundreds of pages. That was not his intention.[82] Degregori's article is longer than the sections in *In Search of an Inca* on the Shining Path. After all, Degregori had done extensive research on the Shining Path, from its origins to the development of the war. In *In Search of an Inca*, Flores Galindo did not intend to write a political history of twentieth-century rural insurgency or on everyday politics in the Andes, topics he knew well. The fact that he did not write this history does not invalidate his arguments; some would disagree.

On the other hand, Degregori correctly criticizes Flores Galindo's dichotomy between more modern towns that rejected the Shining Path and those more 'backwards' (a term used by Flores Galindo and underlined by Degregori) that were more receptive. As Degregori pointed out, the debate about whether to support Shining Path (alternatives often meant flight) usually *divided* towns, something that subsequent studies have confirmed. As noted, social scientists struggled to create models on who supported the Shining Path. Flores Galindo was not alone. Degregori links this critique with a broader debate about modernity in the Andes, which had pitted Flores Galindo against numerous researchers at the Instituto de Estudios Peruanos. I consider them related but distinct debates.

Degregori's third critique is only partially correct: the use of the Andean utopia in the case of Ayacucho in the 1980s seems forced. Degregori deems that 'the Shining Path appears as a nightmarish version of the Andean utopia' or the 'inversion of the world'. In reality, the Andean utopia had little presence in this chapter. In previous chapters, Flores Galindo had examined Ayacucho, often in comparison with Cusco. The fact that the concept of the Andean utopia did not prove germane to understanding the Shining Path does not mean that what Flores Galindo wrote on them is not valuable. In fact, I would argue that his writing on the Shining Path (as well as the chapter 'A Republic without Citizens') form part of his 'authoritarianism' portfolio more than the utopianism project. Flores Galindo's overall project in *In Search of an Inca*, after all, was not to 'find' this strand of utopianism in every episode he studied: it was, as he himself put it, to explore the conflictive relationship between the Andean world and the West, and between socialism/Marxism and the Andes. In that sense, not paying attention to the Shining Path, the war, and the Andes in the

---

82   Rénique noted that Flores Galindo did not accept this critique but took it well. (Conversation with José Luis Rénique, 28 March 2020).

1980s would have been a major omission for a historian who was always connecting past and present.

Finally, Degregori criticizes Flores Galindo for not understanding the Shining Path. In his memoirs, Degregori derides Flores Galindo for 'not having *calle*' or street smarts.[83] At one level, this was somewhat of a callous critique, implicitly contrasting Degregori's Ayacucho and San Marcos University credentials against Flores Galindo, Lima and the posher Catholic University. He also argued that Flores Galindo and the sociologist Gonzalo Portocarrero, a fellow member of SUR, 'needed to meet real Shining Path members'.[84] Certainly, no comparison can be made here – Degregori lived for years in Ayacucho, knew and battled Abimael Guzmán and other Shining Path leaders, and ultimately was a leading if not the leading expert on them.[85] Degregori's arguments, of course, evolved. In the 1970s and early 1980s he disparaged the Shining Path and believed that they would be crushed. His critique of Flores Galindo for not understanding the Shining Path could have been accompanied with a recognition of his own errors and evolution.

Flores Galindo wrote *In Search of an Inca* in Lima primarily in 1985 and 1986, based on wide readings, the sources at hand, and conversations. This was before the Shining Path's 1988 National Congress or the 'interview of the century' with Abimael Guzmán that appeared in July 1989. Both provided documentation on and insights into the armed organisation. Flores Galindo did not conduct research in Ayacucho, virtually impossible at the time. Yet the sections on the Shining Path and the 1980s, as discussed above, are still relevant and at time masterful. I found a subtle and somehow ironic, although not entirely surprising, connection or even reconciliation between Flores Galindo's and Degregori's critical views on the period of violence: Flores Galindo's attention to civil society's action, inaction, and discourse; its members' compliance or complacency; how the press could not or would not cover news in Ayacucho; how different political groups, the Catholic Church, and others avoided the issues; and many facets of authoritarianism and the breakdown of democratic rule all bring to mind the brilliant Final Report of the CVR which Degregori helped orchestrate. Flores Galindo probed the very questions behind the CVR's indignant and inspired denunciation, cited above, of 'ineptitude and indiffer-

---

83 Sandoval and Agüero 2015, p. 141.
84 Sandoval and Agüero 2015, p. 143. It is important to remember that in these interviews, Degregori also had positive comments about Flores Galindo as a person and writer. See also Degregori 2005, where he reiterates his appreciation of Flores Galindo's work, particularly *La agonía de Mariátegui*.
85 Degregori 2014a; see also Degregori 2012.

ence'.[86] Carlos Iván Degregori was an intellectual pillar of the Truth Commission's Final Report. Many of Flores Galindo's arguments echo.

Perhaps their similarities and proximities explain the intensity and passion of the exchanges between them. They both believed in democratic socialism, both had broad cultural interests (literature and cinema), both were dedicated mentors to many students, and both were exquisite and prolific writers. The same Lasallian brothers taught them in high school. In retrospect, they had more in common than not. Like many sibling squabbles, theirs became fierce, despite their mutual respect. Carlos Iván Degregori makes many fine critiques of *In Search of an Inca*, the ultimate respect for an author. Both Flores Galindo and Degregori were capable of biting critiques, but they also received it well. As Flores Galindo wrote in his farewell letter, 'disagreeing is another way of coming together'.[87] In his autobiography, Degregori displayed his characteristic sense of humor and self-deprecation. Flores Galindo's horribly premature death prevented them from further dialogue about utopias, modernity, and the Andes.[88]

5   Time of Plagues

Flores Galindo developed and expressed his ideas about contemporary Peru in his constant contributions to the rich selection of left-leaning journals and magazines that flourished in Lima in the 1980s.[89] One of his concerns was to historicise state violence, not only the repression of the Shining Path but also against multiple forms of day-to-day resistance and protest. He asked in one of his essays, 'What do a maid, the treatment of a prisoner in jail, and mass graves in Ayacucho have to do with one another?' This came from a 1985 review about a book on torture in Chimbote, a northern Peruvian city in which Flores Galindo ruminated on the history of human rights abuses in Peru.[90] He begins by contrasting Peru with Argentina. In the latter, while some could contend that they

---

86   Comisión de la Verdad y Reconciliación 2003, I, p. 13.
87   Flores Galindo 1989f, p. 390.
88   In their published conversations, José Carlos Agüero and Pablo Sandoval as well as Degregori himself referred to the 'interrupted debate' with Flores Galindo. Sandoval and Agüero 2015, pp. 151 and 215. I think Flores Galindo would minimise this, emphasising instead multiple debates and much broader discussions among many people.
89   For a vast collection of texts, photos, and more, see the digital 'Colección Alberto Flores Galindo', organised by the library of the Catholic University. They have articles of his from twenty-four journals. The actual list is longer. https://repositorio.pucp.edu.pe/index/handle/123456789/137486
90   Flores Galindo 1985c, p. 159. The book under review was Renshaw 1985.

did not know of the mass detentions, torture, and disappearance after the 1976 Videla coup, in Peru, in contrast, 'the events were not hidden, it almost seems that they were exhibited'.[91] (Nonetheless, the percentage of people in Lima who would claim that 'I had no idea' if asked about brutalities in Ayacucho would no doubt be shockingly high, especially before the killing of eight journalists in Uchuraccay in January 1983). He pointed out that in Peru the most common justification of repression was that it was an unfortunate but necessary reaction to 'terrorism', a new plague or cancer brought by the Shining Path and manipulated discursively by the state. Yet he asks whether this argument is valid if torture predated the emergence of the Shining Path. He examines Father Renshaw's book to discuss the persistent use of torture by the police throughout Peru against common criminals, well before 1980; 'torture in Peru precedes terrorism'.[92] The state did not understand criminals and prisoners as deserving or meriting the respect of their human rights. Flores Galindo uses a review of a little-known book to rethink the long history of state violence.

He lauds Renshaw's study, reiterating some of its key arguments such as the consequences in the victims, trauma. He notes the prevalence of violence in everyday life via 'domestic servitude'. He cites a study in Cusco that indicated that 22 out of 23 maids interviewed had been 'brutally beaten'.[93] Flores Galindo decries that no one denounces these forms of torture and abuse because everyone has internalised them and the legal system recognises, at least implicitly, 'the abysmal class differences, racism, and above the seemingly compulsive need to impose oneself over the other: total domination at the private level'. He states, 'in this country there is no universal category that grants everyone the same rights and duties'.[94]

Here and elsewhere, Flores Galindo stresses that the roots of the 1980s violence and profound crisis need to be understood historically. His argument that torture did not begin in 1980 or 1982 and that the abuse of political prisoners needs to be compared with that of common prisoners and domestic servants underlines this point (part of what he deemed 'the authoritarian tradition'). Yet this is not fatalistic historical determination – *we are this way and have always been*; far from it. He does not present a Foucaldian reading where power is

---

91   Flores Galindo 1985c, p. 159.
92   Flores Galindo 1985c, p. 160.
93   Flores Galindo 1985c, p. 161.
94   Ibid. This text (originally published in *El Zorro de Abajo*, 2) is the inspiration for a notable article by Carolina Carlessi about domestic violence and servitude (Carlessi 1986). Pushed by feminism and grassroots organisations, the left finally began to consider the wretched status of maids and servants, ubiquitous in middle-class and elite households.

invisible and seemingly inevitable. Instead, he stresses here and elsewhere that authoritarian projects build on racism and other divisive forms of social identification as well as frustration and discontent. He laments the limited notion of democracy, as elections and nothing else.[95] Nonetheless, he reiterates Father Renshaw's call for everyone to denounce the mistreatment and abuse outlined in his book. Flores Galindo believed that knowledge and solidarity could and should confront authoritarianism on all of its many fronts.

Flores Galindo opens another essay, 'Extermination and memory: the prison massacres', with an enlightening epigraph from the detective fiction writer Ross Macdonald, 'I don't know what justice is. Truth interests me, though. Not general truth if there is any, but the truth of particular things. Who did what when why. Especially why'.[96] As Carlos Aguirre shows in chapter 6 of this book, crime novels were one of Flores Galindo's favorite genres. This quote served as a collective and individual call for action, beseeching his readers to not just express befuddlement or indignation regarding the massacre of hundreds of unarmed prisoners, but to learn more, find out what happened, and why. And this is what Flores Galindo set out to do in this essay, published for the first time in *Tiempo de plagas* in 1988. That same year, in a public conversation with Carlos Franco, Hubert Lanssiers, Sinesio López, and Fernando de Trazegnies, he noted that 'violence has its explanations. Its protagonists have faces, the faces of people who live in our country, people like us. The inability to understand the facts is such that we at times must underline the obvious. But explaining is not justifying'.[97] In these years, his participation in two projects pushed Flores Galindo to develop his denunciation of silence and complicity: one on multidisciplinary approaches to understanding violence, coordinated by Father Felipe Mac Gregor, and the other one his collaboration in discussions and publications in psychoanalysis.

The murder of 248 prisoners at El Frontón, Lurigancho, and Santa Bárbara in June 1986 was widely condemned in Peru and internationally. Flores Galindo immediately expressed his indignation: he made declarations to the magazine *Amauta*[98] and later signed a harsh petition against those guilty of the atrocity. Some such as his mentor Ruggiero Romano feared for his safety.[99] Within a year, the Senate's Comisión Ames had released its report on the massacres and Agustín Haya de la Torre and Juan Cristóbal published well-documented books

---

95   Flores Galindo 1985c, p. 163.
96   Flores Galindo 1988e, p. 203. The quote is from Macdonald 1950, p. 156.
97   Instituto de Defensa Legal 1988, p. 10.
98   *Amauta* 1986.
99   Romano 1991b, p. 95.

on the June 1986 events. Flores Galindo used these as well as additional documents provided by APRODEH (Asociación Pro Derechos Humanos) to explore why the prisoners rose up and who they were. He used the macabre statistics to probe the question of the social background of Sendero prisoners. He believed that the condemnations should have been stronger.

In fact, he almost seemed to follow Macdonald's summary of the search for justice: what happened, when, how, and why. He respectfully rejects sociologist Fernando Rospigliosi's explanation of 'cultural inheritance', deeming the term a cliché. Instead, he proposes that the existence of 'Shining Path faces' in Lima and Callao, i.e. real people, the concern about the 'demonstration effect', and what he considers the paranoia of those in power prompted the brutal state reaction. He delves into the background of the dead, concluding that the victims were overwhelmingly young, mestizo, and of lower-class background. Never satisfied with dry sociological categories and statistics, he mentions two victims: Antonio Díaz Martínez, discussed above, and José Valdivia Domínguez, or Jovaldo, a well-known street poet. He poses the question of their aspirations, their 'hopes and dreams'.[100] Shocked by the absence of more public outcry against the massacres and consternated about the lack of information about them, who they were, Flores Galindo seeks to humanise them.

Flores Galindo noted the importance of memory, citing a text by the psychologist César Rodríguez Rabanal, and ended the text examining polls about the massacre. He cited one by APOYO right after the events that showed that only 14% of the respondents were opposed to the government's brutal response. A few days later, as more and more was learned about the events, particularly at El Frontón, a poll from *La República* found that 74% 'condemned the excesses' committed by the military. He ends on a slightly optimistic tone, 'not everyone accepts being an executioner or a victim, nor do they accept authoritarianism o fanaticism'.[101]

6   Human Rights

> Tito tells me we should open a Human Rights section. I respond, *you seem so Christian. That's very petit bourgeois.* He looks at me incredulously and responds, *but rights are violated, they kill people, they disappear them.*[102]

---

100   Flores Galindo 1988e, p. 209.
101   Flores Galindo 1988e, p. 212.
102   Martínez 1997, pp. 223–4.

Flores Galindo wrote about human rights, linking it to his arguments about the long history of authoritarianism and violence in Peru. As the quote above from his dear friend Maruja Martínez captures, some on the left had qualms about the concept. They believed it too bourgeois, too tied to notions of the individual in a capitalist society. Some worried that it would eclipse the broader, structural critique of the inequalities of capitalism that served as the backbone of the struggles of the late 1970s. This debate about whether an approach that focuses on stopping the state from abusing, torturing, and disappearing overlooks broader structural forms of violence remains the leading question today in the global human rights community.[103] The Peruvian left had been reinvigorated by the organised confrontations against the Morales Bermúdez military regime in the late 1970s. Flores Galindo was part of the New Left, less tied to the Soviet Union, China, or Cuba and deeply anti-Stalinist. The fear that the concept of human rights eschewed structural issues and the fight against capitalism discouraged some Peruvians from embracing the concept of human rights. The Shining Path repudiated it. Nonetheless, Flores Galindo understood the denunciation of atrocities in Ayacucho as a humanitarian or ethical obligation and as a valuable rejection of creeping authoritarianism and complacency.[104]

His bonds and ideological affinity with Javier Diez Canseco, a Senator and leader in the human rights community, help explain this enthusiasm for the concept or at least his access to valuable information. His collaboration with the Jesuit Felipe Mac Gregor in the Catholic University and his friendship with the Argentine exile Inés García, a sociologist, were also important. In his 1986 version of 'La guerra silenciosa', he calls for broader attention to human rights, the recuperation of 'shock and indignation with deaths and the disappeared'.[105] He lauds the work of pioneers such as APRODEH, some members of the Catholic Church, and community leaders, but, as mentioned above, decries that the issue was not essential for most of the Peruvian left. He also calls for those not on the left to also embrace the concept and struggle for human rights.[106]

Finally, in this broad-ranging and somewhat disorganised text, he notes that human rights are not limited to state-civilian relations. He underlines Shining Path's lack of respect for human rights – the murder of authorities for

---

103   Moyn 2018, Walker 2020.
104   Youngers 2003, Servicios Populares 1982, Comisión de la Verdad y Reconciliación 2003, III, pp. 293–318.
105   Flores Galindo and Manrique 1986, p. 34.
106   Flores Galindo and Manrique 1986, p. 33.

example – and its use of terror, 'a stark form of authoritarianism'.¹⁰⁷ He underlined that the Shining Path and its tactics were just as much a 'dictatorial threat' as the government's project to extirpate communism and dissent. This was not his only critique of terror from the left. In 1987 he decried the Basque group ETA's killing of 21 people in a bomb placed in the HIPERCOR market in Barcelona on 19 June. He criticised the action itself as well as the failure of ETA and Herri Batasuna to recognise their guilt, their reliance on excuses and euphemisms.¹⁰⁸

Questioning Shining Path from a human rights perspective was a challenge. First, the framework had been developed in the Southern Cone and Central America, where U.S.-funded right-wing governments had committed the vast majority of the atrocities. Human rights activists were accustomed or trained to focus on state actions. Furthermore, little was known about violence by the Shining Path, at least until 1985 or so. As the Truth Commission stressed, three-quarters of the victims were rural, and much of the violence took place in small towns or isolated areas of the Andes. Journalists could not do their job and contradictory reports reached Lima. Many on the left could not fathom that a guerrilla group would unleash such an authoritarian project and murder campesinos. The 1983 Lucanamarca massacre was one wake up call. On 3 April, the Shining Path murdered 69 peasants, men, women, and children.¹⁰⁹

In 'La tradición autoritaria', drafted in 1986 but only published posthumously in 1999, Flores Galindo opens a section on 'racism and servitude' with a burning question: 'All that has happened in recent years reveals the true texture of the republic. Why aren't human rights respected?'¹¹⁰ He discusses the eighteenth-century emergence of the concept and how Peru was born unequal, 'some more equal than others'.¹¹¹ He then examines class structures or *estamentos*, discrimination against the Indigenous, the punishment of slaves and prisoners, and racism, 'a major chapter of authoritarianism'. He contends that 'domestic servitude reproduces in daily life the relationships that in the past marked Andean haciendas, the personal dependence of the serf or *colono* to the lord'.¹¹² He describes here and elsewhere (in *Aristocracia y plebe*, for example) how racism is reproduced within the domestic sphere. In these paragraphs as well as many

---

107 Flores Galindo and Manrique 1986, p. 35.
108 Flores Galindo 1987e.
109 Comisión de la Verdad y Reconciliación 2003, VII, pp. 46–55.
110 Flores Galindo 1986g, p. 442.
111 Flores Galindo 1986g, pp. 442–3.
112 Flores Galindo 1986g, p. 445.

of his essays and books, he addresses the long history of authoritarianism in Peru, using the Shining Path and the dirty war to rethink Peruvian history and vice-versa.

7 Conclusions

Shining Path and the violence of the 1980s might not appear to be among Flores Galindo's principal research topics. Nonetheless, he wrote extensively and emphatically about the period and his essays, long and short, have held up well over time. The violence of the 1980s and the authoritarian project of Sendero were the sources of concern and even anguish for Flores Galindo, a man of the left and a committed public intellectual. In reviewing the volumes of his complete works, one finds a rich collection of essays, dating from his journalism in the late 1970s, especially in *Amauta*, through his denunciations and analyses in the 1980s.

On the one hand, he historicised our understanding of the Shining Path. His examination of torture ruptured the notion that the surge of violence and silencing arose in Chuschi in 1980. This was not an indirect defence of Sendero but instead a reiteration of the deep roots of violence in Peru and a critique of those who abandoned the struggle for social justice in the 1980s.[113] He also used the period to develop his ideas about authoritarianism. As noted, in 'La tradición autoritaria' he linked the situation in the 1980s to the fundamental inequalities in Peru, bolstered over the centuries by slavery, racism, servitude, and the lack of recognition of the rights of others. He stressed the role of the domestic sphere, hinting at but not developing a gendered analysis.

On the other hand, he sought to break through silences and euphemisms, naming names, describing events, and critiquing. In the words of Antonio Melis, Flores Galindo showed 'the need to overcome abstraction, reclaiming the decisive presence of the human factor in history'.[114] He disentangled governmental discourse about the Shining Path (his paragraphs on subversion as disease are outstanding) but also brought up the inadequate response by civil society. Even when lauding the human rights community, he noted that they were a small minority, including within the left.

A review of these writings also deepens our understanding of Flores Galindo as a public intellectual. One is reminded of his nervous, even frenetic pace, how

---

113 Point well made by his former student, Iván Hinojosa. Interview, 2 April 2020.
114 Melis 2005, p. 12.

one article led to another, often bolstered by several public talks or interviews. His projects were not linear; he did not finish one book project to move onto another. Instead, he developed his key areas of interest – the left, violence and authoritarianism, and the search for alternatives – in all of his work, across his different publications. But he also emphasised the need to adopt an ethical stand, a posture that not many on the left accepted or adopted. As such, he felt it was his obligation to examine and write about the dark years of Peru as it 'approached the abyss', even if his interventions caused discomfort to many.

CHAPTER 6

A Requited Passion: Flores Galindo and Literature

Carlos Aguirre

> If you want to know about politics, read literature. Literature provides you with a picture of society, while politics only fragments it. Read Tolstoi and Dostoyevsky.
>
> JOSÉ ARICÓ[1]

∴

1   A Passion for Reading

One of the most outstanding features of Alberto Flores Galindo's intellectual work was its interdisciplinarity. He trained formally as a historian and practiced his trade with the rigour and creativity for which he is widely known, but since his formative years he was also interested in other disciplines. First, it was sociology, which informed his early studies on the labour movement and his collaboration with sociologist Denis Sulmont.[2] After he returned to Peru from France in the mid-1970s, he ventured into anthropology, conducting fieldwork in several locations with colleagues and students. Art and art history were also fields he often explored in his essays and whose study he enthusiastically promoted. In the 1980s he got interested in psychoanalysis, participated in colloquia and discussions around it, and used it in one of his most creative essays, 'Los sueños de Gabriel Aguilar'.[3] Near the end of his life, he embraced environmentalism through his friendship and collaboration with Catalan scholar Juan Martínez Alier.[4] In his writing and teaching, he also engaged with demography

---

[1] Quoted in Cortés 2019, p. 67.
[2] Flores Galindo and Sulmont 1972.
[3] Flores Galindo 1986a, chapter 3. This chapter was not included in the English translation (Flores Galindo 2010).
[4] Flores Galindo and Martínez Alier 1988. Flores Galindo was credited by Martínez Alier for coining the term 'environmentalism of the poor', which was later used by him and other authors. See Martínez Alier 2002, p. 13.

and political science. And while it is true that economics did not have a marked presence in his works, he was always genuinely interested in economic history. It should be noted also that his academic affiliation at the PUCP was through the School of Social Sciences, and not the History Department, which facilitated and stimulated his engagement with other disciplines.

His intellectual curiosity was not limited to the social sciences, however, since Flores Galindo had another great passion, one which has seldom been paid attention to: literature.[5] He was a voracious reader of fiction from a very young age, a devotion that began at home through his father, who introduced him to classics such as *Don Quijote*,[6] and was consolidated at the La Salle school. The philosopher and leftist militant Eduardo Cáceres Valdivia, who attended the same school, offered a recollection of Flores Galindo and the close relationship he developed with books during his school years:

> I first met him at the Colegio La Salle library, which was not a small one: it took up the equivalent of two classrooms under the bleachers of the school stadium, and it was later expanded with an *ad hoc* space in the gym's basement. That is, the book repository and the reading room together were as large as a basketball court or more. This library was headed by a priest from the school, Brother Alberto (who played a key role in the education of several generations of students, including Salomón Lerner, [Enrique] Bernales, [Carlos Iván] Degregori, Alberto Flores Galindo, [Manuel] Dammert, the Iguíñiz brothers [Javier and Manuel], myself ... and many more). This priest taught fourth year Psychology and fifth year Philosophy (and Education at the PUCP) and his classes were very thought provoking. I remember that his favorite author was [José] Ortega y Gasset. He introduced us to academic work: we had to write monograph papers for his courses, for which we had to conduct research, prepare index cards, and so on. And once a week he took us to the library, where we could pick out any book to read. Many of us went to the library more often and we could take out books to read at home.

---

5   Two important exceptions are Elmore 2005 and Portocarrero 2017. In this chapter, I will focus primarily on novels and poetry, but it is worth mentioning that Flores Galindo was also a movie and theater enthusiast. He developed a close friendship and collaboration with the Yuyachkani theater company. Yuyachkani performed at Flores Galindo's funeral in March 1990, and dedicated a booklet on their remarkable play 'Contra el viento' (1989) 'to the people of Puno and to Alberto Flores Galindo'.
6   Portocarrero 2017, p. 110.

Tito is relevant in this story because at some point in high school he became one of the librarians and soon after head librarian. I was his 'assistant' one year. Tito was famous for being a sort of walking catalogue of the library.[7]

Flores Galindo and his fellow high school students started publishing a magazine that they sold in other schools in the Breña district, where several of them lived and where Colegio La Salle was located. One issue of the magazine featured an interview with the prominent *indigenista* writer Enrique López Albújar (1872–1966). Some of Flores Galindo's classmates recall how he helped them write their papers. One of them had to write a paper on Dostoyevsky and remembers being 'overwhelmed with books' on the Russian writer when he asked Flores Galindo for help.[8] By then, Flores Galindo was already an avid reader of the Russian novelist, one of his favorite authors. Cáceres Valdivia remembers reading *The Brothers Karamazov* at a very young age, most likely on Flores Galindo's recommendation. He also recalls that during those years they read many books published in the Populibros Peruanos collection, a project directed by the poet and publisher Manuel Scorza from 1963 to 1965 (the final years of Flores Galindo's secondary education) aimed at bringing books to the Peruvian masses.[9] Among the authors that Flores Galindo read in his school years were Jean-Paul Sartre and the Peruvian novelists José María Arguedas, Ciro Alegría, and Enrique López Albújar.[10]

After enrolling at the PUCP in 1966 Flores Galindo's interest in literature widened. He became good friends with Ricardo González Vigil, who recalls that from the beginning of their friendship they 'talked about history and literature, two passions that always brought us together, although our priorities were reversed: he was a historian in the making, and I was a would-be literary critic and creator'.[11] At the PUCP Flores Galindo took classes with Luis Jaime Cisneros, who was for many years a literary apostle of sorts. González Vigil lists some of Flores Galindo's favorite books during those years: 'we were both voracious and intense readers of literary works, but especially novels. Tito admired

---

7   Author's personal communication with Eduardo Cáceres Valdivia, 27 February 2020. Portocarrero pointed out that Flores Galindo 'was never a regular sports player. In school what he was most interested in was working in the library as assistant to the principal'. Portocarrero 2017, p. 117.
8   The words are by Eduardo Cáceres, whose account is the basis for this reconstruction of Flores Galindo's school years.
9   See also Cáceres Valdivia 1993, p. xiii. On the Populibros collection, see Aguirre 2017b.
10 Coincidently, all these authors were featured in the Populibros Peruanos collection.
11 González Vigil 2015.

Dostoyevsky, Sartre, Camus, and Sabato;' Borges, on the contrary, 'irritated him'. According to González Vigil, Flores Galindo 'found him an aestheticist, too contrived, and fond of arbitrary arguments and sophistry'.[12] He could not finish James Joyce's *Ulysses* and ended up selling his copy to González Vigil. 'He was convinced that it was not worth the effort of putting in the time necessary to understand it'.[13] They closely followed Latin American literature, which was so fashionable at the time, and 'waited anxiously for new Latin American Boom releases (Tito was excited by the works of Arguedas, Carpentier, Sabato, and the Vargas Llosa of those years)'.[14] The early works by the future Peruvian Nobel laureate left their mark: 'Tito and I were so excited when we read *La ciudad y los perros* (1963) [*The Time of the Hero*] ... that we anxiously combed bookstores, in 1966, asking when [his next novel] *La casa verde* [*The Green House*] would arrive (it turned out he didn't like it as much), and, later, in 1969, *Conversación en la Catedral* [*Conversation in the Cathedral*] (which he loved)'.[15] He also enjoyed Vargas Llosa's 1967 novella *Los cachorros* (*The Cubs*).[16] He almost certainly read *Cien años de soledad* (*One Hundred Years of Solitude*), the novel published by Gabriel García Márquez that same year, but there are no accounts that can tell us what he thought of that and other novels by the Colombian writer.[17]

Alberto Adrianzén, another close friend of Flores Galindo during their college years, recalls his interest in Sartre, Marcel Proust, Sabato, and Jorge Semprún. He remembers that Flores Galindo gave him as a gift Borges's short story collection *El informe de Brodie* (*Doctor Brodie's Report*) and read one of the stories together. They also read Sartre's *The Story of a Friendship* together, a book in which the author reflected on his relationship with Maurice Merleau-Ponty.[18] During the two years that Flores Galindo studied in Paris (1972–1974) he attended many seminars and tried to 'read as many books as possible', includ-

---

12 Author's personal communication with Ricardo González Vigil, 10 March 2020.
13 Ibid. Ricardo González Vigil wrote elsewhere that Flores Galindo gave him his copy of *Ulysses* as a gift. See González Vigil 1990.
14 Ibid.
15 González Vigil 2015.
16 Author's personal communication with Ricardo González Vigil, 10 March 2020.
17 I have only found one (very indirect) reference to García Márquez in all his works. Speaking of Arguedas, he wrote that 'he wanted to go beyond national borders. He wanted to be an author like García Márquez. Later he realises – and this will be featured in the press – that he could not be a writer like the Boom authors'. Flores Galindo 1986h, p. 410. García Márquez was probably the only Boom writer whom Flores Galindo saw in person, although from afar, and not once but four times, in Cuba, as noted in chapter 4 of this book.
18 Adrianzén 1990.

ing French literature, while keeping an eye on what was being published in Peru.[19] Upon his return from France he befriended poets such as José Watanabe and Marco Martos, with whom he collaborated in the magazine *Vaca Sagrada*, whose sole issue came out in 1978.[20] Martos notes how he often shared poetry books with Flores Galindo, while his friend 'would sometimes describe the entire plot of a novel while we drove to the beach crammed inside his small German car'. Flores Galindo 'was very oral', according to Martos. One of the novels he recounted in full for Martos was *The Red Orchestra*, by Gilles Perrault, which is based on the true story of a group of Soviet spies in Nazi Germany.[21]

But it was the Peruvian writer José María Arguedas who most interested Flores Galindo, both as a reader and as a historian. González Vigil describes how Flores Galindo 'ordered' his friend Gustavo Benavides, an admirer of Borges, to read Arguedas's novel *Todas las sangres* [1964], and 'succeeded in moving him with the creative power of Arguedas'.[22] Without a doubt, Arguedas's suicide in 1969 deeply affected the young student and voracious reader that Flores Galindo was at the time. References to Arguedas appeared in Flores Galindo's writings as early as 1972, in his undergraduate thesis, and throughout the years the novelist's works featured prominently in the historian's oeuvre to a degree that no other author, except Mariátegui, did. Peter Elmore gives a valuable account of some aspects of Arguedas's work that were of interest to Flores Galindo:

> Arguedas was a recurring presence. He especially liked Arguedas's poems ('A nuestro padre creador Túpac Amaru', 'Katatay', 'Oda al Jet'). Regarding Arguedas's short stories, we once talked about the collection *Amor*

19　Burga 2005, p. 200. In one of the letters that he wrote to Burga from Paris, in April 1974, Flores Galindo requested Julio Ramón Ribeyro's short story *La juventud en la otra ribera* (Ribeyro 1973). Burga 2010, p. 69.

20　The poet Roger Santiváñez remembers that, during those years, Martos regularly had over to his house a group of friends who were mostly connected with literature. Flores Galindo, who lived in the same neighborhood of La Capullana, in the Surco district, often joined those gatherings. Around that time, both Martos and Flores Galindo visited the historian Pablo Macera often. Author's personal communication with Roger Santiváñez, 5 June 2020. It was in such conversations that they came up with the idea to publish *Vaca Sagrada*, whose first and only number featured, among other writings, an article penned by Flores Galindo and José Deustua on the popular response to the 1929 crisis, another piece by Pablo Macera on imperialism, capitalism, and revolution, and two poems also authored by Macera ('Romance del tocino en la cocina' and 'De Ginebra solo una campana').

21　Author's personal communication with Marco Martos, 23 March 2020.

22　González Vigil 2015.

mundo. He was intrigued by Arguedas's sexuality (and, more broadly, eroticism in the Andes), especially because, paradoxically, it is a very obvious theme in the works by Arguedas but hardly discussed by literary criticism.[23]

His final and unfinished project, which he had been maturing for years, was a biography of the author of *Todas las sangres*.[24] Of that project only two unpublished essays remained, which were posthumously released.[25] Flores Galindo was convinced that the life and works of Arguedas could help illuminate the tensions and dilemmas of Peruvian history:

> [I]t might be useful to try to understand the cultural conflict in Peru through Gramsci's notion of historical crossroads, of the moments and places where diverse traditions meet and clash, and the creativity and possibilities of broadening horizons that historical crossroads open up. Arguedas was someone who found himself at one of these historical crossroads, which he experienced with an exceptional intensity, until those conflicts contributed to his suicide. But the personal cost resulted in an outstanding oeuvre that opened up the possibility of thinking about Peruvian society in a different way, while, in other fields, the social sciences remained under other schemes.[26]

Arguedas was to Peru what '[Gustave] Flaubert was for nineteenth century France, Dostoyevsky for the Russia of that same century, or [Robert] Musil for early twentieth century Vienna'.[27] For Flores Galindo, Arguedas was 'the most original Peruvian literary product of our time', and in order to approach his works, he thought, one had to consider the creator, the ethnologist, and the real character, three dimensions that are inseparable.[28] Historian Gustavo Montoya, who was Flores Galindo's research assistant in this project, has offered valuable insight into 'the limits of his academic and intellectual train-

---

23 Author's personal communication with Peter Elmore, 28 February 2020.
24 Martos recalls, 'I once told Tito that I would like to write a biography of Arguedas and he told me that that was also his dream. I immediately thought that he was better suited because of his background, and I told him so. He did not live long enough to fulfill that dream'. Author's personal communication with Marco Martos, 23 March 2020.
25 Flores Galindo 1992. In the prologue, Cecilia Rivera notes that in 1975 Flores Galindo was already thinking of someday writing a biography of Arguedas (p. 3).
26 Flores Galindo 1988f, p. 428.
27 Flores Galindo 1986h, pp. 395–396.
28 Flores Galindo 2010, p. 199.

ing', which, for example, prevented him from interpreting a passage from *El zorro de arriba y el zorro de abajo* (*The Fox From Up Above and the Fox From Down Below*), because it is narrated in '*Quechuañol*' (a mixture of Quechua and Spanish), as he put it. But in addition to the linguistic difficulty, the novel 'is extremely complex in its depiction of the main character's subjectivity, a type of subjectivity that Tito could not tap into'. Montoya adds that Flores Galindo 'demanded an answer' from him, a demand that he made 'dramatically, urgently, with a large dose of irritation'. Montoya's account highlights how rigorous and demanding Flores Galindo was in his work, but also the difficulties he faced in his attempt to incorporate literary sources, and in particular Arguedas, into his work as a historian.[29]

Moreover, Flores Galindo thought he saw in Arguedas's oeuvre, especially in *Todas las sangres*, 'a desire for social revolution', a debatable interpretation but one that allowed him to include Arguedas in the Peruvian socialist tradition, along with major authors such as Mariátegui and César Vallejo.[30] This was perhaps what led him to remark, with obvious satisfaction, on the 'exciting effect' that Arguedas's visit to Cuba in January 1968 had 'on his innermost being'.[31]

In the early 1980s, Flores Galindo forged closer ties with Peruvian writers, especially those associated with *El Caballo Rojo*, the supplement directed by the poet Antonio Cisneros for which Flores Galindo was a frequent collaborator.[32] He became a keen reader of noir fiction, especially the novels of Raymond Chandler, Ross Macdonald, and Dashiell Hammett, a liking he shared with his

---

29 Montoya 2006, pp. 37–8.
30 Flores Galindo 2010, p. 205.
31 Flores Galindo 1987d, p. 195. In that text, Flores Galindo erroneously put 'January 1969' as the date of the visit. The excitement, in fact, transcended his innermost being. In addition to the well-known lines he wrote in the 'first diary' of *El zorro de arriba y el zorro de abajo*, Arguedas referred elsewhere to that visit: '[I]n Cuba I was among men who have triumphed over death, men for whom dying to free mankind from all forms of banishment and deprivation is to live ... [it has] been in Cuba, the island where the sun neither dulls nor destroys but instead inspires and begets, where the Vallejan era in the Americas has begun, the era of the empire of brotherhood of man'. Arguedas 1968, p. 95. And in a letter to Fernández Retamar, he wrote: 'My ideological position is again as clear as it was around 1934–1937, when I started publishing. My trip to Cuba elucidated everything; the circuitous line of the Communist Party affected many intellectuals; Cuba guides and inspires now, as the USSR did when I was young, although it does so at a closer range and in perhaps more difficult times'. Letter from José María Arguedas to Roberto Fernández Retamar, Lima, 17 October 1968, Archivo Casa de las Américas.
32 Cisneros left a memorable depiction of his relationship with Flores Galindo (Cisneros 1988). After Flores Galindo's death in 1990, Cisneros dedicated to him his poem 'Marina'. Cisneros 1992, pp. 31–32.

friend and editor Luis Valera, a great promoter of the genre.[33] His literate taste included both classic and contemporary writers. To his young children he read novels by Jules Verne and other authors.[34] He once gave Maruja Martínez *Memoirs of Hadrian* by Marguerite Yourcenar as a Christmas gift.[35] Elmore recalls conversations with Flores Galindo about authors such as Albert Camus, André Malraux, and Joseph Conrad, but he particularly remembers a book suggestion from Flores Galindo: 'I discovered *Los ilegítimos*, by Hildebrando Pérez Huarancca, thanks to Tito. It's a very brief collection with several good [short] stories. One that attracted special interest from him was 'La oración de la tarde', which (according to Tito) contains a view of violence that provides insight into the sensitivity and imagination of the individuals within the sphere of Sendero Luminoso, although not just theirs. It is a suggestion that I am grateful for'.[36]

Friends of Flores Galindo remember his frustration, and even dismay, with the poor selection of titles found in Lima bookstores, so he used to ask anyone who traveled abroad to bring him books, including novels. He would do the same with friends and colleagues who lived outside Peru. Being as he was,

---

33 Author's personal communication with Peter Elmore, 28 February 2020. Flores Galindo saw a connection between the work of the historian and that of the detectives or policemen featured in crime novels, 'who interrogate one individual after another until they arrive at the truth, or, like Ross Macdonald says, at an exploration of the how and the why something happened'. See Cueto 1986.
34 Ragas and Valdez 2010.
35 Martínez 1997, p. 310.
36 Author's personal communication with Peter Elmore, 28 February 2020. According to Flores Galindo, in the field of *indigenista* literature 'certain high-quality texts such as *Los ilegítimos* have been overlooked'. Flores Galindo 1989b, p. 339. Pérez Huarancca's book, a volume of short stories that take place in a town near Ayacucho plagued by poverty and abuse, was first published by Ediciones Narración in March 1980, just weeks before the start of the Shining Path insurrection. The author's subsequent life has been surrounded by speculation and debates. He was arrested in 1982, accused of being a member of Sendero Luminoso; he later broke out of jail, and, according to testimonies gathered by the Peruvian Truth and Reconciliation Commission, he was the leader of the massacre perpetrated by the guerrilla group in the Andean town of Lucanamarca on 3 April 1983. Other versions argue that there is no evidence of Pérez Huarancca's involvement in that massacre. There is also no information on when and how he died. According to some testimonies he died in combat, but others suggest that he was able to flee the country and went to Spain or France. See, in particular, Cox 2012. Cox does not deny that Pérez Huarancca was an active member of Sendero Luminoso, but he also notes the absence of any evidence of his participation in the Lucanamarca massacre. Some of the short stories in *Los ilegítimos* were later featured in anthologies and the entire collection was reissued in 2004 (Ediciones Altazor) and 2015 (Editorial Amarti).

in the words of Gonzalo Portocarrero, an 'avid reader of novels',[37] he tried to stay up to date on new releases from publishing houses. In June 1989, when he was already suffering from his fatal illness, Flores Galindo asked Esther Pérez, his friend at Casa de las Américas, to send him the Spanish translation of the novel *The Conservationist*, by South African writer Nadine Gordimer, which had been published in Havana the previous year.[38]

But his interest in literature was not limited to works from the lettered tradition and the conventional canon. Quechua culture, in all its expressions (dance, song, poetry, oral tradition, myths), was always of interest for Flores Galindo. This should come as no surprise, given the ethnic, linguistic, and cultural makeup of Peru and his interest in the country's indigenous peoples, both past and present. In this regard, Arguedas's work, both his literary and ethnographic production, again served as a source of inspiration and reflection regarding the indigenous cultures that for centuries existed on the margins of mainstream Peruvian society. Flores Galindo's interest in anthropology was prompted precisely by his need to explore these cultural expressions and try to incorporate them into his interpretations of the past and present of these communities. An example of this is his essay 'Europa y el país de los Incas', in which he used documentary sources to shed light on the origins of the Andean utopia in the sixteenth century, but also material gathered in his fieldwork in Chiquián, in the province of Ancash, during the celebration of a festivity known as 'The Inca and the Captain'.[39]

His interest in Quechua culture was stimulated by his close relationship with the brothers Edwin, Luis, and Rodrigo Montoya, who were prominent Andean music scholars and musicians. In 1987, the Montoyas published the book *La sangre de los cerros*, a compilation of Quechuan songs, which Flores Galindo reviewed in an article revealingly entitled 'Los poetas que no tienen nombre' (The Nameless Poets).[40] These songs, he wrote, were proof of 'a culture that is alive' but whose authors, with few exceptions, were anonymous. Reading and understanding these songs – 'Kechwa singing' in Arguedas's terms, or 'Quechuan poetry' in the words of the Montoya brothers – is impossible, Flores Galindo suggests, 'without making the effort to imagine the singers, feel the

---

37 Portocarrero 2017, p. 111.
38 Letter from Alberto Flores Galindo to Esther Pérez, 13 June 1989, Archivo Casa de las Américas.
39 Essay included in Flores Galindo 2010, pp. 3–52. The description of the Chiquián festivity is on pp. 42–6.
40 Flores Galindo 1987g.

music, and also think about the listeners'.[41] In other words, it is imperative to reconstruct the production, transmission, and reception of these songs-poems in order to capture their deeper meaning.

2 Literature and the Historical Craft

Was his interest in literature useful in his work as a historian? Flores Galindo incorporated literary sources into many of his essays and monograph works, following, in a way, a path taken by Mariátegui, for whom according to Flores Galindo himself, 'literature was a means of acquiring knowledge that was just as important as economics and sociology', and who dedicated the longest of his seven famous essays to tracing the evolution of Peruvian literature.[42] In the case of historical novels, such as Tolstoi's *War and Peace*, Flores Galindo considered them a valid way of approaching the past, as they enabled us to 'see history from various angles: to orchestrate in a work the multiple images of its characters, to reconstruct from within the psychological rhythm of events'.[43] Literature, therefore, was not only a legitimate and important source for the historian, but a valid representation of the past.

The incorporation of literary references into his work as a historian began early and developed throughout the years. Initially, when he was just starting out, Flores Galindo approached literary sources somewhat naively as providers of information that illustrated 'reality' or added a nuance that could not be found in the conventional sources with which historians worked. He treated them 'cautiously' but without distinguishing them from any other kind of historical document. In his undergraduate thesis, mentioned above, Flores Galindo described his literary sources: 'With the caution with which literary works should be treated, we have drawn on Augusto Mateu Cueva, author of *Lampadas de minero*, who lived for many years in Morococha, and on José María Arguedas, who, in *Todas las sangres*, describes how peasants conceived work in the mines. [Manuel] Scorza's novel, *Redoble por Rancas*, its artificial over-ornamentation notwithstanding, describes some events that really happened in the area'.[44] Here literature is a source of *data* that 'describe' aspects

---

41 Flores Galindo 1987g, p. 261.
42 Flores Galindo 1994b, p. 495. Mariátegui's essay, originally titled 'Proceso de la literatura', was translated as 'Literature on Trial'. Mariátegui 1971.
43 Flores Galindo 1983e, p. 15.
44 Flores Galindo 1972, p. 15. When it was published in book form in 1974, the author cut the reference to Arguedas, and in later editions, the section on the sources he used was

of reality, both subjective ('how peasants conceived') and objective ('some events that really happened'). Fictional characters are used to offer a portrayal of 'real' social groups: 'Arguedas, and those who have dealt with the indigenous world, have insisted on the differences between *comuneros* and *colonos* (hacienda Indians). While the latter were generally submissive, staging only sporadic and primitive rebellions (think, for example, of the *colonos* of *Los ríos profundos*[45]), the former, the *comuneros*, are proud men, aware of their rights, and relatively organised 'fierce and aggressive' individuals'.[46]

In later works, his use of literary sources will be more sophisticated. That is the case of *Tradiciones peruanas* by Ricardo Palma,[47] to which he dedicated a section of *Aristocracia y plebe*, under the title: 'A Human Comedy: Traditions', an obvious nod to Honoré de Balzac. In Palma's writings, Flores Galindo noted, 'history is intermingled with fiction, in an attempt to capture an era in an anecdote'.[48] He questioned the idea that Palma had 'invented' Lima, and recalled that the traditionalist considered himself a historian, although he was not as committed to documents as traditional historiography was. Suggesting a relationship between Palma's narrative project and a way of doing history that prioritises *interpretation* over factual reconstruction of events, Flores Galindo added that Palma 'seems to believe that *what is important is not understanding the specific event, exactly as it happened, but the fundamental tendencies of a moment*, for which the narrator can, legitimately, avail himself of the imagination'.[49] Flores Galindo mentions the sources that Palma drew on: manuscripts and papers from the National Library, documents from the National Archive, studies by historians, and oral traditions. It is impossible, he adds, to distinguish in Palma's writings what was the product of his research from that which he invented, but the image of the city that Palma left turned out to be, in a sense, real: 'The Lima of Ricardo Palma is the Lima of the common people'.[50]

---

eliminated in full. The books mentioned are Mateu Cueva 1941, Arguedas 1964, and Scorza 1970.

45 Arguedas 1958. There is an English translation, Arguedas 1971.
46 Flores Galindo, 'Los mineros de la Cerro de Pasco', 22. This quote was removed in the published book version. However, another quote, taken from *Todas las sangres*, was kept (in italics here): 'Penetrating the earth's interior, opening it up, destroying it, was something very different from their traditional activities. Inside the earth dwells the serpent Amaru, who "*determines the droughts or the rains that spoil the earth. And it is said to live in the bottom of lakes or in deep caves, where water drips, the water of the whole body of the hills*"'. Flores Galindo 1974, p. 63, emphasis added.
47 A selection was published in English. Palma 2004.
48 Flores Galindo 1984a, p. 180.
49 Flores Galindo 1984a, p. 181, emphasis added.
50 Flores Galindo 1984a, p. 184.

Flores Galindo's take on Palma clearly shows how distant he was from positivist historians (both conservative and Marxist) and how open and imaginative his conception of history as a discipline was.

Flores Galindo also used fiction to strengthen an argument or the portrait of a society or a historical process, without establishing a solution of continuity between 'real' and 'invented' stories. Writing about the cult of Víctor Raúl Haya de la Torre among APRA activists, for example, Flores Galindo noted that 'the ideas of many activists of the time can be seen reflected in a passage of the novel *Sol: están destruyendo a tus hijos*, written by Serafín Delmar'.[51] When writing about Cuba in 1987, after summarising a 'true' story that illustrated the efforts to rid Cuban society of hierarchical and discriminatory practices, Flores Galindo added: 'Anecdotes like these must have occurred occasionally in those early years. Jesús Díaz includes a similar story in his novel *Las iniciales de la tierra*'.[52] The use of the term 'historia' in Spanish, which translates as both 'story' and 'history', to refer to an anecdote narrated by Díaz in a novel is very revealing, as it seems to suggest that, for Flores Galindo, although it was included in a fictional work, it could have been a 'real' story.

Flores Galindo's books also contain references to writers and works of fiction that are important as they evoke individuals whose lives he was interested in understanding. These are public intellectuals, activists, or political leaders whose works of fiction shed light on their way of thinking and acting. That is the case, for example, of an author such as Mario Vargas Llosa and his novel *La guerra del fin del mundo*, published in 1981.[53] From his reading of that book, Flores Galindo draws conclusions regarding the political views of its author: 'Politics as a misunderstanding, profound or superficial, is the thesis [of the novel]: confused intellectuals and fanatics, all of them alienated, carried away by ideas, are drawn into a bloody conflict. The final *thesis* is that politics are incomprehensible'.[54] The Vargas Llosa of 1981, he adds, is no longer 'a critical intellectual, a malcontent, a 'Sartrecillo valiente'[55] ... he has reconciled with the

---

51 Although this quote comes from a text signed by Flores Galindo and Manuel Burga, it is easy to identify this section as written by the former. Burga y Flores Galindo 1980, p. 230. The book by Serafín Delmar (Reynaldo Bolaños Díaz's pen name) was a short story collection, not a novel (Delmar 1941).
52 Flores Galindo 1987d, p. 191. The quote is from Díaz 1987, p. 112. Díaz's novel was published in June 1987, a mere three or four months before Flores Galindo quoted it, which shows how well informed he was of the latest literary releases.
53 Vargas Llosa 1981. There is an English translation, Vargas Llosa 1984.
54 Flores Galindo 1987a p. 234, emphasis added.
55 Vargas Llosa was called by his youth friends Abelardo Oquendo and Luis Loayza 'el Sartrecillo valiente', a wordplay on the title of the Grimm brothers' famous 'El sastrecillo

Right'.⁵⁶ Similarly, he found in Arguedas' novels insights into the author's social and political views. After referring to 'the rebellion narrated in the final pages of *Todas las sangres*', Flores Galindo sums up how this author saw Peruvian society: 'Thus, Arguedas thinks that Peru, especially Andean Peru, the Peru of the mountains, is a society divided in two. A society governed by impositions and by forms of violence that date back to colonial times'.⁵⁷ Moreover, he suggests 'going back to his novels and stories to see how Arguedas approached the problem of the clash between the Andean world and the West'.⁵⁸ Works of fiction, for Flores Galindo, offer the possibility of tapping into the thinking or ideology of their authors. Incidentally, Vargas Llosa wrote a book about Arguedas based on the same premise, although the conclusions he drew were quite different from those of Flores Galindo regarding Arguedas and the past and future of Andean societies.⁵⁹

As Flores Galindo would say, commenting on Mariátegui's love for novels, 'fiction could provide as much insight into a situation as statistics'.⁶⁰ That's the spirit with which Flores Galindo approached, especially in his more mature years, the challenge of incorporating literary materials into his work as historian. According to Peter Elmore, 'he was a historian who did not seek in literature and its practitioners a confirmation of data provided by statistics or economics; on the contrary, he saw literary texts and the development of the intellectual field as crucial for fully understanding historical processes'.⁶¹ Another literary critic, Antonio Melis, would agree: 'Openness to literature, in a broad sense, is not something secondary, but rather a form of expansion and projection from a solid foundation of knowledge'.⁶² In Flores Galindo, Melis adds, there is not an 'instrumental use' of literature. Novels and stories 'are not considered a mere

---

valiente' ('The Brave Little Tailor') that alluded to Vargas Llosa's admiration for Jean-Paul Sartre.
56   Flores Galindo 1987a, 234. Vargas Llosa himself later said something similar about his novel, although from the other end of the ideological spectrum: 'When I read that book [*Os Sertões*, by Eudides da Cunha] and wrote that novel [*La guerra del fin del mundo*], I had lived through the tremendous trauma of my break with Cuba, my break with Marxism. Actually, I think I had broken with Marxism long ago, but not officially. I made a very radical revision of what had been my political convictions until then and I began to accept the idea of democracy. This book expresses all that, undoubtedly ... all of those experiences are certainly behind the story told in *The War of the End of the World*'. Tusell 1990, p. 76.
57   Flores Galindo 1986h, p. 403.
58   Flores Galindo 1986h, p. 402.
59   Vargas Llosa 1996.
60   Flores Galindo 1994b, p. 568.
61   Elmore 2005, p. 5.
62   Melis 2005, p. 12.

testimony, based on a more or less explicit reflection theory. They are, instead, part of a continuum, of a whole, illuminating hidden crevices of reality through the quality of their writing'.[63]

Flores Galindo's familiarity with literary sources is also reflected in the placement of epigraphs in his books and essays, which were often drawn from poems or narrative works.[64] Verses by poets such as Antonio Cisneros, José Santos Chocano, and Marco Martos, and quotes from novelists such as Dostoyevsky, Camus, and Arguedas, were used very effectively as epigraphs. His book *Tiempo de plagas*, for example, opens with an epigraph taken from Camus's *The Plague*: 'To state quite simply what we learn in time of pestilence: that there are more things to admire in men than to despise'.[65] One of the essays in *In Search of an Inca*, in which he examines peasant mobilisations and the growth of leftist movements, includes as epigraph a verse by Antonio Cisneros: 'And I see (like everyone) the passing of the ship of death'.[66] In his essay on the 1986 prison massacre, first published in *Tiempo de plagas*, Flores Galindo included a quote by Ross Macdonald as an epigraph: 'I don't know what justice is. Truth interests me, though. Not general truth if there is any, but the truth of particular things. Who did what when why. Especially why'.[67] Perhaps one of the most memorable is the epigraph he included in his essay 'Vivir en el Perú', which revealed an effort to remain optimistic amid the bleak Peruvian reality of the late 1980s, marked by political violence, inflation, unemployment, and crime. For that epigraph, Flores Galindo chose a poem by another one of his close friends, Marco Martos:

> This country is not your country
> because you know its borders,
> nor does a shared language
> or the names of the dead make it yours.
> What makes this country yours
> is that if you had to
> you would again choose
> to build here all your dreams.[68]

---

63   Ibid.
64   Melis also mentioned this in the essay cited above.
65   Flores Galindo 1988c, p. 15.
66   Flores Galindo 2020, p. 197.
67   Flores Galindo 1988e, p. 203. The quote is from Macdonald 1950, p. 156.
68   Flores Galindo 1986i.

3   The Forging of a Style

Flores Galindo's frequent engagement with literature was reflected in his narrative style. His prose is widely regarded as being both captivating and polemical. One of the best descriptions of Flores Galindo's writing style was that by Gonzalo Portocarrero: 'When reading his works, the eyes glide effortlessly over the lines, as the internal melody flows; there are almost no breaks in rhythm, the phrases are short and forceful. They connect together to form persuasive arguments'.[69] His writing, Portocarrero would say in another text, had 'a rhythm that made reading easy'.[70] Martos described it as 'pleasing, brisk, and nervous'.[71] His use of the infinitive and of short sentences, while at times departing from grammar conventions, is quite effective and contributes to achieve the desired emphasis. Melis highlighted the 'continuous recourse to questions as a stylistic device'.[72] Several critics have underlined the imprint that Flores Galindo's familiarity with literature left in his narrative style. Portocarrero stated it directly: 'Where did that ease of expression come from? That compelling ability to convince? Without intending to give a definitive answer, I think it is important to note his ongoing engagement with literature and, perhaps, especially his desire to communicate, to reach wider audiences'.[73] In his prologue to *Tiempo de plagas*, Antonio Cisneros placed Flores Galindo's prose within Peru's 'literary tradition', in which he also included Raúl Porras Barrenechea, Pablo Macera, and José de la Riva Agüero, who 'clearly exhibit a healthy and familiar relationship with literature'.[74]

Cisneros could have also included Mariátegui in that list, who was a major source of inspiration for Flores Galindo in so many aspects, including his interest in literature, his skills as a writer, and the frequent choice of the essay form, a genre 'situated midway between fiction and erudite studies', as Flores Galindo would define it.[75]

Journalism also contributed to forge Flores Galindo's narrative style. Since the mid-1970s, he was a regular contributor to newspapers, supplements, and magazines, while continuing to write essays, book chapters, and historical monographs. We can say of Flores Galindo what he said of Mariátegui: that he

---

69 Portocarrero 2005.
70 Portocarrero 2017, p. 108.
71 Martos 2005, p. 8.
72 Melis 2005, p. 105.
73 Portocarrero 2005, p. 21.
74 Cisneros 1988.
75 Flores Galindo 1994b, p. 558.

produced works at 'the rapid, brisk, and hammering [pace] of his typewriter'.[76] As Alejo Carpentier once observed with respect to novelists, journalism 'can help 'loosen the pen' of the writer'.[77] The pen of the historian as well, we could add, as Flores Galindo's case proves. In the abovementioned prologue to *Tiempo de plagas*, Cisneros noted Flores Galindo's enthusiastic participation in journalistic adventures and his willingness to write 'under urgent circumstances and deadlines'.[78] Flores Galindo's incursions into journalism had important precedents among early twentieth century intellectuals, a period that he studied as a historian: 'The journalistic style – he wrote – infected even the scholars at the university: short phrases, precision qualified by somber adjectives; it was also the style that José Carlos Mariátegui would gradually develop'.[79] The influence of journalism is not without some potential costs. Carpentier, remembering Flaubert, warned against the risk of 'getting comfortable with using too loose a pen', something that, in Flores Galindo's case, can be detected in some of his writings, produced at frenzied speed, as we saw in chapter 3 of this book.

Flores Galindo's approach to history always showed an interest in humanising the reconstruction of past events and processes by offering fleshed-out portraits of many of its characters. As in the best novels, his readers are left with very vivid images of some of the protagonists and episodes featured in his essays and books. History, as practiced by Flores Galindo, was not dry, hyperspecialised, or stark, even less a narrative without human agents. Telling good stories was one of the virtues of his work as a historian and essayist. Melis argued that Flores Galindo reflected 'a view of the historian's task where the scientific method meets the art of the storyteller'.[80] A good example of this is the essay 'Los sueños de Gabriel Aguilar', an innovate effort to use psychoanalysis in historical interpretation, and, at the same time, a captivating account that seduces and keeps the reader's interest. The opening line could very well be the beginning of a novel: 'For a whole afternoon, on 5 December 1805, the bodies of two convicts swung from the gallows of the Plaza Mayor of Cusco'.[81] His careful biographical sketch of Aguilar reveals his grasp of the novelist's technique for building characters. *La agonía de Mariátegui* is another example of narrative effectiveness. Flores Galindo succeeded in offering a human and empathetic portrayal of his character, while at the same time reconstructing

---

76 Flores Galindo 1994b, p. 377.
77 Arias 1997, p. 20.
78 Cisneros 1988.
79 Flores Galindo 1994b, p. 445.
80 Melis 2005, p. 101.
81 Flores Galindo 1986a, p. 141.

the development of his thinking, placing it within the intellectual and political coordinates of his time, and examining the heated debates and many projects in which he was engaged (the magazine *Amauta*, the socialist party, labour solidarity, transnational network building). The book is both biography and history, individual and collective portrait, a study of the man and his circumstances. Mariátegui's Marxism, Flores Galindo wrote, was 'developed far from any academicism, caught up in events, immersed in everyday life, an offspring of those same streets and crowds that fueled the journalistic craft of the young Mariátegui'.[82] The use of metaphors is an enormously effective mechanism for seducing readers. 'Europe was a world in which the convictions, certainties, and sureties that had ushered in the 1900s had been shattered, like the shells that destroyed the trenches at Verdun or Caporetto', Flores Galindo writes describing Mariátegui's visit to the continent.[83] The quality prose was not the only element that likened this book to literary works. Flores Galindo allowed himself to 'play with time' – a device of the modern novel that no doubt influenced his decision to use it –, despite this being 'objectionable in a historian'.[84] The book does not follow a strictly chronological sequence of events, which actually works very effectively in constructing a story that moves back and forth in time and keeps the reader engaged.

4   The Impossible Library

Reconstructing Flores Galindo's wide range of literary readings is an impossible task, in part because we do not have a list of the books that he had in his library nor do we know all those titles that he read in other libraries. The accounts by his friends and colleagues mentioned above give us a glimpse of the authors and titles the historian was in contact with at different moments of his life and those he shared with friends and colleagues. To enhance this information I compiled a list of the authors and titles he mentions in his works. Although Flores Galindo obviously did not mention or quote in his writings all the poetry books and novels that he read, nor did he necessarily read all the authors he mentioned, this exercise allows us to draw some conclusions regarding his reading habits and his knowledge of the process of writing literature. I have included two tables at the end of this chapter. The first contains the names of the writers that Flores Galindo mentioned in at least one of his works, along

---

82   Flores Galindo 1994b, p. 391.
83   Flores Galindo 1994b, p. 553.
84   Flores Galindo 1994b, p. 396.

with the titles he cited, and the volume and pages of his *Obras Completas* where he mentions or quotes them. The second is a list of writers mentioned without any specific reference to any of his works.[85]

The lists are quite eclectic and broad. The variety of books he read or at least was familiar with was truly diverse. However, with very few exceptions, they were all works by canonical authors, from Cervantes to Carpentier and from Dostoyevsky to Borges. Not surprisingly, Peruvian writers outnumber foreign authors in both lists, and José María Arguedas is the most often cited writer, which is consistent with Flores Galindo's interest in his works and life. The vast majority of authors are twentieth century writers. Notable absences among Latin American authors include Pablo Neruda, Octavio Paz, and Carlos Fuentes, which obviously does not mean he did not read any of their works, but Vargas Llosa does appear repeatedly. He was an author that, as we saw, Flores Galindo read with great interest in the 1960s, but with whom he became disenchanted over the years. As González Vigil recounted, Flores Galindo enjoyed *La ciudad y los perros* (1963), *Los cachorros* (1967), and *Conversación in La Catedral* (1969). Flores Galindo's personal copy of the first volume of the latter novel,[86] which I was able to review, gives us an opportunity to glimpse how the historian read a novel. The book contains numerous markings and underlining, particularly in passages that relate to politics (the Odría dictatorship, the San Marcos university Communist cell), class distinctions (social status of characters, descriptions of specific locations), and racial issues (expressions of racism, racial terminology). On the blank page at the end of the book, Flores Galindo listed a series of themes ('workers', 'Aprista martyrs', 'working-class ideals', 'working-class housing', 'Communist Party', and others) and the pages where they were mentioned, but also wrote notes of a general character, such as 'influence of Salazar Bondy' or 'Benedetti, *Gracias por el fuego*', which show that, while reading Vargas Llosa's novel, he was somehow placing it within a broader literary and intellectual context, looking for influences and connections and also thinking about the usefulness of those characters and passages for future historical projects.

---

85 I have also included a few references to works of literary criticism, because of their obvious importance for the subject at hand.

86 The copy is of the second edition, published in Barcelona by Seix Barral in 1970.

5   Signs of a Bygone Era

Was Flores Galindo's affinity with literature a personal trait of his or was it more a characteristic of his generation? Answering this would require more extensive and detailed research, but the evidence is clear: historians, political scientists, sociologists, and other intellectuals trained in the 1960s and 1970s had a very close relationship with literature. In some cases, this was due to their education or family influence, but it is more generally explained by the favorable environment created by the proliferation of publishing houses and accessible collections and by the impact that the Latin American literary Boom and its offshoots had on this generation. We should also bear in mind that, during that period, fiction writers became visible participants in intellectual and political debates, so engaging with them and their works was inevitable for social scientists.[87] Locally, the limited and not very creative historiographic production in Peru during Flores Galindo formative years (which he would harshly criticise in his essay 'La imagen y el espejo')[88] also prompted the search for and tapping into other forms of intellectual creation and work. It was more intellectually gratifying to read Vargas Llosa's *La ciudad y los perros*, Arguedas's *Todas las sangres*, or Sabato's *El túnel* than any traditional history book loaded with facts but lacking a critical horizon. Flores Galindo would often say that Peruvian historiography was lagging literature. The 'autonomy that our literature achieved years ago (at least since Vallejo and Arguedas) is still to be attained by our historians', he wrote in 1981.[89] In a 1982 interview, when asked about the lack of historical studies on sex, for example, he observed that it was 'another area in which history lags behind literature' and cited the novel *Canto de sirena*, by Gregorio Martínez, as an example of a literary work that addressed this issue.[90]

Literature became in the 1960s a very important sphere of cultural production, consumption, and discussion for anyone with even a passing interest in intellectual matters and politics. There are many well-known cases of intellectuals close to Flores Galindo's generation, from different disciplines and with different ideological leanings, for whom literature was not their main activity but who, nonetheless, developed a very strong inclination for it. Some names that come to mind are the anthropologist Carlos Iván Degregori (1945–

---

87   On this, see Gilman 2003.
88   Flores Galindo 1988b.
89   Flores Galindo 1981d.
90   Aguirre and Ruiz Zevallos 2011, p. 205.

2011), the journalist César Hildebrandt (b. 1948), the sociologist Gonzalo Portocarrero (1949–2019), and the essayist Alfredo Barnechea (b. 1952), who were known for being not only consumers of literary works, but also, in one way or another, practitioners of the trade.[91] A member of a younger generation, Magdalena Chocano (b. 1957) is also a noteworthy case; while developing an important career as a historian, she has also produced first-rate and acclaimed poetry. Moreover, she has also ventured into intellectual and literary history, thus succeeding, in a way, in merging those two dimensions of her creative work.[92]

I want to highlight the case of Degregori, in many ways comparable to Flores Galindo. They studied at the same school, were prominent public Leftist intellectuals, contributed to many of the same magazines and supplements, maintained a respectful and unfinished debate regarding the Shining Path and violence in Peru, and were both avid readers of fiction and poetry. As has been highlighted many times, Degregori was also a great prose writer, one of the best to come out of Peru's social sciences tradition. In his book of conversations with Pablo Sandoval and José Carlos Agüero, his relationship with literature was touched on extensively: his favorite books and authors (Arguedas, the Latin American Boom writers – especially Cortázar –, science fiction novels), his forays into poetry, the relationship between literature and anthropology, and the construction of a narrative style inspired by novels and plays. The comparison with Flores Galindo was inevitable:

---

91   Hildebrandt wrote poetry and published a novel (Hildedrandt 1994); Degregori wrote poetry (Degregori 1970, among other publications), Portocarrero penned numerous texts about literary authors and works, many of which were compiled in Portocarrero 2010, and Barnechea published a collection of interviews with Latin American writers (Barnechea 1997). This familiarity with and passion for literature was not limited to Peruvian intellectuals. The great Argentine historian Juan Carlos Garavaglia (1944–2017), who was only a few years older than Flores Galindo, mentions or cites in his memoirs the names of the authors he had read (Lope de Vega, Jules Verne, Alexandre Dumas, Stendhal, Lawrence Durrell, Antonio Machado, Camus, Sartre, Javier Marías, Carlos Fuentes, Grossman, Primo Levi, Lampedusa, Ricardo Piglia) and the Argentine writers whom he interacted with as a result of his publishing and political work: Roberto Walsh, David Viñas, and Francisco Urondo, among others (Garavaglia 2015). Another influential author in Flores Galindo's studies on Mariátegui, the Argentine José Aricó, who belonged to an earlier generation, was also an avid reader of novels, which he claimed had the ability to offer an all-encompassing portrait of society, as can be read in this chapter's epigraph.

92   Chocano 2011.

Q. – I have heard and read that in recent decades it is Flores Galindo and yourself who are producing and constructing a literary style in the social sciences. A more literary prose, with images, metaphors, sentence construction, powerful symbolism: *Buscando un Inca*. And, curiously, it is the two of you who have an unfinished debate.

A. – Funny, isn't it? I hadn't thought about either of those things. *La agonía de Mariátegui* is a very good title; *Tiempo de plagas, La ciudad sumergida* ...[93]

Flores Galindo's connection with literature went in a different direction in the case of his relationship with another contemporary author, the poet Tulio Mora (1948–2019), a conspicuous member of the Hora Zero group. Mora wrote a poetry book entitled *Cementerio general*, in which he offers an overview of Peruvian history through a series of imaginary monologues by different characters from the past.[94] Prominent and widely known men and women (the chronicler Guaman Poma, the anticolonial rebel Túpac Amaru, the writer and activist Flora Tristán) parade through its pages, alongside others who are less visible in history books, but whose lives illuminate other dimensions of the Peruvian historical experience. These include Ku-Chío, a Chinese immigrant who led a coolie rebellion in 1870; Ernesto (Sánchez) Silva, a.k.a. 'Poncho negro' (Black Poncho), leader of land invasions in mid-twentieth century Lima; Guillermo Cárdenas, a.k.a. 'Mosca Loca' (Crazy Fly), a drug lord active in the 1980s; and Lucha Reyes, an Afro-Peruvian singer who rose from poverty to stardom but could not escape a tragic destiny and met an early death at 37. They are featured besides guerrilla fighters, poets, conquistadores, and hacienda owners. The idea, as Mora would say years later, was to showcase a wide range of characters, 'the good, the naive, the wicked, the torturers'.[95]

Mora confessed, somewhat hyperbolically, that when he was writing *Cementerio general* he used Flores Galindo's history books 'as if they were mine'.[96] The

---

93   Sandoval and Agüero 2015, p. 214.
94   Mora 1989. The book was awarded the CICLA (Latin American Cultural Integration Council) prize in 1988, by a jury formed by Carlos Germán Belli, Alberto Escobar, and Enrique Lihn. The prologue to the first edition, which had 30 poems, was penned by a historian, Pablo Macera, who observes that Mora 'strives to be doubly rigorous: historically and imaginatively'. Each subsequent edition contained additional poems, reaching a total of 77 in the most recent one (Mora 2018). There is an English translation (Mora 2001).
95   Casa de la Literatura Peruana, 'Video homenaje a Tulio Mora y los 30 años de *Cementerio general*', https://bit.ly/2XqME4z.
96   Mora 1990.

relationship between history and literature that I have explored in this chapter was thus inverted: this time it was Flores Galindo's historical work that left its imprint in Mora's poetic project, and not just as a source of facts, but as a way of understanding the study and representation of the past as part of a commitment to the oppressed of yesterday and today. Flores Galindo and Mora shared an outrage over the injustices that plagued the history of Peru, but also a view of the past that sought to rescue the voices of the subordinate, the forgotten, the marginalised. The two had met in March 1986, when Mora interviewed Flores Galindo after he received the Casa de las Américas prize.[97] Shortly after that interview, more than 240 prisoners accused of belonging to Sendero Luminoso were massacred by the government. Flores Galindo denounced the 'extermination' logic applied in that military operation.[98] For Mora, the horror and outrage it produced in him triggered the writing of *Cementerio general*.[99]

The poems in *Cementerio general*, like the works by Flores Galindo, contain a denunciation of racism, violence, invisibility, and marginalisation, but also represent an effort to recover the voices and reconstruct the experiences of those 'without history'. In fact, someone even 'accused' Mora of 'versifying Alberto Flores Galindo'.[100] Nothing could be further from the truth: there is no mechanical correspondence between one and the other, and Mora drew on a much greater number of sources. The confluence of perspectives on the past and the present in both authors, however, is palpable. In January 1989, shortly after the book was published, the two spoke on the telephone. According to Mora, Flores Galindo asked him for a copy of the book, because 'he knew that

---

97 Mora 1986.
98 *Amauta* 1986, Flores Galindo 1988e.
99 The last poem of the first edition of *Cementerio general* was dedicated to Antonio Díaz Martínez, an agricultural engineer associated with Sendero Luminoso who was among the victims of the massacre. The poem ends with the following lines: 'On the fresh lime of the tombstones / shadows etch two guilty letters: N.N. / the true name of Peru'. According to Jorge Pimentel, a friend and colleague of Mora's in Hora Zero, the CICLA award panel called him to announce that they were going to give him the prize, but that they wanted him to remove one of the poems. Mora refused. It is likely that the poem in question was the one dedicated to Díaz Martínez. Ironically, the CICLA had been established in 1986 by the same APRA government that perpetrated the mass killing and which was still in power. So perhaps the award panel was trying to avoid a potential political scandal. Years later, Mora published a book on the massacre (Mora 2003). It should be noted that in the second edition of the book Mora included a poem dedicated to Barbara D'Achille, an environmentalist activist and journalist killed by Sendero Luminoso.
100 Freyre 2000, p. 141.

two or three of the characters I had featured in it belonged to him'.[101] Mora took the opportunity to invite him to participate at the book launch, along with the poets Washington Delgado and Hildebrando Pérez. Flores Galindo accepted the invitation, but in the end was unable to attend. Just before the event, he was stricken with the illness he would succumb to a year later.[102]

∴

The portrait I have sketched in this chapter is part of a greater challenge: rediscovering 'Flores Galindo, the reader'. That is, reconstructing his reading habits, the ways in which he acquired information, his obsessions and interests, how he documented his research, the annotations and comments on the margins, the order (or disorder) that guided his path through books and periodicals. Reconstructing his library (now an impossible task) would have contributed significantly to profiling his formation as an intellectual, as Harry Vanden, for example, did with Mariátegui.[103]

I have highlighted not only Flores Galindo's passion for literature, but also the ways in which he used literary sources in his historical works, how his close connection to literature left a mark on his narrative style, and even, I would venture to say, how it shaped his conception of history as a complex, human, and multidimensional process. As José Aricó suggested in the phrase I used as an epigraph, literature allows for a more comprehensive understanding of society than the social sciences. It is not an exaggeration to suggest that Flores Galindo would not have become the sharp, insightful, and creative historian he was without his close engagement with literature, which was seen by him and by other intellectuals of his generation as not just a source of aesthetical pleasure, but as a bearer of ideas, images, and representations.

---

101   In some of the brief biographical sketches that accompany the book, Mora mentions the authors he drew on to write the poems. Flores Galindo is featured in the entries for Jorge Gobea, an informer murdered in what was known as the 'Amancaes Conspiracy', in the mid-eighteenth century, and for Gabriel Aguilar, to whom he dedicated a chapter of *Buscando un Inca*. Mora's book, however, includes other figures who were studied by Flores Galindo, such as Túpac Amaru and Antonio, a slave that committed suicide.
102   Mora 1990. Mora recalls that during the months that Flores Galindo was battling the disease they talked on several occasions, discussing, in particular, Gabriel Aguilar, about whom Mora was writing a movie script.
103   Vanden 1975.

TABLE 1   Literary texts cited or mentioned in Alberto Flores Galindo's writings

Author	Title[104]	Location of the quotes or references in Flores Galindo's *Obras Completas* (volume, page number) or other publications
Martín Adán	*La casa de cartón*, Lima: Biblioteca Amauta, 1927.	II, 151, 527, 575
Ciro Alegría	*El mundo es ancho y ajeno* [1941].	IV, 119; IV, 355
Anónimo	*Libro del caballero Zifar* [c. 1300].	III (I), 30
José María Arguedas	'Warma Kuyay' [1933].	III (I), 315
José María Arguedas	*Agua* [1935].	III (I), 313; VI, 393; VI, 399; VI, 402; VI, 403, 422
José María Arguedas	*Yawar Fiesta* [1941].	III (I), 318; VI, 393; VI, 399
José María Arguedas	*Mitos, leyendas y cuentos peruanos*, Lima: Ministerio de Educación, 1947.	VI, 393
José María Arguedas	*Canciones y cuentos del pueblo quechua*, Lima: Editorial Huascarán, 1949.	VI, 393
José María Arguedas	'Orovilca' [1954].	III (I), 315; VI, 420
José María Arguedas	*Los ríos profundos*, Buenos Aires: Losada, 1972 [1958].	III (I), 307–8, 321; IV, 355; V, 208; VI, 391; VI, 393; VI, 397; VI, 405; VI, 417, 418, 422
José María Arguedas	*El sexto*, Lima: Editorial Horizonte, 1986 [1961].	II, 327 (epigraph); IV, 183; VI, 393, 399
José María Arguedas	*Todas las sangres*, Buenos Aires: Losada, 1964.	I, 70; III (I), 321; IV, 183; V, 234; V, 308; VI, 223; VI, 393; VI, 397; VI, 403; VI, 405–6
José María Arguedas	*El sueño del pongo* [1965].	III (I), 25, 375; IV, 217
José María Arguedas	*El zorro de arriba y el zorro de abajo* [1969].	III (I), 314; IV, 187 (epigraph); IV, 207; V, 234, 274; VI, 255, 385, 386, 393, 399, 407, 412, 414, 424]
José María Arguedas	*Obras completas*, Lima: Editorial Horizonte, 1983.	III (I), 315; VI, 397
José María Arguedas	*'¿He vivido en vano?' Mesa redonda sobre* Todas las sangres, Lima: Instituto de Estudios Peruanos, 1985.	III (I), 320
Henri Barbusse	*El fuego* [1916].	IV, 92
Pedro Calderón de la Barca	*La aurora de Copacabana* [1672].	III (I), 51
Albert Camus	*La peste* [1947].	IV, 16 (epigraph)
Alejo Carpentier	*La ciudad de las columnas* [1964].	III (II), 98
Alejo Carpentier	[*Concierto barroco*, 1974].	II, 421 (epigraph)
Miguel de Cervantes	*Los trabajos de Persiles y Segismunda* [1617].	III (I), 51

104   In this column I include the references (title, publisher, year) that Flores Galindo offered for each of the quotes or mentions listed in the table. I have only added, in brackets, the year of the publication when Flores Galindo did not include it or the year of the first edition when the citation referred to a different edition.

TABLE 1 Literary texts cited or mentioned in Alberto Flores Galindo's writings (cont.)

Author	Title	Location of the quotes or references in Flores Galindo's *Obras Completas* (volume, page number) or other publications
José Santos Chocano	['Los caballos de los conquistadores', 1906].	IV, 171 (epigraph)
José Santos Chocano	*Ayacucho y los Andes* [1924].	II, 254
Magdalena Chocano	'La palabra en la piedra: una lectura de Martín Adán', *Socialismo y participación*, 32, July–December 1985.	III (I), 308
Antonio Cisneros	*Como higuera en un campo de golf*, Lima: Instituto Nacional de Cultura, 1972.	VI, 215 (epigraph)
Antonio Cisneros	*Monólogo de la casta Susana y otros poemas*, Lima: Instituto Nacional de Cultura, 1986.	III (I), 313 (epigraph); VI, 224
Antonio Cornejo Polar	*Los universos narrativos de José María Arguedas*, Buenos Aires: Losada, 1973.	III (I), 313
Julio Cortázar	*62. Modelo para armar* [1968].	V, 270
Cristóbal María Cortés	*Atahualpa* [1784].	III (I), 51
Washington Delgado	*Historia de la literatura republicana*, Lima: Rikchay Perú, 1980.	III (I), 303
Serafín Delmar	*Sol: están destruyendo a tus hijos*, Huancayo: Concejo Provincial de Huancayo, 1967 [1941].	II, 331
Jesús Díaz	*Las iniciales de la tierra* [1987].	IV, 191
Fedor Dostoievski	[*Los hermanos Karamazov*, 1880].	VI, 88 (epigraph)
Roland Forgues	'José María Arguedas: del pensamiento dialéctico al pensamiento trágico. Historia de una utopía' (1982, unpublished). [Was released in book format in 1988].	III (I), 317–8
Inca Garcilaso de la Vega	*Comentarios reales* [1607, 1619].	III (I), 49, 50; VI, 176
Fedor Gladkov	*El cemento* [1928].	II, 479
Alberto Hidalgo	*Panoplia lírica* [1917].	II, 540
Franz Kafka	*América* [1927].	IV, 194
Martin Lienhard	*Cultura popular andina y forma novelesca*, Lima: Tarea, 1981.	III (I), 314
Artur London	*La confesión*, Caracas: Monte Ávila, 1969 [1968].	I, 117; IV, 95
Enrique López Albújar	*Cuentos andinos*, Lima: Mejía Baca, 1980 [1920].	II, 153
Marco Martos	['El Perú', 1990].	IV, 198 (epigraph)
Augusto Mateu Cueva	*Lampadas de minero*, Lima: Compañía de impresiones y publicidad, 1941.	I, 65
Ross Macdonald	*La piscina de los ahogados* [1950].	IV, 203 (epigraph)
Gregorio Martínez	*Canto de sirena* [1977].	Interview with Carlos Aguirre and Augusto Ruiz Zevallos (1982)
Joanot Martorell	*Tirant lo Blanc* [1490].	III (I), 30

TABLE 1 Literary texts cited or mentioned in Alberto Flores Galindo's writings (cont.)

Author	Title	Location of the quotes or references in Flores Galindo's *Obras Completas* (volume, page number) or other publications
Mariano Melgar	*Poesías completas*, Lima: Academia Peruana de la Lengua, 1971.	III (I), 205
Herman Melville	[*Moby Dick*, 1851].	VI, 163 (epigraph)
Tirso de Molina	*Amazonas en las Indias* [1635].	III (I), 51
George Orwell	[*Homenaje a Cataluña*, 1938].	IV, 30
Ricardo Palma	*Tradiciones peruanas completas*, Madrid: Aguilar, 1953.	III (II), 213
Felipe Pardo y Aliaga	*Los frutos de la educación* [1830].	VI, 277
Hildebrando Pérez Huarancca	*Los ilegítimos* [1980].	VI, 339
Julio Ramón Ribeyro	*Atusparia* [1981].	V, 352; VI, 62–63
Julio Ramón Ribeyro	'La piel de un indio no cuesta caro' [1961].	III (1), 366
Julio Ramón Ribeyro	*Crónica de San Gabriel*, Lima: Milla Batres, 1975.	III (I), 271
Rainer Maria Rilke	['Requiem', 1908].	VI, 137 [An essay coauthored with Magdalena Chocano]
Garci Rodríguez de Montalvo	*Amadís de Gaula* [1508].	III (I), 30
Garci Rodríguez de Montalvo	*Las sergas de Esplandián* [1510].	III (I), 30
Carlos Augusto Salaverry	*El pueblo y el tirano* [1862].	III (I), 230
Carlos Augusto Salaverry	'La conquista del Perú' [1858].	III (I), 230
Luis Alberto Sánchez	*La literatura peruana*, Lima: P.L. Villanueva, 1965.	II, 267
Jean-Paul Sartre	*Las palabras* [1963].	IV, 41
Jean-Paul Sartre	[*Historia de una amistad*, 1968].	II, 13 (epigraph)
Jean-Paul Sartre	[*El escritor y su lenguaje*, 1971].	II, 511
Manuel Scorza	*Redoble por Rancas* [1970].	BA thesis; this quote was deleted in the version published in *Obras completas*
Jorge Semprún	['Las rutas del sur', screenplay, 1978].	II, 13 (epigraph)
Lev Tolstoi	*Guerra y paz* [1869].	VI, 14
Abraham Valdelomar	*El caballero Carmelo* [1913].	II, 266
Abraham Valdelomar	*Obras: textos y dibujos*, Lima: Editorial Pizarro, 1979.	II, 521
Mario Vargas Llosa	*Los cachorros* [1967].	VI, 225
Mario Vargas Llosa	*Conversación en La Catedral* [1969].	V, 328; VI, 234
Mario Vargas Llosa	*La guerra del fin del mundo* [1981].	III (I), 72, 359; V, 352; VI, 63, 234
Mario Vargas Llosa	*Historia de Mayta* [1984].	VI, 233

TABLE 1   Literary texts cited or mentioned in Alberto Flores Galindo's writings (cont.)

Author	Title	Location of the quotes or references in Flores Galindo's *Obras Completas* (volume, page number) or other publications
César Vallejo	*Los heraldos negros* [1918].	II, 543
César Vallejo	*Trilce* [1922].	III (I), 303
Francisco Vásquez	*Palmerín de Oliva* [1511].	III (I), 30
Peter Weiss	*Trotsky en el exilio*, México, 1972.	VI, 215 (epigraph)
Emilio Adolfo Westphalen	['Poetas en la Lima de los años treinta', 1974].	II, 13 (epigraph)

TABLE 2   Other writers mentioned but without direct reference to their works[105]

Peruvian authors		
Xavier Abril de Vivero	Abelardo Gamarra	Estuardo Núñez
Augusto Aguirre Morales	Ventura García Calderón	Carlos Oquendo de Amat
Armando Bazán	Percy Gibson	Clemente Palma
Alfredo Bryce Echenique	Manuel González Prada	Juan Parra del Riego
César Calvo	Javier Heraud	Magda Portal
Juan Cristóbal	Alberto Hidalgo	Juan Gonzalo Rose
Gamaliel Churata	Enrique López Albújar	Felipe Santiago Salaverry
Nicanor de la Fuente	Clorinda Matto de Turner	Sebastián Salazar Bondy
Washington Delgado	César Miró	Abelardo Sánchez León
Carlos Doig y Lora	César Moro	Manuel Ascencio Segura
José María Eguren	Luis Nieto	Alcides Spelucín

Non-Peruvian authors		
Charles Baudelaire	Johan von Goethe	Marcel Proust
Jorge Luis Borges	Maximo Gorki	José Enrique Rodó
Blanca Luz Brum	Julien Green	Romain Rolland
Rubén Darío	Panait Istrati	Paul Valéry
Gustave Flaubert	Lope de Vega	Voltaire
Gabriel García Márquez	Robert Musil	
André Gide	Paul Nizan	

105   I do not include in this list authors who appear in Table 1.

Acknowledgements

I would like to thank Alberto Adrianzén, Eduardo Cáceres Valdivia, Peter Elmore, Ricardo González Vigil, Marco Martos, and Roger Santiváñez for sharing valuable accounts with me for this chapter; Víctor Peralta and Chuck Walker for carefully reading it and providing feedback; and Laura Pérez Carrara for her translation.

Bibliography

Adrianzén, Alberto (ed.) 1987, *Pensamiento político peruano*, Lima: DESCO.
Adrianzén, Alberto 1990, 'Elogio de la amistad', *La República*, April 1.
Adrianzén, Alberto 2011, 'La izquierda derrotada', in *Apogeo y crisis de la izquierda peruana. Hablan los protagonistas*, edited by Alberto Adrianzén, Lima: IDEA and Universidad Ruiz de Montoya, pp. 45–60
Aguirre, Carlos 1993, *Agentes de su propia libertad. Los esclavos de Lima y la desintegración de la esclavitud, 1821–1854*, Lima: Pontificia Universidad Católica del Perú.
Aguirre, Carlos 2005a, 'Aristocracia y plebe', *Libros & Artes*, 11: 27–9.
Aguirre, Carlos 2005b, *The Criminals of Lima and Their Worlds. The Prison Experience, 1850–1935*, Durham: Duke University Press.
Aguirre, Carlos 2007, 'Cultura política de izquierda y cultura impresa en el Perú contemporáneo (1968–1990): Alberto Flores Galindo y la formación de un intelectual público', *Histórica*, 31, 1: 171–205.
Aguirre, Carlos 2011, 'Terruco de m ... Insulto y estigma en la guerra sucia peruana', *Histórica*, 35, 1: 103–39.
Aguirre, Carlos 2013, 'Punishment and Extermination: The Massacre of Political Prisoners in Lima, Peru, June 1986', in *Murder and Violence in Modern Latin America*, edited by Eric A. Johnson, Ricardo Salvatore, and Pieter Spierenburg, London: Wiley-Blackwell.
Aguirre, Carlos 2017a, 'The Second Liberation? Military Nationalism and the Sesquicentennial Commemoration of Peruvian Independence, 1821–1971', in *The Peculiar Revolution. Rethinking the Peruvian Experiment Under Military Rule*, edited by Carlos Aguirre and Paulo Drinot, Austin: University of Texas Press.
Aguirre, Carlos 2017b, '"Vamos a quitarle el frac al libro, vamos a ponerlo en mangas de camisa". El proyecto editorial Populibros Peruanos (1963–1965)', *Políticas de la memoria*, 17: 204–22.
Aguirre, Carlos 2022, 'Apuntes sobre la "guerrillerización" de la cultura: *Las venas abiertas de América Latina*, el Premio Casa de las Américas y los debates sobre los intelectuales y la revolución', *Histórica*, 46, 1: 131–76.
Aguirre, Carlos 2025, '"La plebeiade": la colección Biblioteca Peruana y el proyecto nacionalista de Velasco Alvarado', in *El Estado editor en América Latina. Libros, política y cultura*, edited by Carlos Aguirre, Martín Bergel, and Sebastián Rivera Mir, Buenos Aires: Tren en movimiento.
Aguirre, Carlos and Paulo Drinot (eds.) 2017, *The Peculiar Revolution. Rethinking the Peruvian Experiment Under Military Rule*, Austin: University of Texas Press.
Aguirre, Carlos and Augusto Ruiz Zevallos 2011, '"La historia es una necesidad colectiva". Entrevista a Alberto Flores Galindo (1982)', *Histórica*, 35, 1: 187–209.

Aguirre, Carlos and Charles Walker (eds.) 1990, *Bandoleros, abigeos y montoneros. Criminalidad y violencia en el Perú, siglos XVIII–XX*, Lima: Instituto de Apoyo Agrario.

Ali, Tariq 2008, 'Where has all the rage gone?', *The Guardian*, March 22.

Aljovín de Losada, Cristóbal and Nils Jacobsen (eds.) 2007, *Cultura política en los Andes (1750–1950)*, Lima: Universidad Nacional Mayor de San Marcos, Embajada de Francia, and Instituto Francés de Estudios Andinos.

Aljovín de Losada, Cristóbal and Marcel Velásquez (eds.) 2017, *Voces de la modernidad: Perú, 1750–1870*, Lima: Fondo Editorial del Congreso.

Alonso, Félix Julio 2017, 'Fernando, asaltador del cosmos', UNEAC, https://bit.ly/2XnE6eq.

Altshuler, Ernesto et al. 2005, 'Controversia. El debate de ideas en la cultura y el pensamiento en Cuba', *Temas*, 41–42: 132–51.

Amauta 1986, 'Políticos e intelectuales condenan la masacre', June 23: 7.

Ángeles Loayza, César 2015, *Cortes intensivos: Entrevistas y crónicas, 1986–2014*, Lima: Alpiedelorbe Producciones & Posición Editores.

Angell, Alan 1982, 'Classroom Maoists: The Politics of Peruvian Schoolteachers under Military Government', *Bulletin of Latin American Research*, 1, 2: 1–20.

Araníbar, Carlos et al. 1979, *Nueva historia general del Perú*, Lima: Mosca Azul.

Arguedas, José María 1958, *Los ríos profundos*, Buenos Aires: Losada.

Arguedas, José María 1964, *Todas las sangres*, Buenos Aires: Losada.

Arguedas, José María 1968, 'En el trigésimo aniversario de la muerte de Vallejo', *Amaru*, 6: 95.

Arguedas, José María 1971, *Deep Rivers*, translated by Frances Horning Barraclough, Austin: University of Texas Press.

Arguedas, José María 1981, 'Carta de José María Arguedas a John Murra', *Allpanchis*, 17–18: 164–6.

Arias, Salvador (comp.) 1997, *Recopilación de textos sobre Alejo Carpentier*, Havana: Casa de las Américas.

Aricó, José (ed.) 1978, *Mariátegui y los orígenes del marxismo latinoamericano*, México: Siglo XXI.

Aricó, José 2014 [1986], 'Debemos reinventar América Latina, pero ... ¿desde qué conceptos 'pensar' América?', interview with Waldo Ansaldi, in *José Aricó. Entrevistas 1974–1991*, edited by Horacio Crespo, Córdoba: Universidad Nacional de Córdoba.

Aroni, Renzo 2020, 'Huamanquiquia: The Indigenous Peasant Counter-Rebellion and the Fall of the Shining Path in Peru', PhD dissertation, University of California, Davis.

Aroni, Renzo 2023, 'Pacto de alianzas entre pueblos: coaliciones campesinas contra Sendero Luminoso, 1983–1986', in *Una revolución precaria: Sendero Luminoso y la guerra en el Perú, 1980–1992*, edited by Renzo Aroni and Ponciano del Pino, Lima: Instituto de Estudios Peruanos.

Aroni, Renzo and Ponciano del Pino (eds.) 2023, *Una revolución precaria: Sendero Luminoso y la guerra en el Perú, 1980–1992*, Lima: Instituto de Estudios Peruanos.

Arrelucea Barrantes, Maribel 2018, *Sobreviviendo a la esclavitud. Negociación y honor en las prácticas cotidianas de los africanos y afrodescendientes. Lima, 1750–1820*, Lima: Instituto de Estudios Peruanos.

Arroyo, Eduardo 1986, 'La generación del 68', *Los Caminos del Laberinto*, 3: 41–7.

Barnechea, Alfredo 1997, *Peregrinos de la lengua: confesiones de los grandes autores latinoamericanos*, Madrid: Alfaguara.

Basadre, Jorge 1990 [1931], *Perú, Problema y posibilidad*, Lima: Banco Internacional del Perú.

Bazán Díaz, Marissa 2017, 'El impacto de los panfletos y los rumores en la rebelión de Huánuco, 1812: 'Los Incas' y la interpretación hecha en el caso de Juan de Dios Guillermo', in *El Perú en revolución. Independencia y guerra: un proceso 1780–1826*, edited by Manuel Chust and Claudia Rosas, Castelló de la Plana: Universitat Jaume I, Pontifica Universidad Católica del Perú, and El Colegio de Michoacán.

Benedetti, Mario 1981, 'Los intelectuales se unen contra Reagan', *El Día*, September 17.

Benvenuto, Sergio 1987, 'Violencia y utopía en los Andes', *Casa de las Américas*, 27, 162: 142–4.

Bonilla, Heraclio (ed.) 1972, *La independencia en el Perú*, Lima: Instituto de Estudios Peruanos.

Bonilla, Heraclio 1981, 'Clases populares y Estado en el contexto de la crisis colonial', in *La independencia en el Perú*, 2nd edition, edited by Heraclio Bonilla, Lima: Instituto de Estudios Peruanos.

Bonilla, Heraclio 2007, *Metáfora y realidad de la independencia en el Perú*, Lima: Fondo Editorial del Pedagógico San Marcos.

Bonilla, Heraclio and José Matos Mar 1972, 'Presentación', in *La independencia en el Perú*, edited by Heraclio Bonilla, Lima: Instituto de Estudios Peruanos.

Bryce Echenique, Alfredo c. 1986, 'Una vez más, el premio Casa de las Américas', ALASEI (Agencia latinoamericana de servicios especiales de información), Archivo Vertical, Casa de las Américas.

Bryce Echenique, Alfredo 1993, *Permiso para vivir. Antimemorias*, Barcelona: Anagrama.

Burga, Manuel 1988, *Nacimiento de una utopía. Muerte y resurrección en los Andes*, Lima: Instituto de Apoyo Agrario.

Burga, Manuel 2005, *La historia y los historiadores en el Perú*, Lima: Universidad Nacional Mayor de San Marcos and Universidad Inca Garcilaso de la Vega.

Burga, Manuel (ed.) 2010, *Alberto Flores Galindo, Cartas de Francia, 1973–1974. Homenaje, dos décadas después*, Lima: SUR and Asamblea Nacional de Rectores.

Burga, Manuel and Alberto Flores Galindo 1980, *Apogeo y crisis de la república aristocrática*, Lima: Rikchay Peru.

Burga, Manuel and Alberto Flores Galindo 1982a, 'La utopía andina. Ideología y lucha campesina en los Andes. Siglos XVI–XX', in Alberto Flores Galindo, *Obras Completas V*, Lima: SUR, 1997.

Burga, Manuel and Alberto Flores Galindo 1982b, *La utopía andina. Ideología y lucha campesina en los Andes. Siglos XVI-XX*, Lima: Programa Académico de Ciencias Sociales, Pontificia Universidad Católica del Perú.

Burga, Manuel and Alberto Flores Galindo 1982c, '¿Qué es la utopía andina?', *El Caballo Rojo*, III, 111: 12–13, and III, 113: 12–13.

Burga, Manuel and Alberto Flores Galindo 1982d, 'La utopía andina', *Allpanchis*, 12, 20, pp. 85–101.

Cáceres Valdivia, Eduardo 1993, 'Introducción', in Alberto Flores Galindo, *Obras Completas I*, Lima: Fundación Andina and SUR.

Cáceres Valdivia, Eduardo 2000, ''No hay tal lugar': Utopía, ucronía, e historia', *Márgenes*, 17: 11–27.

Caravedo, Baltazar 1977, *Clases, lucha política y gobierno en el Perú, 1919–1933*, Lima: Retama.

Carlessi, Carolina 1986, 'Pensando el horror', *El Zorro de Abajo*, 4: 33–5.

Casa de las Américas 1981, 'Del primer encuentro de intelectuales por la soberanía de los pueblos de Nuestra América', 129: 4–42.

Casa de las Américas 1986, 'Del segundo encuentro de intelectuales por la soberanía de los pueblos de Nuestra América', 155/156: 14–132.

Casa de las Américas 1990, 'Flores Galindo: testamento político', 180: 148–52.

Casañas, Inés and Jorge Fornet 1999, *Premio Casa de las Américas. Memoria 1960–1999*, Havana: Casa de las Américas.

Chavarría, Jesús 1979, *José Carlos Mariátegui and the Rise of Modern Peru*, Albuquerque: University of New Mexico Press.

Chocano, Magdalena 2001, 'Presentación', in Alberto Flores Galindo, *Los rostros de la plebe*, Barcelona: Crítica.

Chocano, Magdalena et al. (eds.) 2011, *Huellas del mito prehispánico en la literatura latinoamericana*, Madrid and Frankfurt: Iberoamericana and Vervuert.

Chust, Manuel and Claudia Rosas (eds.) 2017, *El Perú en revolución. Independencia y guerra: un proceso 1780–1826*, Castelló de la Plana: Universitat Jaume I, Pontifica Universidad Católica del Perú, and El Colegio de Michoacán.

Cioran, E.M. 1976, *The Trouble with Being Born*, New York: Viking Press.

Cisneros, Antonio 1988, 'Tito Flores, periodista', in Alberto Flores Galindo, *Tiempo de plagas*, Lima: El Caballo Rojo.

Cisneros, Antonio 1992, *Las inmensas preguntas celestes*, Lima: Jaime Campodónico.

Cisneros, Antonio and Marco Martos 1980, '28 de Julio. La Independencia que no culminó', *El Caballo Rojo*, 11: 6–7.

Colectivo por el Bicentenario de la Revolución del Cusco 2015, *La revolución de 1814 en la ciudad del Cusco*, Cusco: Ministerio de Cultura, Dirección Desconcentrada de Cultura de Cusco.

Colectivo por el Bicentenario de la Revolución del Cusco 2016, *El Cusco insurrecto. La revolución de 1814, doscientos años después*, Cusco: Ministerio de Cultura, Dirección Desconcentrada de Cultura de Cusco.

Comisión de la Verdad y Reconciliación 2003, *Informe final*, Lima: Comisión de la Verdad y Reconciliación.

Comisión investigadora de los sucesos de Uchuraccay 1993, *Informe de la comisión investigadora de los sucesos de Uchuraccay*, Lima: Editora Perú.

Contreras, Carlos 2007, 'La independencia del Perú: Balance de la historiografía contemporánea', in *Debates sobre las independencias iberoamericanas*, edited by Manuel Chust and José Antonio Serrano, Madrid: Iberoamericana-Vervuert.

Contreras, Carlos 2015, 'Menos plata pero más papas: consecuencias económicas de la independencia del Perú', in *La Independencia del Perú: ¿Concedida, conseguida, concebida?*, edited by Carlos Contreras and Luis Miguel Glave, Lima: Instituto de Estudios Peruanos.

Contreras, Carlos and Luis Miguel Glave (eds.) 2015, *La Independencia del Perú: ¿Concedida, conseguida, concebida?*, Lima: Instituto de Estudios Peruanos.

Cortázar, Julio 1972, *62: A Model Kit*, translated by Gregory Rabassa, New York: Pantheon Books.

Cortés, Martín 2018, 'José Aricó y el coloquio mariateguiano (1980) de la Universidad Autónoma de Sinaloa', *Cuadernos Americanos*, 165: 65–82.

Cortés, Martín 2019, *Translating Marx. José Aricó and the New Latin American Marxism*, Leiden: Brill.

Cortés, Martín and Diego García (eds.) 2023, *Redescubriendo a Mariátegui. El Coloquio de México (1980)*, Lima: Universidad Nacional Mayor de San Marcos.

Cosamalón, Jesús A. 1999, *Indios detrás de la muralla*, Lima: Pontificia Universidad Católica del Perú.

Cox, Mark 2012, *La verdad y la memoria. Controversias en la imagen de Hildebrando Pérez Huarancca*, Lima: Pasacalle.

Crespo, Horacio 2023, 'En torno a "Cuadernos de Pasado y Presente" (1968–1983)', in *Edición y revolución en Argentina*, edited by Ezequiel Saferstein and Lucas Domínguez Rubio, Buenos Aires: Tren en Movimiento.

Cueto, Alonso et al. 1986, 'Las aventuras de Clío en el Perú', *Posible*, 5: 30–5.

Debray, Régis 2007, 'Socialism: A Life-Cycle', *New Left Review*, 46: 5–28.

De Cárdenas, Federico and Peter Elmore, 'Alberto Flores Galindo: No soy un francotirador', *El Observador*, 31: 4–6.

Degregori, Carlos Iván 1970, *Para aplacar la ira de los dioses*, Trujillo: Cuadernos Trimestrales de Poesía, 1970.

Degregori, Carlos Iván 1985, *Sendero Luminoso: los hondos y mortales desencuentros*, Lima: Instituto de Estudios Peruanos.

Degregori, Carlos Iván, Ponciano del Pino, Orin Starn and José Coronel 1996, *Las rondas campesinas y la derrota de Sendero Luminoso*, 2nd edition, Lima: UNSCH and Instituto de Estudios Peruanos.

Degregori, Carlos Iván 2005, 'Otro mundo es posible', *Libros & Artes*, 11: 3–4.
Degregori, Carlos Iván 2007, 'A Dwarf Star', *NACLA*, 24, 4: 10–38.
Degregori, Carlos Iván 2012, *How Difficult it is to Be God: Shining Path's Politics of War in Peru, 1980–1999*, Madison: University of Wisconsin Press.
Degregori, Carlos Iván 2014a, *El surgimiento de Sendero Luminoso*, Lima: Instituto de Estudios Peruanos (3rd edition).
Degregori, Carlos Iván 2014b, 'Del mito mariateguista a la utopía andina', in Carlos Iván Degregori, *¿Cómo despertar a la bella durmiente? Por una antropología en el Perú*, Lima: Instituto de Estudios Peruanos.
DeGroot, Gerard J. 2008, *The Sixties Unplugged: A Kaleidoscopic History of a Disorderly Decade*, Cambridge, MA: Harvard University Press.
Deler, Jean Paul and Yves Saint-Geours (eds.) 1986, *Estados y naciones en los Andes: hacia una historia comparativa. Bolivia, Colombia, Ecuador, Perú*, Lima: Instituto Francés de Estudios Andinos and Instituto de Estudios Peruanos.
Delmar, Serafín 1941, *Sol: están destruyendo a tus hijos*, Buenos Aires: Americalee.
Del Pino, Ponciano 2017, *En nombre del Gobierno. El Perú y Uchuraccay. Un siglo de política campesina*, Lima: La Siniestra Ensayos.
DESCO 1989, *Violencia política en el Perú, 1980–1988*, Lima: DESCO.
De Soto, Hernando et al. 1986, *El otro sendero. La revolución informal*, Lima: El Barranco.
Díaz, Jesús 1987, *Las iniciales de la tierra*, Madrid: Alfaguara.
Díaz, Jesús 2000, 'El fin de otra ilusión. A propósito de la quiebra de *El Caimán Barbudo* y la clausura de *Pensamiento Crítico*', *Encuentro de la cultura cubana*, 16/17: 106–19.
Díaz Martínez, Antonio 1969, *Ayacucho: hambre y esperanza*, Ayacucho: Waman Puma.
Di Meglio, Gabriel 2016, *1816: La verdadera trama de la independencia*, Buenos Aires: Planeta.
Di Meglio, Gabriel 2021, 'La participación política de las clases populares en la América del Sur hispana, 1780–1850', in *Repúblicas sudamericanas en construcción: Hacia una historia común*, edited by Natalia Sobrevilla Pérez, Lima: Fondo de Cultura Económica.
Drinot, Paulo 2004, 'Historiography, Historiographic Identity, and Historical Consciousness in Peru', *Estudios Interdisciplinarios de América Latina*, 15, 4: 65–88.
Drinot, Paulo 2023, 'Entrevista a Nelson Manrique', *Histórica*, 47, 2: 176–209.
Dunbar Temple, Ella (ed.) 1971a, *La acción patriótica del pueblo en la emancipación. Guerrillas y montoneras*, Colección Documental de la Independencia del Perú, 6 vols., Lima: Comisión Nacional del Sesquicentenario de la Independencia del Perú.
Dunbar Temple, Ella (ed.) 1971b, *Conspiraciones y rebeliones en el siglo XIX*, III, *La revolución de Huánuco, Panatahuas y Huamalíes de 1812*. Lima: Comisión Nacional del Sesquicentenario de la Independencia del Perú.
El Zorro de Abajo 1987, 'Conversación a puerta cerrada', 6: 11–15.
Echeverri, Marcela, Francisco A. Ortega, and Tomás Straka (eds.) 2018, 'La invención

de la república: La Gran Colombia', Special Issue, *Anuario Colombiano de Historia Social y de la Cultura*, 45, 2.

Elmore, Peter 2005, 'La urgencia del tiempo', *Libros & Artes*, 11: 5–6.

Escanilla Huerta, Silvia 2018, 'Hacia una nueva cronología de la guerra de la independencia del Perú', in *Tiempo de guerra. Estado, nación y conflicto armado en el Perú, siglos XVII–XIX*, edited by Carmen McEvoy and Alejandro M. Rabinovich, Lima: Instituto de Estudios Peruanos.

Evora, José Antonio 1987, 'Con Alberto Flores Galindo, jurado del Premio Especial Ernesto Guevara', *Juventud Rebelde*, February 9.

Favre, Henri 1984, 'Perú: Sendero Luminoso, horizontes oscuros', *Quehacer*, 31: 25–34.

Flores Galindo, Alberto 1972, 'Los mineros de la Cerro de Pasco: 1900–1930 (Un intento de caracterización social y política)', B.A. thesis, Pontificia Universidad Católica del Perú.

Flores Galindo, Alberto 1974, *Los mineros de la Cerro de Pasco, 1900–1930. (Un intento de caracterización social)*, Lima: Pontificia Universidad Católica del Perú, Departamento Académico de Ciencias Sociales, Área de Sociología.

Flores Galindo, Alberto 1975, *El carácter de la sublevación de Túpac Amaru: algunas aproximaciones*, Lima: Departamento de Ciencias Sociales, Pontificia Universidad Católica del Perú.

Flores Galindo, Alberto (ed.) 1976a, *Sociedad colonial y sublevaciones populares. Túpac Amaru II-1780. Antología*, Lima: Retablo de papel.

Flores Galindo, Alberto 1977a, *Arequipa y el sur andino. Ensayo de historia regional, siglos XVIII–XX*, Lima: Horizonte.

Flores Galindo, Alberto 1977b, 'La nación como utopía. Túpac Amaru 1780', *Debates en Sociología*, 1, 1: 139–57.[1]

Flores Galindo, Alberto 1978a, 'El marxismo peruano de Mariátegui', in Alberto Flores Galindo, *Obras Completas V*, Lima: SUR, 1997.

Flores Galindo, Alberto 1978b, 'Presentación de *Allpanchis* No. 11/12', in Alberto Flores Galindo, *Obras Completas V*, Lima: SUR, 1997.

Flores Galindo, Alberto 1980a, *La agonía de Mariátegui. La polémica con la Komintern*, Lima: DESCO.

Flores Galindo, Alberto 1980b, 'Mariátegui: ¿Un nacionalista burgués? ¿Partido Comunista o Partido Socialista?', in Alberto Flores Galindo, *Obras Completas V*, Lima: SUR, 1997.

Flores Galindo, Alberto 1980c, 'Mariátegui y el PC', in Alberto Flores Galindo, *Obras Completas V*, Lima: SUR, 1997.

---

1 In this bibliography, Flores Galindo's articles and essays published in periodicals will be identified with the year of their original publication and the volume of his *Obras Completas* in which they were reproduced, unless they were not included.

Flores Galindo, Alberto 1980d, 'La heterodoxia de Mariátegui', in Alberto Flores Galindo, *Obras Completas v*, Lima: SUR, 1997.

Flores Galindo, Alberto 1980e, 'Mariátegui y los indigenistas', in Alberto Flores Galindo, *Obras Completas v*, Lima: SUR, 1997.

Flores Galindo, Alberto 1980f, 'Haya, Mariátegui y el europeísmo', in Alberto Flores Galindo, *Obras Completas v*, Lima: SUR, 1997.

Flores Galindo, Alberto 1980g, 'Mariátegui: imagen de un político', in Alberto Flores Galindo, *Obras Completas v*, Lima: SUR, 1997.

Flores Galindo, Alberto 1980h, 'Socialismo y problema nacional en el Perú', in Alberto Flores Galindo, *Obras Completas v*, Lima: SUR, 1997.

Flores Galindo, Alberto 1980i, 'Mariátegui, cincuenta años de actualidad', in Alberto Flores Galindo, *Obras Completas v*, Lima: SUR, 1997.

Flores Galindo, Alberto 1980j, 'Usos y abusos de Mariátegui', in Alberto Flores Galindo, *Obras Completas v*, Lima: SUR, 1997.

Flores Galindo, Alberto 1981a, 'Utopía andina y socialismo', in Alberto Flores Galindo, *Obras Completas v*, Lima: SUR, 1997.

Flores Galindo, Alberto 1981b, 'La pesca y los pescadores en la costa central (siglo XVIII)', *Histórica*, 5, 2: 159–65.

Flores Galindo, Alberto 1981c, 'La revolución tupamarista y los pueblos andinos', *Allpanchis*, 17/18: 253–65.

Flores Galindo, Alberto 1981d, '¿Historia peruana o historia sobre el Perú?', in Alberto Flores Galindo, *Obras Completas v*, Lima: SUR, 1997.

Flores Galindo, Alberto 1982a, 'La historia y el tiempo. Miseria de la teoría', in Alberto Flores Galindo, *Obras Completas v*, Lima: SUR, 1997.

Flores Galindo, Alberto 1982b, 'La antropología como encono', in Alberto Flores Galindo, *Obras Completas v*, Lima: SUR, 1997.

Flores Galindo, Alberto 1982c, 'Independencia y clases populares: el mundo al revés', in *El Caballo Rojo*, 3, 121: 12–13.

Flores Galindo, Alberto 1982d, 'La nueva izquierda: sin faros ni mapas', in Alberto Flores Galindo, *Obras Completas IV*, Lima: CONCYTEC and SUR, 1996.

Flores Galindo, Alberto (ed.) 1982e, *El pensamiento comunista. 1917–1945*, Lima: Mosca Azul.

Flores Galindo, Alberto 1982f, 'Independencia y clases sociales', *Debates en Sociología*, 7: 99–114.

Flores Galindo, Alberto 1983a, 'Para una historia inteligente', in Alberto Flores Galindo, *Obras Completas VI*, Lima: SUR, 2007.

Flores Galindo, Alberto 1983b, 'La aristocracia mercantil limeña', *Banca*, 3.

Flores Galindo, Alberto 1983c, 'Vida de esclavos: un suicidio en Lima colonial', *El Caballo Rojo*, 3, 150: 5.

Flores Galindo, Alberto 1983d, 'Los rostros de la plebe', *Revista Andina*, 1, 2: 315–52.

Flores Galindo, Alberto 1983e, 'Tolstoi y Trotski. Historia y literatura', in Alberto Flores Galindo, *Obras Completas VI*, Lima: SUR, 2007.

Flores Galindo, Alberto 1984a, *Aristocracia y plebe. Estructura de clases y sociedad colonial, Lima 1760–1830*, Lima: Mosca Azul.

Flores Galindo, Alberto 1984b, 'Marxismo y religión. Para situar a Mariátegui', in Alberto Flores Galindo, *Obras Completas VI*, Lima: SUR, 2007.

Flores Galindo, Alberto 1984c, 'Un motín: 5 de julio de 1821. El ocaso de la aristocracia colonial', *El Búho*, 11: 63–6.

Flores Galindo, Alberto 1984d, 'Un historiador para el futuro', in Alberto Flores Galindo, *Obras Completas VI*, Lima: SUR, 2007.

Flores Galindo, Alberto 1985a, 'Historia: La pregunta incómoda', *La República*, July 28: 39.

Flores Galindo, Alberto 1985b, 'Clases populares e independencia. Realidad y mistificación', in Alberto Flores Galindo, *Obras Completas VI*, Lima: SUR, 2007.

Flores Galindo, Alberto 1985c, 'Pensando el horror', in Alberto Flores Galindo, *Obras Completas IV*, Lima: CONCYTEC and SUR, 1996.

Flores Galindo, Alberto 1986a, *Buscando un Inca. Identidad y utopía en los Andes*, Havana: Casa de las Américas.

Flores Galindo, Alberto 1986b, *Europa y el país de los Incas. La utopía andina*, Lima: Instituto de Apoyo Agrario.

Flores Galindo, Alberto 1986c, 'La revolución tupamarista y los pueblos andinos', in *Perú: El problema agrario en debate*, Lima: SEPIA.

Flores Galindo, Alberto 1986d, 'Soldados y montoneros', *Los Caminos del Laberinto*, 3: 15–30.

Flores Galindo, Alberto 1986e, 'El horizonte utópico', in *Estados y naciones en los Andes: hacia una historia comparativa. Bolivia, Colombia, Ecuador, Perú*, edited by Jean Paul Deler and Yves Saint-Geours, Lima: Instituto Francés de Estudios Andinos and Instituto de Estudios Peruanos.

Flores Galindo, Alberto 1986f, '¿Es posible la utopía?', in Alberto Flores Galindo, *Obras Completas VI*, Lima: SUR, 2007.

Flores Galindo, Alberto 1986g, 'La tradición autoritaria. Violencia y democracia en el Perú', in Alberto Flores Galindo, *Obras Completas VI*, Lima: SUR, 2007.

Flores Galindo, Alberto 1986h, 'Arguedas y la utopía andina', in Alberto Flores Galindo, *Obras Completas VI*, Lima: SUR, 2007.

Flores Galindo, Alberto 1986i, 'Vivir en el Perú', in Alberto Flores Galindo, *Obras Completas II*, Lima: Fundación Andina and SUR, 1994.

Flores Galindo, Alberto 1987a, 'Generación del 68: Ilusión y realidad', in Alberto Flores Galindo, *Obras Completas VI*, Lima: SUR, 2007.

Flores Galindo, Alberto (ed.) 1987b, *Independencia y revolución, 1780–1840*, Lima: Instituto Nacional de Cultura.

Flores Galindo, Alberto 1987c, 'La crisis de la independencia: El Perú y Latinoamérica', in *Independencia y revolución, 1780–1840*, edited by Alberto Flores Galindo, Lima, Instituto Nacional de Cultura.

Flores Galindo, Alberto 1987d, 'El socialismo a la vuelta de la esquina', in Alberto Flores Galindo, *Obras Completas IV*, Lima: CONCYTEC and SUR, 1996.

Flores Galindo, Alberto 1987e, 'Moral y política: una carta', in Alberto Flores Galindo, *Obras Completas VI*, Lima: SUR, 2007.

Flores Galindo, Alberto 1987f, 'El Che Guevara en la imaginación popular', in Alberto Flores Galindo, *Obras Completas VI*, Lima: SUR, 2007.

Flores Galindo, Alberto 1987g, 'Los poetas que no tienen nombre', in Alberto Flores Galindo, *Obras Completas VI*, Lima: SUR, 2007.

Flores Galindo, Alberto 1988a, 'La utopía andina: esperanza y proyecto', in Alberto Flores Galindo, *Obras Completas IV*, Lima: CONCYTEC and SUR, 1996.

Flores Galindo, Alberto 1988b, 'La imagen y espejo: la historiografía peruana 1910–1986', in Alberto Flores Galindo, *Obras Completas VI*, Lima: SUR, 2007.

Flores Galindo, Alberto 1988c, *Tiempo de plagas*, Lima: El Caballo Rojo.

Flores Galindo, Alberto 1988d, 'Los caballos de los conquistadores, otra vez (*El otro sendero*)', in Alberto Flores Galindo, *Obras Completas IV*, Lima: CONCYTEC and SUR, 1996.

Flores Galindo, Alberto 1988e, 'El exterminio y el recuerdo: la masacre de los penales', in Alberto Flores Galindo, *Obras Completas IV*, Lima: CONCYTEC and SUR, 1996.

Flores Galindo, Alberto 1988f, 'Los últimos años de Arguedas. Intelectuales, sociedad e identidad en el Perú', in Alberto Flores Galindo, *Obras Completas VI*, Lima: SUR, 2007.

Flores Galindo, Alberto 1989a, 'Redescubriendo lo andino', in *Encuentros. Historia y movimientos sociales en el Perú*, edited by Carlos Arroyo, Lima: MemoriAngosta.

Flores Galindo, Alberto 1989b, 'El rescate de la tradición', in Alberto Flores Galindo, *Obras Completas VI*, Lima: SUR, 2007.

Flores Galindo, Alberto 1989c, 'Las revoluciones tupamaristas. Temas en debate', in Alberto Flores Galindo, *Obras Completas VI*, Lima: SUR, 2007.

Flores Galindo, Alberto 1989d, 'La gran rebelión: Recuerdos e historia social', in Alberto Flores Galindo, *Obras Completas VI*, Lima: SUR, 2007.

Flores Galindo, Alberto 1989e, 'Presentación a *Invitación a la vida heroica*', in Alberto Flores Galindo, *Obras Completas VI*, Lima: SUR, 2007.

Flores Galindo, Alberto 1989f, 'Reencontremos la dimensión utópica. Carta a los amigos', in Alberto Flores Galindo, *Obras Completas VI*, Lima: SUR, 2007.

Flores Galindo, Alberto 1991, *La ciudad sumergida. Aristocracia y plebe en Lima, 1760–1830*, Lima: Horizonte.

Flores Galindo, Alberto 1992, *Dos ensayos sobre José María Arguedas*, Lima: SUR.

Flores Galindo, Alberto 1993, *Obras Completas I*, Lima: Fundación Andina and SUR.

Flores Galindo, Alberto 1994a, *Obras Completas II*, Lima: Fundación Andina and SUR.

Flores Galindo, Alberto 1994b [1980], *La agonía de Mariátegui*, in Alberto Flores Galindo, *Obras Completas II*, Lima: Fundación Andina and SUR.

Flores Galindo, Alberto 1996, *Obras Completas IV*, Lima: CONCYTEC and SUR.

Flores Galindo, Alberto 1997, *Obras Completas V*, Lima: SUR.

Flores Galindo, Alberto 2001, *Los rostros de la plebe*, Barcelona: Crítica.

Flores Galindo, Alberto 2005, *Obras Completas III (I)*, Lima: SUR.

Flores Galindo, Alberto 2007, *Obras Completas VI*, Lima: SUR.

Flores Galindo, Alberto 2010, *In Search of an Inca. Identity and Utopia in the Andes*, edited and translated by Carlos Aguirre, Charles F. Walker, and Willie Hiatt, New York: Cambridge University Press.

Flores Galindo, Alberto 2011, *Obras Completas III (II)*, Lima: SUR.

Flores Galindo, Alberto 2021, *La agonía de Mariátegui*, Lima and Havana: Pontificia Universidad Católica del Perú and Casa de las Américas.

Flores Galindo, Alberto and Nelson Manrique 1986, *Violencia y campesinado*, Lima: Instituto de Apoyo Agrario.

Flores Galindo, Alberto and Juan Martínez Alier 1988, 'Agricultura, alimentación y medio ambiente en el Perú', *Mientras Tanto*, 34: 79–89.

Flores Galindo, Alberto and Denis Sulmont 1972, *El movimiento obrero en la industria pesquera. El caso de Chimbote*, Lima: Programa de Ciencias Sociales de la Pontificia Universidad Católica del Perú.

Flores Guzmán, Ramiro Alberto 2010, 'Fiscalidad y gastos de gobierno en el Perú Borbónico', in *Economía del periodo colonial tardío*, edited by Carlos Contreras, Lima: Banco Central de la Reserva and Instituto de Estudios Peruanos.

Flórez-Estrada, María 1988, 'No hay molde para el socialismo peruano', *Cambio*, 3, 30: 12–13.

Fontana, Josep 1983, 'Para leer a Manuel Moreno Fraginals', prologue to Manuel Moreno Fraginals, *La historia como arma y otros estudios sobre esclavos, ingenios y plantaciones*, Barcelona: Crítica.

Formisano, Ronald 2001, 'The Concept of Political Culture', *Journal of Interdisciplinary History*, 31, 3: 393–426.

Fornet, Ambrosio 2004, 'La década prodigiosa. Un testimonio personal', in *Mirar a los 60. Antología cultural de una década*, Havana: Museo Nacional de Bellas Artes.

Fornet, Ambrosio 2007, 'El quinquenio gris: revisitando el término', in *La política cultural del período revolucionario: memoria y reflexión*, edited by Eduardo Heras León and Desiderio Navarro, Havana: Centro Teórico-Cultural Criterios.

Fradkin, Raúl (ed.) 2015, *¿Y el pueblo dónde está?: Contribuciones para una historia popular de la revolución de independencia en el Río de la Plata*, Buenos Aires: Prometeo Libros.

Fradkin, Raúl and Jorge Gelman 2015, *Juan Manuel de Rosas. La construcción de un liderazgo político*, Buenos Aires: EDHASA.

Franco, Carlos 1981, 'La agonía de Mariátegui: una lectura', Socialismo y Participación, 13: 51–62.

Franco, Carlos (ed.) 1986, El Perú de Velasco, Lima: CEDEP.

Freyre, Maynor 2000, 'Hora Zero en su cuarto de siglo', in Altas voces de la literatura peruana y latinoamericana. Segunda mitad del siglo XX Entrevistas – comentarios – reportajes, Lima: San Marcos.

Garavaglia, Juan Carlos 2015, Una juventud en los años sesenta, Buenos Aires: Prometeo.

García Márquez, Gabriel 1975, 'Cuba de cabo a rabo', in Gabriel García Márquez, Por la libre. Obra periodística (1974–1995), Barcelona: Random House and RBA, 2004.

García Márquez, Gabriel 1981, '300 intelectuales juntos', El País, September 16.

Gavilán Sánchez, Lurgio 2015, When Rains Became Floods: A Child Soldier's Story, Durham: Duke University Press.

Germaná, César 1980, La polémica Haya de la Torre-Mariátegui. Reforma o revolución en el Perú, Lima: Cuadernos de Sociedad y Política.

Gilman, Claudia 2003, Entre la pluma y el fusil. Debates y dilemas del escritor revolucionario en América Latina, Buenos Aires: Siglo XXI.

Goldman, Noemí 2016, Mariano Moreno. De reformista a insurgente, Buenos Aires: EDHASA.

Gonzales, Osmar 1994, 'La seducción de la democracia. Socialismo y nueva izquierda en el Perú', Perfiles Latinoamericanos, 5: 145–66.

González Vigil, Ricardo 1990, 'Recuerdo de Flores Galindo', Suplemento Dominical, El Comercio, April 15.

González Vigil, Ricardo 2015, 'El amigo Flores Galindo', El Comercio, April 5.

Gordimer, Nadine 1988, El conservador, Havana: Arte y Literatura.

Gorriti, Gustavo 1999, The Shining Path: A History of the Millenarian War in Peru, Chapel Hill: University of North Carolina Press.

Gould, Jeffrey 2009, 'Solidarity under Siege: The Latin American 1968', American Historical Review, 114, 2: 348–75.

Granma 1986, 'Premio Casa de las Américas 1986', April 13: 6.

Grenier, Yvon 2017, Culture and the Cuban State. Participation, Recognition, and Dissonance under Communism, Boulder: Lexington Books.

Guerra, François-Xavier 1992, Modernidad e independencias: Ensayos sobre las revoluciones hispánicas, Madrid: MAPFRE.

Guevara, Luis and Adrián Gechelín 2001, Historia de la gráfica en el Perú, Lima: Kartel.

Guha, Ranajit 1983, Elementary Aspects of Peasant Insurgency in Colonial India, Delhi: Oxford University Press.

Guha, Ranajit and Gayatri Chakravorty Spivak (eds.) 1988, Selected Subaltern Studies, New York: Oxford University Press.

Hildebrandt, César 1994, Memoria del abismo, Lima: Jaime Campodónico.

Hinojosa, Iván 1998, 'On Poor Relations and the Nouveau Riche: Shining Path and the

Radical Peruvian Left', in *Shining and Other Paths. War and Society in Peru, 1980–1995*, edited by Steve J. Stern, Durham: Duke University Press.

Huerta Vera, María Claudia 2019, 'La palabra impresa durante la guerra de independencia peruana', in *España en Perú (1796–1824): Ensayos sobre los últimos gobiernos virreinales*, edited by Víctor Peralta Ruiz and Dionisio de Haro, Madrid: Marcial Pons and Universidad Michoacana San Nicolás de Hidalgo.

Iguíñiz, Javier (ed.) 1979, *La investigación en ciencias sociales en el Perú: economía, historia social, ciencia política, problemática laboral, problemática rural*, Lima: Tarea. Centro de Publicaciones Educativas.

Instituto de Defensa Legal 1988, *La violencia en el Perú: Aproximaciones desde la cultura y la política*, Lima: Instituto de Defensa Legal.

Kapsoli Escudero, Wilfredo 1976, *Las luchas obreras en el Perú, 1900–1919*, Lima: Delva Editores.

Klaiber, Jeffrey (comp.) 1987, *Violencia y crisis de valores en el Perú: trabajo interdisciplinario*, Lima: Pontificia Universidad Católica del Perú.

Kurlansky, Mark 2004, *1968: The Year That Rocked the World*, New York: Ballantine Books.

Lévano, César 1981, 'La agonía de Mariátegui o la muerte de dos tesis', *Marka*, 186: 39.

Loayza Pérez, Alex 2016, 'Del Perú mestizo a la 'idea crítica'. Historiografía, nación e Independencia, 1920–1980', in *La independencia peruana como representación. Conmemoración, historiografía y escultura pública*, edited by Alex Loayza Pérez, Lima: Instituto de Estudios Peruanos.

López, Sinesio 1991, 'Pancho Aricó', *Socialismo y participación*, 56: 5–7.

López, Sinesio 2005, 'El historiador de los vencidos', *Libros & Artes*, 11: 2.

López, Sinesio 2009, 'La reinvención de la historia desde abajo', *Libros & Artes*, 22/23: 1–12.

López Soria, José Ignacio 1982a, 'La vuelta a Mariátegui', *Análisis*, 10: 104–10.

López Soria, José Ignacio 1982b, 'Mariátegui, Túpac Amaru y la Revolución', *El Caballo Rojo*, 101: 12–13.

Lynch, Nicolás 1990, *Los jóvenes rojos de San Marcos*, Lima: El Zorro de Abajo.

Macdonald, Ross 1950, *The Drowning Pool*, New York: Knopf.

Macera, Pablo 1955, *Tres etapas en el desarrollo de la conciencia nacional*, Lima: Fanal.

Macera, Pablo 1983, *Las furias y las penas*, Lima: Mosca Azul.

Machuca Castillo, Gabriela 2006, *La tinta, el pensamiento y las manos. La prensa popular anarquista, anarcosindicalista y obrera-sindical en Lima, 1900–1930*, Lima: Universidad de San Martín de Porres.

Manco, Jorge 1990, 'Alberto Flores Galindo: Hay un divorcio entre la intelectualidad y el movimiento social', *Actualidad Económica*, 117: 38–41.

Manrique, Nelson 1986–88, 'Historia y utopía en los Andes', *Debates en Sociología*, 12/14: 201–11.

Manrique, Nelson 2005, 'Alberto Flores Galindo. Cambiar el mundo, cambiar la vida', *Libros & Artes*, 11: 9–11.

Mariátegui, José Carlos 1971 [1928], *Seven Interpretive Essays on Peruvian Reality*, translated by Marjory Urquidi, Austin: University of Texas Press.

Mariátegui, José Carlos 2011 [1929], 'The Problem of Race in Latin America', in *José Carlos Mariátegui. An Anthology*, edited by Harry E. Vanden and Marc Becker, New York: Monthly Review Press.

Martínez, Maruja 1997, *Entre el amor y la furia. Crónicas y testimonio*, Lima: SUR.

Martínez Alier, Juan 2002, *The Environmentalism of the Poor: A Study of Ecological Conflicts and Valuation*, Cheltenham: Edward Elgar.

Martínez Heredia, Fernando 1988, *Desafíos del socialismo cubano*, Havana: Centro de Estudios sobre América.

Martínez Heredia, Fernando 1989, *Che, el socialismo y el comunismo*, Havana: Casa de las Américas.

Martínez Heredia, Fernando 1991, 'Cuba: problemas de la liberación, el socialismo, la democracia', in *Pensar en tiempo de revolución. Antología esencial*, Buenos Aires: CLACSO.

Martínez Heredia, Fernando 1998, 'Trazando el mapa político de la América Latina', in *Pensar en tiempo de revolución. Antología esencial*, Buenos Aires: CLACSO.

Martínez Heredia, Fernando 2005, 'Palabras de Fernando Martínez Heredia en "El autor y su obra"', December 28, https://bit.ly/3fwmt2E.

Martínez Heredia, Fernando 2007, 'Pensamiento social y política de la Revolución', in *La política cultural del período revolucionario: memoria y reflexión*, edited by Eduardo Heras León and Desiderio Navarro, Havana: Centro Teórico-Cultural Criterios.

Martínez Heredia, Fernando 2008, 'A cuarenta años de *Pensamiento Crítico*', *Crítica y emancipación*, 1: 237–50.

Martínez Heredia, Fernando 2000, 'Problemas de la historia del pensamiento marxista: los tiempos de Mariátegui', in *Pensar en tiempo de revolución. Antología esencial*, Buenos Aires: CLACSO.

Martínez Heredia, Fernando 2018, *Pensar en tiempo de revolución. Antología esencial*, Buenos Aires: CLACSO.

Martínez Riaza, Asención 2018, '"Contra la independencia". La guerra en el Perú según los militares realistas (1816–1824)', in *Tiempo de guerra. Estado, nación y conflicto armado en el Perú, siglos XVII–XIX*, edited by Carmen McEvoy and Alejandro M. Rabinovich, Lima: Instituto de Estudios Peruanos.

Martos, Marco 2005, 'La utopía andina en debate', *Libros & Artes*, 11: 7–8.

Mateu Cueva, Augusto 1941, *Lampadas de minero*, Lima: Baluarte.

Mazzeo, Cristina 2010, 'El comercio colonial a la largo del siglo XVIII y su transformación frente a las coyunturas del cambio', in *Economía del periodo colonial tardío*, edited by Carlos Contreras, Lima: Banco Central de Reserva and Instituto de Estudios Peruanos.

McEvoy, Carmen 2015, 'De la república imaginada a la República en armas: José Faustino Sánchez Carrión y la forja del republicanismo-liberal en el Perú, 1804–1824', in *La Independencia del Perú: ¿Concedida, conseguida, concebida?*, edited by Carlos Contreras and Luis Miguel Glave, Lima: Instituto de Estudios Peruanos.

Mejía Baca, Juan (ed.) 1980, *Historia del Perú*, Lima: Mejía Baca.

Melis, Antonio 1968, 'Mariátegui, primer marxista de América', *Casa de las Américas*, 8, 48: 16–31.

Melis, Antonio 2005, 'Apuntes sobre el estilo', *Libros & Artes*, 11: 12–14.

Méndez, Cecilia 2005, *The Plebeian Republic: The Huanta Rebellion and the Making of the Peruvian State, 1820–1850*, Durham: Duke University Press.

Merino Vigil, Germán Enrique 2008, '*Marka* y la 'pequeña prensa' de los setenta: ¿Te acordás, hermano?', Portal Libros Peruanos, April, https://bit.ly/3i2RFIb.

Miró Quesada, Francisco, Franklin Pease, and David Sobrevilla (eds.) 1978, *Historia, problema y promesa. Homenaje a Jorge Basadre*, Lima: Pontificia Universidad Católica del Perú.

Montoya, Gustavo 2006, 'Revolución, socialismo y utopía. Historia, política e ideología en la obra de Alberto Flores Galindo Segura (1949–1989)', *Socialismo y Participación*, 101: 35–51.

Mora, Tulio 1986, 'Un buscador de incas', *Visión peruana*, March 30.

Mora, Tulio 1989, *Cementerio general*, Lima: Lluvia editores.

Mora, Tulio 1990, 'La pasión según Flores Galindo. Itinerario de un historiador', *La República*, April 1.

Mora, Tulio 2003, *La matanza de los penales. Días de barbarie*, Lima: Asociación Pro Derechos Humanos.

Mora, Tulio 2018, *Cementerio general*, Barcelona: Sin Fin.

Mora, Tulio, 2001, *A Mountain Crowned by a Cemetery*, translated by C.A. de Lomellini and David Tipton, Bradford: Redbeck.

Morán, Daniel 2007, 'Borrachera nacionalista y diálogo de sordos. Heraclio Bonilla y la historia de la polémica sobre la independencia peruana', *Praxis*, 6: 25–40.

Morán, Daniel 2013, *Batallas por la legitimidad. La prensa de Lima y Buenos Aires durante las guerras de la independencia*. Lima: UCH.

Morote Best, Efraín 1988, *Aldeas sumergidas. Cultura popular y sociedad en los Andes*, Cusco: Centro Bartolomé de Las Casas.

Moyn, Samuel 2018, *Not Enough: Human Rights in an Unequal World*, Cambridge, MA: Belknap, Harvard University Press.

Najarro, Margareth 2017, 'Los veinticuatro electores incas y los movimientos sociales y políticos. Cusco: 1780–1814', in *El Perú en revolución. Independencia y guerra: un proceso 1780–1826*, edited by Manuel Chust and Claudia Rosas, Castelló de la Plana: Universitat Jaume I, Pontifica Universidad Católica del Perú, and El Colegio de Michoacán.

Oliart, Patricia and Gonzalo Portocarrero 1989, *El Perú desde la escuela*, Lima: Instituto de Apoyo Agrario.

O'Phelan Godoy, Scarlett 1984, 'El mito de la "independencia concedida": los programas políticos del siglo XVIII y del temprano siglo XIX en el Perú y el Alto Perú, 1730–1814', in *Problemas de la formación del Estado y de la nación en Hispanoamérica*, edited by Inge Buisson et al., Cologne: Böhlau Verlag.

O'Phelan Godoy, Scarlett 1985, *Rebellions and Revolts in Eighteenth-Century Peru and Upper Peru*, Cologne: Böhlau Verlag.

Ortemberg, Pablo 2014, *Rituales del poder en Lima (1735–1828). De la monarquía a la república*, Lima: Pontificia Universidad Católica del Perú.

Oshiro, Jorge 1990, 'Reencontrar a Mariátegui', *Amauta*, 6, 60: 8–9.

Palma, Ricardo 2004, *Peruvian Traditions*, edited by Christopher Conway and translated by Helen Lane, New York: Oxford University Press.

Panfichi, Aldo and Felipe Portocarrero (eds.) 1995, *Mundos interiores: Lima 1850–1950*, Lima: Universidad del Pacífico.

Pareja, Piedad 1978, *Anarquismo y sindicalismo en el Perú, 1904–1929*, Lima: Rikchay Perú.

Paris, Robert et al. 1973, *El marxismo latinoamericano de Mariátegui*, Buenos Aires: Crisis.

Peralta Ruiz, Víctor 2002, *En defensa de la autoridad. Política y cultura bajo el gobierno del virrey Abascal, Perú 1806–1816*, Madrid: CSIC.

Peralta Ruiz, Víctor 2010, *La independencia y la cultura política peruana (1808–1821)*, Lima: Instituto de Estudios Peruanos and Fundación M.J. Bustamante de la Fuente.

Pita, Alfredo 2000, *El cazador ausente*, Barcelona: Seix Barral.

Ponce Suárez, Vilma 2014, 'Multimedia *Pensamiento Crítico*: una revista cubana para el ejercicio de pensar', *Bibliotecas. Anales de investigación*, 10, 10: 273–76.

Ponza, Pablo 2008, 'Comprometidos, orgánicos y expertos: Intelectuales, marxismo y ciencias sociales en Argentina (1955–1973)', *A Contracorriente*, 5, 2: 74–98.

Portocarrero, Gonzalo 2005, 'La hazaña de Alberto Flores Galindo. El deber del héroe', *Libros & Artes*, 11: 19–22.

Portocarrero, Gonzalo 2010, *Oído en el silencio. Ensayos de crítica cultural*, Lima: Red para el desarrollo de las ciencias sociales.

Portocarrero, Gonzalo 2017, 'La escritura y el legado de Alberto Flores Galindo', in *Circuit circus. Circos, intelectuales y payasos*, edited by Eduardo Subirats, Valencia: Universitat de València.

Postero, Nancy 2007, 'Andean Utopias in Evo Morales's Bolivia', *Latin American and Caribbean Ethnic Studies*, 2: 1–28.

Rabinovich, Alejandro M. 2017, *Anatomía del pánico. La Batalla de Huaqui, o la derrota de la revolución (1811)*, Buenos Aires: Sudamericana.

Ragas, José and Jorge Valdez, 2010, 'La vigencia de la utopía', *La República*, March 28.

Ramos, César 1987, 'Buscando un Inca. Servicio especial para el periódico *Granma*', Casa de las Américas, Servicio Especial de Prensa, January.

Rénique, José Luis 1988, 'La utopía andina hoy (un comentario a *Buscando un Inca*)', *Debate Agrario*, 2: 131–46.

Rénique, José Luis 2007, 'Una larga marcha andina: tradición radical y organización revolucionaria en el Perú', in *El comunismo: otras miradas desde América Latina*, edited by Elvira Concheiro, Massimo Modonesi, and Horacio Crespo, Mexico City: Universidad Nacional Autónoma de México.

Rénique, José Luis 2016, *La batalla por Puno: Conflicto agrario y nación en los Andes peruanos*, Lima: La Siniestra Ensayos.

Rénique, José Luis 2019, *Incendiar la pradera. Un ensayo sobre la revolución en el Perú*, Lima: La Siniestra Ensayos.

Renshaw, Ricardo 1985, *La tortura en Chimbote. Un caso en el Perú*, Chimbote: IPEP.

Revista Andina 1984, 'Debate en torno a "Los rostros de la plebe"', *Revista Andina*, 2, 3: 57–72.

Rey Yero, Luis 1987a, 'Recital de poesía hoy en la Casa de la Cultura espirituana', *Escambray*, 9, 23, January 30: 1.

Rey Yero, Luis 1987b, 'El Che está presente en el Perú', *Escambray*, 9, 23, January 30: 2.

Ribeyro, Julio Ramón 1973, *La juventud en la otra ribera*, Lima: Mosca Azul.

Ricca, Guillermo 2015, *Nada por perdido. Política en José M. Aricó*, Córdoba: Universidad Nacional de Río Cuarto and CLACSO.

Rivera, Omar 2019, *Delimitations of Latin American Philosophy. Beyond Redemption*, Bloomington: Indiana University Press.

Rivera Cusicanqui, Silvia and Rossana Barragán (eds.) 1997, *Debates post coloniales: Una introducción a los estudios de la subalternidad*, La Paz: Historias, SEPHIS, and Aruwiyiri.

Rivera Serna, Raúl 1958, *Los guerrilleros del centro en la emancipación peruana*, Lima: P.L. Villanueva.

Rochabrún, Guillermo 2007, *Batallas por la teoría. En torno a Marx y el Perú*, Lima: Instituto de Estudios Peruanos.

Rodríguez Rivera, Guillermo 2017, *Decirlo todo. Políticas culturales (en la Revolución cubana)*, Havana: Ojalá.

Romano, Ruggiero 1991a, 'Prefazione', in Alberto Flores Galindo, *Perù: identità e utopia. Cercando un Inca*, Florence: Ponte alle Grazie.

Romano, Ruggiero 1991b, 'Buscando un inca se encontró un gran historiador', *Márgenes*, IV, 8: 89–97.

Romero, Emilio et al. 1979, *7 ensayos: 50 años en la historia*, Lima: Biblioteca Amauta.

Rosas Lauro, Claudia 2006, *Del trono a la guillotina. El impacto de la Revolución Francesa en el Perú (1789–1808)*, Lima: Instituto de Estudios Peruanos, Instituto Francés de Estudios Andinos, and Embajada de Francia.

Rosas Lauro, Claudia (ed.) 2005, *El miedo en el Perú. Siglos XVI al XX*, Lima: Pontificia Universidad Católica del Perú.

Ruiz Zevallos, Augusto 2011, 'Alberto Flores Galindo: marco sociopolítico, fronteras teóricas y proyecto político', *Histórica*, 35, 1: 11–51.

Said, Edward 1996, *Representations of the Intellectual*, New York: Random House.

Sandoval, Pablo and José Carlos Agüero 2015, '*Aprendiendo a vivir se va la vida*'. *Conversaciones con Carlos Iván Degregori*, Lima: Instituto de Estudios Peruanos.

Scorza, Manuel 1970, *Redoble por Rancas*, Barcelona: Planeta.

Servicios Populares 1982, *Derechos humanos y ley terrorista*, Lima: Servicios Populares.

Sobrevilla Perea, Natalia 2015a, 'La nación subyacente: de la monarquía hispánica al Estado en el Perú', in *La Independencia del Perú: ¿Concedida, conseguida, concebida?*, edited by Carlos Contreras and Luis Miguel Glave, Lima: Instituto de Estudios Peruanos.

Sobrevilla Perea, Natalia 2015b, 'Loyalism and Liberalism in Peru, 1810–1824', in *The Rise of Constitutional Government in the Iberian Atlantic World: The Impact of the Cádiz Constitution of 1812*, edited by Scott Eastman and Natalia Sobrevilla Perea, Tuscaloosa: University of Alabama Press.

Sorensen, Diana 2007, *A Turbulent Decade Remembered: Scenes from the Latin American Sixties*, Stanford, CA: Stanford University Press.

Sorrilha Pinheiro, Marcos 2013, *Utopia andina. Socialismo e historiografia em Alberto Flores Galindo*, São Paulo: Annablume.

Spitta, Silvia 2003, 'Prefacio. Más allá de la ciudad letrada', in *Más allá de la ciudad letrada: crónicas y espacios urbanos*, edited by Silvia Spitta and Boris Muñoz, Pittsburgh, Instituto Internacional de Literatura Iberoamericana.

Starn, Orin 1999, *Nightwatch: The Politics of Protest in the Andes*, Durham: Duke University Press.

Suárez, Luis and Dirk Kruijt 2012, 'Una necesidad de la proyección internacionalista de la Revolución Cubana', interview with Fernando Martínez Heredia, http://www.alainet.org/pt/node/186373.

Suárez Salazar, Luis 2022, 'El Centro de Estudios sobre América (CEA): Apuntes para su historia', *La Tizza*, May 30, https://medium.com/la-tiza/el-centro-de-estudios-sobre-am%C3%A9rica-cea-apuntes-para-su-historia-527c81c566d2.

Sulmont, Denis 1975, *El movimiento obrero en el Perú, 1900–1956*, Lima: Pontificia Universidad Católica del Perú.

Szeminski, Jan, Alberto Flores Galindo, and Manuel Burga 1981, 'Túpac Amaru y los conflictos del mundo andino', *Tarea*, 3: 9–16.

Tamayo Herrera, José 1988, *Regionalización: mito o realidad e identidad nacional: utopía o esperanza*, Lima: Centro de Estudios País.

Thompson, E.P. 1964, *The Making of the English Working Class*, New York: Pantheon Books.

Trabajadores 1987, 'El jurado en tertulia periodística', January 30.
Trimboli, Javier 2024, *Alberto Flores Galindo. La escritura de la historia*, Buenos Aires: Universidad Nacional de General Sarmiento.
Truth and Reconciliation Commission 2014, *Hatun Willakuy. Abbreviated Version of the Final Report of the Truth and Reconciliation Commission. Peru*, Lima: Transfer Commission of the Truth and Reconciliation Commission of Peru.
Tusell, Javier 1990, *Retrato de Mario Vargas Llosa*, Barcelona: Círculo de Lectores.
Urbano, Henrique 1982, 'Representaciones colectivas y arqueología mental en los Andes', *Allpanchis*, 17, 20: 33–83.
Urbano, Henrique 1986, *'Europa y el país de los Incas. La utopía andina'* (Review), *Revista Andina*, 4, 1: 282–4.
Valderrama, Lucila 2004, *Alberto Flores Galindo: Biobibliografía*, Lima: Biblioteca Nacional.
Vallega, Alejandro 2024, 'Latin American Thought as a Path toward Philosophizing from Radical Exteriority', in *Philosophizing the Americas*, edited by Jacoby Adeshei Carter and Hernando Arturo Estévez, New York: Fordham University Press.
Vanden, Harry E. 1975, *Mariátegui. Influencias en su formación ideológica*, Lima: Biblioteca Amauta.
Varese, Stefano 2020, *The Art of Memory: An Ethnographer's Journey*, translated by Margaret Randall, Raleigh, NC: A Contracorriente.
Vargas Llosa, Mario 1996, *La utopía arcaica. José María Arguedas y las ficciones del indigenismo*, Mexico City: Fondo de Cultura Económica.
Vargas Llosa, Mario 1981, *La guerra del fin del mundo*, Barcelona: Seix Barral.
Vargas Llosa, Mario 1984, *The War of the End of the World*, translated by Helen Lane, New York: Farrar, Straus & Giroux.
Vergara Arias, Gustavo 1974, *Montoneros y guerrillas en la etapa de la emancipación del Perú (1820–1825)*, Lima: Salesiana.
Walker, Charles 2017, 'The General and His Rebel: Juan Velasco Alvarado and the Reinvention of Túpac Amaru II', in *The Peculiar Revolution. Rethinking the Peruvian Experiment Under Military Rule*, edited by Carlos Aguirre and Paulo Drinot, Austin: University of Texas Press.
Walker, Charles 2020, 'The Shining Path and the Emergence of the Human Rights Community in Peru', *Berkeley Review of Latin American Studies*, Fall: 76–83.
Wasserman, Fabio 2011, *Juan José Castelli. De súbdito de la corona a líder revolucionario*. Buenos Aires: EDHASA.
Weinberg, Liliana 2002, *El ensayo. Entre el paraíso y el infierno*, Mexico City: Universidad Nacional Autónoma de México.
Weinberg, Liliana 2007, *Pensar el ensayo*, Mexico City: Siglo XXI.
Wilson, Fiona 2007, 'Transcending Race? Schoolteachers and Political Militancy in Andean Peru, 1970–2000', *Journal of Latin American Studies*, 39, 4: 719–46.

Youngers, Coletta 2003, *Violencia política y sociedad civil en el Perú: Historia de la Coordinadora Nacional de Derechos Humanos*, Lima: Instituto de Estudios Peruanos.

Zolov, Eric 2014, 'Introduction: Latin America in the Global 1960s', *The Americas*, 70, 3: 349–62.

Index

Page numbers in *italics* refer to tables and figures.

Acevedo, Juan   82
Adrianzén, Alberto   62, 76, 142
Aguilar, Gabriel   42, 43, 44, 45, 139, 154
Aguirre, Carlos   40
Ali, Tariq   1
Alianza Popular Revolucionaria Americana (APRA)   11, 15, 17, 19, 48, 65, 150
Allende, Salvador   11
Allpanchis (journal)   23, 59, 62, 65, 71, 108, 113
Altshuler, Ernesto   105
Amauta (magazine)   14, 15, 17, 62, 67–68, 72, 133, 137, 155
Amazon   43
American Popular Revolutionary Alliance. *See* Alianza Popular Revolucionaria Americana
Andes, the   23, 27, 32, 35, 41, 43, 47, 48n4, 113, 120, 129, 136
   Andean cultures   4, 9–11, 21
   Andean peoples   9, 89
   eroticism in   144
   millenarianism and messianism in   20
   modernity in   128, 131
Andean utopia   20–27, 31–32, 36, 37, 42–46, 69–70, 118, 128–129, 147
Ángeles Loayza, César   125
Annales school   7, 23, 37, 42
Ansión, Juan   65, 114
APRA. *See* Alianza Popular Revolucionaria Americana
Aprismo   13, 19–20, 21
Archivo de Indias (Sevilla)   34, 36, 41
Archivo General de la Nación   41
Arguedas, José María   21, 103, 141, 142–145, 147–149, 151–152, 156, 157, 158
   El zorro de arriba y el zorro de abajo   103
   Flores Galindo's study of   4, 10, 110, 111, 114, 117, 122, 128–129
   Todas las sangres   143, 144, 145, 148, 151, 157
Aricó, José   12–15, 161
Arrelucea, Maribel   40

Arroyo, Eduardo   57, 64
Arze, René   88–89
Asalto al Cielo (supplement)   125
Asociación Pro Derechos Humanos (APRODEH)   118, 134, 135
Atahualpa, Juan Santos   4, 36, 42, 43
'authentic revolutions'   35, 99
authoritarianism   4, 26, 28, 58, 72, 82, 109, 122, 124, 129, 130, 132–138
   in Cuba   6, 76, 85
   of the Shining Path   21, 27, 110, 116–117, 121
Autonomous University of Barcelona   15, 96

Bakhtin, Mikhael   23
Balzac, Honoré de   149
Barrantes Lingán, Alfonso   48
Basadre, Jorge   22, 32, 33, 61
Bastidas, Micaela   36
Bedoya Reyes, Luis   48
Béjar, Héctor   52, 87
Benavides, Gustavo   143
Benedetti, Mario   78, 79, 80, 91, 156
Benjamin, Walter   7, 23
Benvenuto, Sergio   88, 95
Betto, Frei   91
Biblioteca Nacional de Madrid   41
Blanco, Hugo   48, 75
Blondet, Cecilia   128
Boletín del Instituto Riva-Agüero (journal)   31
Bolívar, Simón   32, 41
Bonilla, Heraclio   29–30, 33, 35, 39, 57–58
Borges, Luis   19, 142, 143, 156
Bosch, Juan   78, 79
Bourbons   41, 44
Braudel, Fernand   3, 4, 58, 61
Britto García, Luis   80
Bryce Echenique, Alfredo   79, 87, 89
Buarque, Chico   79
Burga, Manuel   9, 20, 22, 33, 36, 44, 56, 60, 63–64, 68–71, 88, 108

Buscando un Inca (*In Search of an Inca*)
(Flores Galindo) 4–5, 10, 20, 61, 65, 75, 82, 93, 95, 101, 159
  Andean utopia and 20–27, 31–32, 36, 37, 42–46, 69–70, 118, 128–129
  awards and prizes 25, 71, 75, 87–91
  Casa de las Américas edition 90
  Cuban edition 71, 75
  Degregori's critiques of 127–131
  editions and translations of 25
  impact and influence of 25–27, 40
  methodology and themes in 22–24
  origins and writing of 69–71
  Peruvian War of Independence and 42–46
  publication of 10, 20
  reviews of 65, 95–96
  on Shining Path 108–111, 121–131

Cáceres Valdivia, Eduardo 56, 140, 141
Camus, Albert 142, 146, 152
Caravedo, Baltazar 11
Cardenal, Ernesto 79
Carpentier, Alejo 152, 154, 156
Carrera Damas, Germán 40
Casa de las Américas 71, 77, 107, 147
  Ernesto Che Guevara Extraordinary Essay Prize jury 91–96
  literary prizes 87–91
Casa de las Américas (journal) 96
Castor, Suzy 79
Castro, Fidel 76, 78, 84, 93, 95, 101n89, 106
Castro, Raúl 86–87n41
Catholic University. *See* Pontificia Universidad Católica del Perú
censorship 124
Centro de Estudios sobre América (CEA) 84, 85, 91, 93
Cerro de Pasco Copper Corporation 7, 12, 58
Chandler, Raymond 145
Chatterjee, Partha 24
Chavarría, Jesús 12, 14
Chocano, Magdalena 5, 38, 124, 152, 158
Christian Popular Party (Partido Popular Cristiano) 48
Chust, Manuel 29n3, 33
Cisneros, Antonio 59, 79, 80, 87, 145, 152–154

Cisneros, Luis Jaime 141
Coatsworth, John 5
colonialism 4, 9, 42, 45, 46
Comisión de la Verdad y Reconciliación (CVR) 115, 121, 130–131, 136, 146n36
  Informe Final 114n23, 121, 130
Conrad, Joseph 146
Contreras, Carlos 41
Coordinadora Nacional de Derechos Humanos 115
Corcuera, Arturo 82
Cornejo Polar, Antonio 79
Cortázar, Julio 79
Córtes de Cádiz 31
coup of October 3 1968, 1–2. *See also* Velasco Alvarado, Juan
COVID-19 pandemic 33
Cristóbal, Juan 133
Cuba 75–77. *See also* Casa de las Américas; Castro, Fidel; Guevara, Ernesto
  Communist Party of 85, 93, 145n31
  Edición Revolucionaria and 84
  first Encounter of Intellectuals for the Sovereignty of the Peoples of Our America 78
  Flores Galindo's 1981 visit to 78–81
  Flores Galindo's 1985 visit to 81–87
  Flores Galindo's 1987 visit to 91–96
  Reagan and 78–79, 81
  second Encounter of Intellectuals for the Sovereignty of the Peoples of Our America 76, 81, 88
  socialism and democracy in 98–101
Cuban Revolution 1, 6, 18, 47, 75–77, 86, 87, 102
Cultural Studies 24
Cusco uprisings of 1814–15 32

Damonte, Humberto 61
Dancourt, Óscar 14–15, 18
Degregori, Carlos Iván 18, 25–26, 64, 109, 113–114, 116, 125–131, 157–158
de la Peña, Sergio 88–89
Delgado, Carlos 52
Delgado, Washington 41, 79, 161
Delmar, Serafín 150
Dependency Theory 8
de Soto, Hernando 55, 65, 126
Deutscher, Isaac 81

Díaz, Jesús 150
Díaz Martínez, Antonio 112, 134, 160n99
Di Meglio, Gabriel 39
Dostoyevsky, Fyodor 141, 142, 144, 152, 156
Dunbar Temple, Ella 40
Durant, Alberto 79, 80

École des hautes études en sciences sociales (EHESS) 37
École pratique des hautes études 33, 58
Editorial Horizonte 61, 69, 72
El Búho (magazine) 59, 62
El Caballo Rojo (supplement) 33, 34, 53, 59, 62, 71, 72, 145
El Diario de Marka (newspaper) 34, 53, 62, 79, 125
El Frontón prison 112n13, 133, 134
Elgueta, Belarmino 91–92
Elmore, Peter 63, 143–144, 146, 151
El País (newspaper) 78
El Zorro de Abajo (journal) 59, 62, 127
Engels, Federico 35
Escobar, Alberto 122
Espino Prieto, Mayra 105
Espinoza García, Manuel 87

Fanon, Franz 1
federalism 32, 46
Fernández Retamar, Roberto 80, 91, 104, 145n31
Flores Galindo, Alberto
   affinity with literature of 157–161
   bibliography of 60–61
   collaborative relationships 61–62
   death of 3, 59, 104
   education 2–3, 57–58
   farewell letter by 64, 102–104, 126, 131
   in front of Lenin monument 94
   on Guevara 97–98
   illness of 102–104
   jury member for Ernesto Che Guevara Extraordinary Essay Prize 91–96
   literary texts in writings of *162–165*
   with Manrique 83
   member of Ernesto Che Guevara Extraordinary Essay Prize jury 92
   reading and interdisciplinarity of 139–148, 155–156
   research and essay writing of 109–111
   role of literature in historical craft of 148–152
   on socialism and democracy in Cuba 98–101
   visits to Cuba 78–87, 91–96
   writers mentioned by *165*
   writing style and practices of 63–73, 153–155
Flores Galindo, Alberto, works of
   Apogeo y crisis de la república aristocrática (with Manuel Burga) 20, 60, 63, 69
   Arequipa y el sur andino 7–8, 60
   Aristocracia y plebe 9, 37–42, 44, 60, 65, 68, 69, 86, 136, 149
   La agonía de Mariátegui 5, 13–16, 18–19, 60, 68, 110, 113, 154, 159
   'La tradición autoritaria. Violencia y democracia en el Perú' 109, 136–137
   Los mineros de la Cerro de Pasco 60, 61, 70
   Los rostros de la plebe 5
   'Soldados y montoneros' 44–45
   Tiempo de plagas 60, 72–73, 125, 133, 152–154, 159
   See also Buscando un Inca
Fontana, Josep 4, 77n10
Fornet, Ambrosio 105, 106
Franco, Carlos 19, 62, 133
Freire, Paulo 1
Frente Revolucionario de Estudiantes Socialistas (FRES) 2, 56, 75
Fuentes, Manuel Atanasio 64
Fujimori, Alberto 4, 47, 55

Galeano, Eduardo 80, 87
Gálvez, William 91, 102
García, Alan 48, 101, 112n13, 125
García, Inés 135
García Canclini, Néstor 80
García Márquez, Gabriel 78, 79, 80n20, 82, 91, 92, 142
Garcilaso de la Vega, Inca 21, 26, 44
Generation of 1968 22, 56–60, 77, 127
Geremek, Bronislaw 42, 81
Germaná, César 11, 68
German Peasant Wars 35

Gilroy, Paul   24
Ginzburg, Carlo   23
Glave, Luis Miguel   113
globalisation   4
Góngora, Mario   40
González, Raúl   115
González Casanova, Pablo   79
González Prada, Manuel   64
González Vigil, Ricardo   141–143, 156
Gordimer, Nadine   103–104, 147
Gorriti, Gustavo   112, 114–115
Gramsci, Antonio   2, 4, 7, 13, 23, 110, 144
Granados, Manuel Jesús   114
Granma (newspaper)   90, 93
Guaman Poma de Ayala, Felipe   21, 26, 159
Guayasamín, Oswaldo   78
Guerra, François-Xavier   31
guerrillas   1, 3–4, 9, 47, 52, 91, 111, 118–119, 122, 136, 159. *See also* Guevara, Ernesto; Movimiento Revolucionario Túpac Amaru; Shining Path
and wars of Independence   40, 42–45
Guevara, Ernesto (Che)   1, 47, 77, 84, 91–93, 96–98, 102, 104
Guha, Ranajit   24
Gutiérrez, Gustavo   2, 56, 57
Guzmán, Abimael   130
Guzmán, Ramiro   41

Hall, Stuart   24
Hammett, Dashiell   145
Hart, Armando   78, 91
Haya de la Torre, Agustín   133–134
Haya de la Torre, Víctor Raúl   11, 16, 17, 19, 48, 58, 64, 150
Hebdige, Dick   24
Hernández, Max   122
Hernández, Rafael   104–105
Hidalgo, Alberto   64
Hildebrandt, César   58, 158
Hill, Christopher   24
Histórica (journal)   31, 62
historiography   25, 29–33, 38–43, 45–46, 89, 126, 149, 157
Hobsbawm, Eric   4, 24, 40
Huánuco uprisings of 1812   32, 45
Huari   113, 117
human rights   122–123, 134–137
violations of   3, 27, 66, 72

Iguíñiz, Javier   62
Incas   21, 25, 33, 45, 113, 117
invocations of   111, 117
reimagining of   43
inequalities   4, 111, 112, 135, 137
Instituto de Apoyo Agrario   61, 68, 71–72, 75, 88, 90
Instituto de Pastoral Andina   59, 62
Instituto Libertad y Democracia (ILD)   126

July 1821 riots   38
Juventud Rebelde (newspaper)   89, 93

Kapsoli, Wilfredo   11, 53
Katz, Friedrich   5
Klaiber, Jeffrey   62
Komintern   16–17, 18, 19, 68, 110
Kruijt, Dirk   86

Lagos, Edith   117
La Jornada (supplement)   58, 62
Lamming, George   79
La Palabra del Pueblo (magazine)   58, 62
La Prensa (newspaper)   58, 62
Larco, Juan   79, 80
La República (newspaper)   33, 62, 65, 134
La Salle school   56, 127, 140–141
Lauer, Mirko   58, 61
Lecaros, Fernando   56, 61
Leftist Revolutionary Movement. *See* Movimiento de Izquierda Revolucionaria
Lenin, Vladimir   1, 11, 50, *94*
Lentz, Vera   115
Lévano, César   13, 19, 58, 68
Liberation Theology   1, 2, 56
Lohmann, Guillermo   39
longue durée   4, 7, 26
López, Sinesio   13, 25, 79, 80, 133
López Albújar, Enrique   141
López Soria, José Ignacio   11, 82
Los Caminos del Laberinto (journal)   62, 71
Lucanamarca massacre of 1983   136, 146n36
Luna Vegas, Ricardo   13, 68
Lurigancho prison uprising of 1986   112, 133
Lynch, Nicolás   49n5, 52, 128

Macdonald, Ross   133, 134, 145, 152
Macera, Pablo   22, 33, 41, 54, 63, 143n20, 153, 159n94

INDEX   191

Machado, Antonio   18
Mallon, Florencia   5
Malraux, André   146
Manrique, Nelson   25–26, 82, *83*, 84, 107, 121–122, 124
   on trip to Havana   82–83
Maoism   2, 3, 9, 11, 14, 21, 57, 109, 110, 111, 117
Mao Zedong   1, 11, 15, 50
Marcuse, Herbert   1
Márgenes (journal)   10, 59, 95n64, 96, 108, 127
Mariátegui, José Carlos   2, 52, 64, 86, 102, 108, 118, 143, 145, 148
   fiftieth anniversary of death of   15
   Flores Galindo on   5, 9, 13–19, 60, 67–68, 110–113, 151, 154–155, 159
   influence on Flores Galindo   4, 8, 153
   'The Problem of Race in Latin America'   18
   Siete ensayos   13, 62, 67
Marka (magazine)   53
Martí, José   78
Martínez, Gregorio   157
Martínez, Maruja   14, 59, 72, 96, 112–113, 135, 146
Martínez Alier, Juan   139–140
Martínez Heredia, Fernando   5, 83–87n41, 91, 95, 95n64, 100–105
Martos, Marco   59, 63–64, 143, 152, 153
Marx, Karl   1, 11, 12, 14, 50, 56, 100
Marxism   2–5, 8, 11–13, 17, 18, 20–24, 39, 48, 49n5, 56, 64n58, 68, 72, 76, 77n10, 86, 101, 110, 111, 129, 151n56, 155
Mateu Cueva, Augusto   148
Matos Mar, José   35, 39
Matta, Roberto   79
Mayer, Eric   65
Mazzeo, Cristina   41
Medrano, Oscar   115
Mejía Baca, Juan   52, 62
Melis, Antonio   12, 64, 123–124, 137, 151, 153
Mendoza, Juan   72
Merino Vigil, Germán   53
Merleau-Ponty, Maurice   142
messianism   20, 26, 58, 115
millenarianism   20, 25, 118, 125n66
Millones, Luis   65
MIR. *See* Movimiento de Izquierda Revolucionaria

Miró Quesada, Francisco   61
modernity   23, 26, 113, 116–117
   in the Andes   128–129, 131
monarchism   41, 46
Moncloa, Francisco   79, 80
Montoya, Edwin   147
Montoya, Gustavo   144–145, 147
Montoya, Luis   147
Montoya, Rodrigo   82, 147
Mora, Tulio   159–161
Moreno Fraginals, Manuel   4, 77
Morote Best, Efraín   112
Movimiento de Izquierda Revolucionaria (MIR)   2, 56, 75–76
Movimiento Revolucionario Túpac Amaru (MRTA)   97

Nanterre University   68
Naranjo, Reynaldo   79
'national question'   3, 11, 12n17, 58, 60
national strike of 1977   47–48
Neira, Hugo   58, 87
Neo-Liberalism   3–4, 125, 126
New Left   2, 23, 57, 76, 110, 135

Ollé, Carmen   82
O'Phelan Godoy, Scarlett   29, 33, 34–35, 113
Oquendo, Abelardo   61, 150
Otero Silva, Miguel   79

Pachacuti   37
Padilla affair   84
Palma, Ricardo   149–150
Panfichi, Aldo   40
Pareja, Piedad   11
Paris, Robert   12
Partido Popular Cristiano   48
Pease, Franklin   61, 64
Peirano, Luis   79, 80
Pensamiento Crítico (journal)   83–85
Pérez, Esther   93, 95, 102–104, 107, 147
Pérez Grande, Hildebrando   102
Pérez Huarancca, Hildebrando   102n94, 146
   Los ilegítimos   146
Perrault, Gilles   142
Peruvian Communist Party   2, 12n17, 13, 68
Peruvian Truth and Reconciliation Commission. *See* Comisión de la Verdad y Reconciliación

Peruvian War of Independence   28–31
  Aristocracia y plebe (Flores Galindo) and   37–42, 44
  historiographical approaches   31–33
  In Search of an Inca (Flores Galindo) and   42–46
  teleology and   32
  Túpac Amaru uprising   4, 8–9, 21, 26, 33–37, 58, 108, 118, 159
Pino Santos, Oscar   88
Pita, Alfredo   51
Pontificia Universidad Católica del Perú (PUCP)   2, 13, 56–58, 61–62, 71, 127, 140–141
Poole, Deborah   5
popular history   58
Porras Barrenechea, Raúl   22, 63, 153
Portocarrero, Felipe   25, 40
Portocarrero, Gonzalo   130, 147, 153
Portocarrero, Ricardo   107
Portuondo, José Antonio   82
print culture   47–56
  cultural magazines   50–51, 55, 67
  Generation of 1968 and   56–60
  leftwing activism and   52
  leftwing political culture and   47–49, 51–56, 63–67
  limited-circulation newspapers and supplements   62–63
  mass circulation newspapers and supplements   62
  public intellectuals and   73–74
  study groups and   51–52
propaganda   49n7, 57, 67, 73
Proust, Marcel   142
publishing houses   61
PUCP. *See* Pontificia Universidad Católica del Perú

Quechua (language)   10, 23, 43, 145
Quechua culture   147

racism   4, 43, 58, 65, 108, 114, 122, 132–133, 136–137, 160
Ramos, César   93–94
rebellion   8–9, 43, 51n12. *See also* Túpac Amaru II
  of coolies   159
  led by Angulo   46

led by Túpac Amaru   21, 26, 34–37, 58
  primitive   149
Reagan, Ronald   78–79, 81
Remy, María Isabel   113
Rénique, José Luis   57, 128
Renshaw, Ricardo   132, 133
republicanism   32, 42, 46, 113
Revista Andina (journal)   23, 59, 62
Revolutionary Front of Socialist Students. *See* Frente Revolucionario de Estudiantes Socialistas
Revolutionary Government of the Armed Forces   2. *See also* Velasco Alvarado, Juan
Revolutionary Left Movement. *See* Movimiento de Izquierda Revolucionaria
Revolutionary Túpac Amaru Movement   97
Revolutionary Vanguard (VR)   2, 57, 76–77
Riva-Agüero, José de la   41, 63
Rivera, Cecilia   69, 104
Rivera Serna, Raúl   45
Rochabrún, Guillermo   56, 59–60, 64, 107
Rodríguez, Mariano   79
Rodríguez Rabanal, Cesar   82, 134
Rodríguez Rivera, Guillermo   106
Romano, Ruggiero   34, 37, 65, 66, 81, 133
rondas campesinas   119
Rosas, Claudia   29n3, 33, 41
Rospigliosi, Fernando   134
royalism   32, 39, 46
Rudé, George   24, 40

Sabato, Ernesto   142, 157
Said, Edward   54n24
Salazar, Oswaldo (Jorge)   87
Salazar Bondy, Sebastián   99, 156
Sánchez, Luis Alberto   64
San Martín, José de   32, 41, 45
Santa Bárbara prison   133
Santiváñez, Roger   82
Sartre, Jean-Paul   1, 2, 56, 141–142, 164
Scorza, Manuel   141, 148
Semprún, Jorge   142
Sendero Luminoso. *See* Shining Path
Shining Path   3, 4, 9, 14, 21. *See also* Peruvian Truth and Reconciliation Commission
  authoritarianism and   27, 109, 110, 111, 115–117, 121–122, 124–125, 129, 137
  complicit silence and   120–124
  costs of war   117

debates, controversies, and polemics 124–131
emergence and expansion of 111–118
human rights and 122–123, 134–137
Lucanamarca massacre of 1983 136, 146n36
peasant resistance and 121
torture and 131–132
Uchuraccay massacre of 1983 45, 114, 120, 132
violence of 118–124
SINAMOS 2
Sindicato Unitario de Trabajadores de la Educación Peruana (SUTEP) 47, 50
slavery 37–38, 40, 136, 137
Sobrevilla, David 61–62
socialism 1–3, 6–9, 11–12, 15, 18, 20, 27, 48, 52, 55–57, 66, 68, 72–73, 75, 92, 97, 100–102, 104–106, 110, 128, 131
  in the Andes 129
  in Cuba 76–77, 80, 82, 86, 93, 95n64, 98n74, 107
  Soviet model of 84
Socialist Students Revolutionary Front. See Frente Revolucionario de Estudiantes Socialistas
Sorrilha Pinheiro, Marcos 5
Spalding, Karen 5, 29, 33
Spivak, Gayatri Chakravorty 24
Stalin, Joseph 50
Stalinism 110
Stern, Steve 5
Suárez, Luis 86
Subaltern Studies 4, 24
Sulmont, Denis 11, 53, 58, 139
SUR Casa de Estudios del Socialismo 10, 59, 95
Szeminski, Jan 36, 65

Tablada Pérez, Carlos 91
Tacna uprisings of 1811 32, 45
Tamayo Herrera, José 124
Taqui Onqoy 118, 119
Tauro, Alberto 82
Temas (journal) 104
Textual (magazine) 51
Third International 13, 15–16, 19. *See also* Komintern
30 Días (magazine) 59, 62

Thompson, E.P. 4, 7, 23–24, 27, 38, 42, 81
Tolstoi, Lev 81, 148
Torres, Javier 128n79
torture 66, 120, 131–132, 137
Tristán, Flora 159
Trotsky, Leon 11, 81
Trotskyism 11, 14, 48, 75
Túpac Amaru II 4, 8–9, 21, 26, 33–37, 58, 108, 118, 159

Ubalde, Manuel 43, 44, 45
Uchuraccay massacre of 1983 45, 114, 120, 132
  Comisión Investigadora 120n48
Unanue, Hipólito 41
UNESCO 20
Universidad Nacional San Cristóbal de Huamanga 112
University of Havana 84
Urbano, Henrique 26, 64
Urrutia, Carlos 82
utopia. *See* Andean utopia

Vaca Sagrada (magazine) 59, 143
Valera, Luis 61, 71, 72, 75, 146
Vanden, Harry 12, 161
Vanguardia Revolucionaria. *See* Revolutionary Vanguard
Vargas Llosa, Mario 55, 65, 142, 150, 151, 156, 157
Vega, Juan José 64, 65
Velasco Alvarado, Juan 47, 51, 52, 53, 58
  coup of 3 October 1968 1–2, 47, 57
  fall of 3
  reforms 11, 111
  Revolutionary Government of the Armed Forces 2
  Túpac Amaru studies and 33–34
Velasquismo 76n7
Vidaurre, Manuel Lorenzo de 41
Vilar, Pierre 3, 4, 33, 34, 58, 81
Violencia y campesinado (pamphlet) 72n92, 123
Vitier, Cintio 80
Vuskovic, Pedro 91–92

War of Independence. *See* Peruvian War of Independence
Watanabe, José 59, 143

www.ingramcontent.com/pod-product-compliance
Lightning Source LLC
Chambersburg PA
CBHW070624030426

42337CB00020B/3903